Palgrave Studies in Cyberpsychology

Palgrave Studies in Cyberpsychology aims to foster and to chart the scope of research driven by a psychological understanding of the effects of the 'new technology' that is shaping our world after the digital revolution. The series takes an inclusive approach and considers all aspects of human behaviours and experiential states in relation to digital technologies, to the Internet, and to virtual environments. As such, Cyberpsychology reaches out to several neighbouring disciplines, from Human-Computer Interaction to Media and Communication Studies. A core question underpinning the series concerns the actual psychological novelty of new technology. To what extent do we need to expand conventional theories and models to account for cyberpsychological phenomena? At which points is the ubiquitous digitisation of our everyday lives shifting the focus of research questions and research needs? Where do we see implications for our psychological functioning that are likely to outlast short-lived fashions in technology use?

Richard James • Lucy Hitcham

Critical Perspectives on Smartphone Addiction

palgrave
macmillan

Richard James
School of Psychology
University of Nottingham
Nottingham, Nottinghamshire, UK

Lucy Hitcham
School of Medicine
University of Nottingham, Nottingham,
Nottinghamshire, UK

ISSN 2946-2754 ISSN 2946-2762 (electronic)
Palgrave Studies in Cyberpsychology
ISBN 978-3-031-96187-8 ISBN 978-3-031-96188-5 (eBook)
https://doi.org/10.1007/978-3-031-96188-5

This Palgrave Macmillan imprint is published by the registered company Springer Nature Switzerland AG.
The registered company address is: Gewerbestrasse 11, 6330 Cham, Switzerland

Acknowledgements

This book is the product of several projects exploring the role of smartphone use and smartphone addiction. We would like to thank the participants who have taken part in our studies over the last four years for their time and insights in this endeavour. Several colleagues and collaborators, Richard Tunney and Alex Bradley in particular, have acted as sounding boards and shaped the thinking behind this research. As an alumnus and current student, we would like to thank the Horizon Centre for Doctrol Training for the training and support they have provided in forming us as researchers. This work also wouldn't have been possible without the data collection undertaken by project students and volunteers, and we wish to thank them for their contributions. We would like to give a special mention to Hannah Jackson for her valuable contributions and inspiration during the outset of these projects.

Lucy would like to pay tribute to her late father, David Hitcham. You are gone but not forgotten, and I will continue trying to make you proud.

Richard dedicates the book to the memory of his grandmothers, and his dogs Tima and Rubes.

Finally, we would like to thank our partners and family.

From Lucy: To my mum, Karen, for always believing in me and encouraging me through all my pursuits. And importantly, to Cameron for all your love and support, and patience in acting as a sounding board for my constant internal monologue.

From Richard: To Tima, Rubes, Freyja, and Nyx as an endless source of joy, inspiration, and barking throughout the process of writing this book. And to Cherry for her patience, thoughtfulness, and most importantly, for introducing me to Freyja and Tima. Best dogs ever.

Competing Interests The authors declare the following as potential competing interests: Richard James currently receives research funding from GREO Evidence Insights and UKRI for gambling-related projects, and from the 1001 Critical Days Foundation for a project on perinatal technology use. In the past three years, he has also received funding from the Academic Forum for the Study of Gambling. The funds from these grants are ultimately sourced from regulatory settlements levied by the Gambling Commission in lieu of penalties. The funding for primary data collection related to smartphone addiction research was supported by internal startup and pump-priming funding from the School of Psychology, University of Nottingham. Lucy Hitcham is currently funded by the Engineering and Physical Sciences Research Council (EPSRC) on a PhD Studentship scholarship [Grant Number EP/S023305/1].

Contents

About the Authors

Richard James is Assistant Professor of Psychology at the University of Nottingham and incoming Senior Lecturer in Psychology at the School of Sports, Exercise and Health Sciences at Loughborough University. His research focuses on understanding addictive behaviours (gambling, smartphone use) using intensive logged data, external records, social media behaviour, and psychometric modelling. He has also published papers on understanding heterogeneity in chronic pain and autistic traits. He has published on these topics in journals such as *Addiction*, *Journal of Behavioral Addictions, Computers in Human Behavior*, and *Addictive Behaviours.*

Lucy Hitcham is a PhD candidate at the University of Nottingham as part of the EPSRC Horizon Centre for Doctoral Training. Her research focuses on smartphone use and addiction, and more recently, her PhD research focuses on the use and responsible design of digital mental health interventions. She has published research related to smartphone addiction in journals such as *Computers in Human Behavior* and *Addictive Behaviors.*

Abbreviations

AA	Alcoholics Anonymous
ACT	Acceptance and Commitment Therapy
ADHD	Attention Deficit Hyperactivity Disorder
AI	Artificial Intelligence
APA	American Psychological Association
CBT	Cognitive Behaviour Therapy
CFA	Confirmatory Factor Analysis
CMA	Components Model of Addiction
DSM	Diagnostic and Statistical Manual of Mental Disorders
EAI	Exercise Addiction Inventory
EFA	Exploratory Factor Analysis
EMA	Ecological Momentary Assessment
FOMO	Fear Of Missing Out
GA	Gamblers Anonymous
GSP	General Scale of Phubbing
I-PACE	Interaction of Person-Affect-Cognitive-Execution
IA	Internet Addiction
IAT	Internet Addiction Test
ICD	International Classification of Diseases
IGD	Internet Gaming Disorder
IPD	Individual Patient Data
IS	Information Systems
LLMs	Large Language Models

ITAA	Internet and Technology Addicts Anonymous
MBCT	Mindfulness Based Cognitive Therapy
MBSR	Mindfulness Based Stress Reduction
MBIs	Mindfulness Based Interventions
MG-CFA	Multiple Group Confirmatory Factor Analysis
MPAI	Mobile Phone Addiction Index
MPIQ	Mobile Phone Involvement Questionnaire
MPPUS	Mobile Phone Problem Use Scale
NICE	National Institute of Care Excellence
NMP-Q	Nomophobia Questionnaire
OCD	Obsessive Compulsive Disorder
PCA	Principal Component Analysis
PGSI	Problem Gambling Severity Index
PHQ9	Patient Health Questionnaire (9 items)
PIU	Problematic Internet Use
PLS-SEM	Partial Least Squares—Structural Equation Modelling
PMPUQ	Problematic Mobile Phone Use Questionnaire
PPI	Patient and Public Involvement
PSU	Problematic Smartphone Use
QMP	Questionable Measurement Practice
ROC	Receiver Operating Characteristic
SA	Smartphone Addiction
SABAS	Smartphone Application-Based Addiction Scale
SAPS	Smartphone Addiction Proneness Scale
SAS / SAS-SV	Smartphone Addiction Scale / - Short Version
SEM	Structural Equation Modelling
SPAI	Smartphone Addiction Inventory
UK	United Kingdom
US(A)	United States (of America)
WEIRD	White, Educated, Industrialized, Rich, and Democratic
WHO	World Health Organization

List of Figures

List of Tables

1

The Importance of Understanding Smartphone Addiction

Abstract Smartphones are one of the groundbreaking technological developments of the last 20 years and their introduction has led to rapid changes in the way we work, socialise, and behave. However, there has been significant concern about potential harms associated with smartphones, including the possibility of smartphone addiction. This introductory chapter is designed to provide context to the importance of understanding smartphone use within our society and its proposed addictive properties. We explore why smartphone addiction has been proposed as a public health matter, how it overlaps with other proposed behavioural addictions, and the ongoing parallel consideration of 'screen time'. This chapter further contextualises the current political and legislative climate around smartphone use, addiction, and the impact they may have on mental health.

Keywords Smartphone Addiction • Screen time • Technology • Policy • Context • Harm

R. James, L. Hitcham, *Critical Perspectives on Smartphone Addiction*, Palgrave Studies in Cyberpsychology, https://doi.org/10.1007/978-3-031-96188-5_1

Introduction

The proliferation of smartphones has been among the most significant technological developments of the early twenty-first century. Following the release of the iPhone in 2007, sales of smartphones rapidly increased and, since 2014, have stabilised at 1 to 1.5 billion devices sold per year (IDC, 2024). The distinguishing feature of the smartphone compared to earlier mobile phones is its increased computational sophistication, enabling numerous activities and services on a handheld device that can be taken with the user wherever they go. Smartphones have facilitated a larger share of the world's population to access the benefits of the internet, enabling opportunities for people to connect, learn, and share (Tsetsi & Rains, 2017). Consequently, the increased capabilities of smartphones have radically changed how we interact with ourselves, each other, and the world around us (Fortunati, 2023).

While many of these changes are undeniably for the better, most reflections on the impact of the smartphone express significant ambivalence (Harmon & Mazmanian, 2013). These dramatic changes have raised concerns about the negative effects of smartphone usage that may outweigh these positives. Over the last decade, a mounting body of research has examined whether smartphone use is harmful and how harms could occur. In some cases, these harms might be situational, where smartphones distract people while doing things that require attention, such as walking, driving, or holding a conversation ('phubbing') (Chotpitayasunondh & Douglas, 2016). Others may be physiological, with impacts on posture, eye strain, and hormones regulating sleep (Lee & Seo, 2014; Wang et al., 2020). There is also concern that phone use might displace other necessary and beneficial activities, such as sleep, social activity, or exercise (Demirci et al., 2015; Carter et al., 2016; Chu et al., 2023; Han et al., 2024). Many proposed harms have been psychological, linked with deleterious effects on mental health, well-being, and cognitive function, especially among children, adolescents, and young adults (Thomee, 2018; Twenge et al., 2018).

One of the most prominent concerns is the possibility that people can become addicted to their smartphones and develop a condition called 'smartphone addiction' (SA). This term suggests that people can engage with their smartphones in problematic ways, experiencing impaired control due to psychological dependence and feeling intense distress when parted from their phones, sometimes called 'nomophobia' (Yildirim & Correia, 2015; King et al., 2013). This dependence may result in negative consequences such as interference with everyday activities, conflicts with close contacts, and impaired behavioural control. Smartphone addiction is linked with multiple adverse psychosocial outcomes, including heightened levels of depression, anxiety, and distress (Hussain et al., 2017; Augner et al., 2023; Osorio-Molina et al., 2021). At present, smartphone addiction is not considered a psychiatric disorder. However, researchers have highlighted similarities with other behavioural addictions and the presence of addiction symptoms (e.g. Eichenberg et al., 2021; Sha et al., 2019). Therefore, some researchers have proposed that smartphone addiction could be added to future iterations of the Diagnostic and Statistical Manual of Mental Disorders (DSM) and the International Classification of Diseases (ICD). Potential diagnostic criteria (Lin et al., 2015) and measures based on DSM and ICD criteria have since been developed (e.g. Su et al., 2024). The proposed impacts are widespread, with current instruments identifying 25% to 33% of the population worldwide as potentially meeting the criteria for smartphone addiction (Meng et al., 2022). Recent meta-analyses of studies using these instruments have suggested that the prevalence and severity of smartphone addiction are increasing (Olson et al., 2022; Lu et al., 2024) but may vary based on factors such as sex, age and country (Olson et al., 2023).

However, many of the claims regarding the impact of smartphone use and smartphone addiction are deeply contested and controversial. Several converging lines of critique have highlighted problems at each stage of conceptualising, measuring, and researching smartphone addiction and its potential impact on broader society (e.g. Panova & Carbonell, 2018; Ellis et al., 2019; Shaw et al., 2020; Davidson et al., 2022). These critiques question whether (a) an addiction perspective is an appropriate way to approach smartphone use, (b) what smartphone addiction ought to be defined as, (c) how researchers should measure smartphone addiction, and consequently, (d) the conclusions we can draw about key findings (i.e., prevalence, treatment, risk factors, and outcomes) linked to smartphone addiction.

With these controversies in mind, the purpose of this book is to critically examine key conceptual and methodological issues in smartphone addiction. This first chapter explains the importance of understanding these issues in a wider societal context, providing a broad overview of the concerns about smartphone use, antecedents of the addiction approach in other technologies, and how these converge into pressure for policy change. The following four chapters tackle some of the most salient issues in the field: the conceptualisation of smartphone addiction, how smartphone addiction is measured, the research methodologies commonly applied in smartphone addiction research, and finally, how researchers, clinicians, and authors writing for the general public have proposed how we might treat smartphone addiction. In the concluding chapter, we reflect on possible solutions to overcome these challenges or use them to consider different ways to discuss our relationships with new technology.

Why Does Smartphone Addiction Matter?

This chapter focuses on the wider context surrounding smartphone addiction. It is necessary to consider why we should treat smartphone use and addiction as an important issue. We propose two reasons for doing so. First, it sheds light on how researchers, policymakers, and the public express concerns about technology. Understanding this process has important implications for our thinking about new and emerging technologies and how we should respond to them as a society, irrespective of whether there is compelling evidence that smartphone use should be considered an addictive behaviour. The second focuses on the implications of the introduction of a novel addictive disorder and what this would mean as a result.

Understanding Our Relationship with Technologies Through Smartphone Addiction

Concerns about the impacts of new technologies and whether people might become addicted to them are not new. Orben (2020) highlights how these concerns have recurred throughout history, with fears about addiction created by emerging entertainment media, including books and later comics, radio, and television. In doing so, Orben proposes a 'Sisyphean' cycle of moral panics around new technologies, illustrating a process where public concern about a new technological development drives pressure on policymakers, who then prioritise these issues. Politicians then frequently emphasise the need for research, thereby outsourcing this problem to academia. This need is picked up by researchers, either through increased funding opportunities, reputation/career incentives, or personal motivation, who then conduct studies on the subject. The body of research examining these impacts is typically inconclusive, often because of a lack of solid theory, methodological inconsistency, and limited research designs. By this point, the public discourse has moved on, either because concerns about the technology have receded due to public acceptance or because they have been replaced by the emergence of a new technology or 'threat', which begins the cycle anew. This shift can already be seen in how public discourse is moving onto concerns about Artificial Intelligence (AI), including generative and conversational AI or chatbots (Hu et al., 2023; Salah et al., 2024; Huang et al., 2024). Within this cycle, Orben notes that similar concerns (e.g. addiction, harm to health and society) recur with each new technology, along with the same flawed research programmes. Consequently, this process generates limited insights that cannot translate into actions that address public concerns or allow policymakers to monitor and assess the risks posed by emerging technologies.

Thinking about technological addictions in this 'Sisyphean' cycle is informative for understanding concerns about smartphone addiction. The last 45 years have seen the growth of new technologies facilitated by the Internet and personal computers. This has included activities such as computer gaming, social media, and video streaming. At various junctures, researchers have proposed that all these activities could become addictive and have examined them through the lens of establishing symptoms of behavioural addiction (e.g. Sun & Zhang, 2021; Billieux et al., 2021; Zhang et al., 2019). There is a significant overlap between the proposed symptoms of many of these candidate addictions. Indeed, the features of a new addiction are often translated from earlier examples (i.e. gambling disorder and internet addiction). Assessments of new candidate behavioural addictions commonly adapt questionnaire items from older ones, with wording changes to accommodate the new behaviour (see Chap. 3). The practice of adapting and reusing criteria and assessment items exemplifies how this cycle perpetuates. Smartphone use continues in this tradition; many of the concepts and assessments of addiction are drawn from other technologies. Like internet addiction, smartphone addiction is proposed as a broad category that includes many activities that have been part of this cycle as well.

In parallel, other developments have made thinking about these new technologies easier through an addiction lens. There has been a marked change in consensus with how psychiatrists and medical professionals conceptualise addiction, which led to gambling becoming categorised as the first behavioural addiction in 2013. Behavioural addictions are not a new concept themselves, with traditions of considering exercise (De Coverley Veale, 1987; Berczik et al., 2012), sex (Irvine, 1995; Gold & Heffner, 1998; Carnes, 2001), and food (Gearhardt et al., 2009, 2023) as potential addictions going back to the 1970s and beyond (Morgan, 1979; Orford, 2001). However, they have only been considered seriously as a broader category in the last ten to twenty years, spearheaded by the case of gambling disorder.

The observation that some people experience debilitating gambling-related harms predates modern conceptualisations of addiction by centuries (Reith, 2002). Nonetheless, while addictions to alcohol and substance use became psychiatric disorders during the 20th century, it took longer for a consensus to emerge on gambling. Pathological Gambling was classified as an impulse control disorder in the DSM-III (APA, 1980), primarily focused on the consequences of gambling (Rosenthal, 2020). These criteria were then amended in the 1987 revision using criteria from substance use disorders (Lesieur, 1988). In 2013, it was reclassified as the sole behavioural addiction disorder in the DSM-5 (APA, 2013). This shift, in turn, has led to serious consideration of other behaviours, specifically gaming, culminating in the codification of Gaming Disorder in the ICD-11 (WHO, 2024).

These developments have accelerated the cycle of public concern about technology. The speed at which new technologies have emerged has meant that this process is rarely complete before more addictions are thrown into the mix and similar concerns arise. This acceleration has happened with the internet, smartphones, several forms of social media (i.e. Facebook, WhatsApp, WeChat, TikTok), and, most recently, large language models (e.g. Hu et al., 2023; Yu et al., 2024). There are now parallel sub-disciplines on each of these topics. The emergence of behavioural addiction disorders such as gambling and gaming has given researchers a framework to study technology effects by drawing comparisons from these behaviours. This blueprint produces research that appears to demonstrate credible harms, without necessarily doing so conclusively or rigorously, in a confirmatory framework. Finally, the practice of translating symptoms from existing models not only perpetuates this cycle but also enables researchers to anticipate policy needs by applying these to new technologies at the first stage of the process. Thus, instead of being conducted to respond to public needs, this research increasingly contributes to generating initial public concern.

Nonetheless, there are limits to this analysis. The case of gambling is again informative here.

The cycle explores the interplay between three sets of actors: the public, policymakers, and academic/clinical researchers. A notable absence is the role of the industries harnessing these technologies. Because these technologies have significant potential to generate revenue, the sectors that benefit from this technology are often stakeholders in this process, who act to collaborate with academics and influence policy. The economic potential of these industries frequently creates tensions between policymakers, for example, balancing opportunities for economic growth against public health concerns. Tech industries also have greater direct control over the way online media reaches the public than older forms of entertainment. Although treated as relatively neutral, it has not been uncommon in popular media for people affiliated with tech industries to draw comparisons between these products and gambling. Often, this relies heavily on concepts that focus on randomised reinforcement and preoccupation. With new technologies, the role of industry is critical as they hold and control data that can directly examine many of the questions posed by policymakers and researchers (Livingstone et al., 2023). Indeed, many companies have collaborated with behavioural scientists for this purpose (Guess et al., 2023a, 2023b; Gonzalez-Bailon et al., 2023; Nyhan et al., 2023). However, it is also an area where there is little consensus or movement towards developing guidelines that enable high-quality science to proliferate (Livingstone et al., 2023). A lack of guidance on appropriate practices could become deleterious, for example, if public and political sentiment towards the tech industry changes and these interactions become adversarial.

The role of industry is also essential because industries can lobby, shape discourse, and, in extreme cases, prevent legitimate concerns from being addressed. In the case of gambling, as with alcohol and tobacco in the past, concerted actions from these industries have successfully influenced both the outsourcing of policy problems to scientific research and the research process itself (Cassidy et al., 2013). The main concern raised with this perspective is that it situates addiction as the focus of policy intervention and an absence of consideration concerning other harms (Langham et al., 2016). The responsible gambling approach promotes the central importance of individual responsibility and individual differences in adverse outcomes. Thus, harms are framed in terms of a failure of self-control and severe addiction problems attributed to personal factors that are independent of the product being promoted.

Smartphone Addiction as a Clinical Disorder

The claim that people can become addicted to these technologies has broad implications. The most obvious is that this claim assumes that the technologies themselves are addictive, as opposed to specific patterns or motivations of use that are maladaptive. Harmful or unhealthy behaviours are not simply the result of bad habits and poor decision-making (i.e. how they are used) but are determined by the device or the content accessed through the device. As the object of addiction, smartphones would take some responsibility for the harms that emerge from dependent usage. It means that something about smartphones, whether intrinsic to the device itself or the content that characterises smartphone use, impinges on people's ability to control their interactions with them. These impairments create a rationale for intervention or regulation on devices to prevent or limit practices associated with the greatest harm. This claim positions the smartphone as the focus of the addiction, and promotes actions that intervene broadly on phone use rather than specific harmful behaviours.

The second implication is that if there is a smartphone addiction disorder, there are likely to be people more vulnerable to developing smartphone addiction. Addiction disorders are characterised by a transition from impulsive to compulsive use of a behaviour (Everitt et al., 2008). Certain groups, especially those with greater tendencies towards impulsivity, neuroticism and negative affect, are often at greater risk (Settles et al., 2012). Consequently, this emphasises a need to intervene early or in specific groups, such as children and young people, to prevent the most severe harms from emerging. Interventions or measures to limit access to addictive products are a central component of public health strategies to mitigate the harms of alcohol, smoking, illicit substances, and, increasingly, gambling (Clune et al., 2024). This strategy of limiting access is now extending to smartphones with the proposed 'bans' for young people in schools despite limited evidence of efficacy (Campbell et al., 2024; King et al., 2024).

The third is that the codification of a psychiatric disorder implies that people will require intervention to remediate these difficulties, and this necessitates the provision of treatment. The form of treatment may vary, but may consist of psychotherapy, medication, or behavioural interventions designed to change the person's interaction with the addictive behaviour. It may also begin to tackle other issues that exacerbate or motivate the use of an addictive substance or behaviour to create the conditions for recovery. The ubiquity of smartphones, as with other online technologies, raises issues around the focus and goal of treatment. For gambling, alcohol, and substance use disorders, the goal of treatment is to promote recovery with abstinence as the desired outcome. This goal might be harder for certain candidate addictions, such as smartphone or internet addiction, because it is becoming impossible not to engage with them for many everyday activities. These issues are explored in Chap. 5.

Both of these perspectives highlight the importance of exploring the issue of smartphone addiction. Seriously considering the possibility that smartphone addiction could become a psychiatric disorder highlights several implications for the public and policymakers, especially when thinking about intervention and prevention. Irrespective of scepticism about this construct, looking at smartphone addiction through the lens of a cycle of concerns about technology demonstrates there is value in critically exploring these issues because it illuminates the processes we use when adapting to new technologies. These ideas can also be translated into how we think about smartphones more generally, and the concept of 'screen time'.

Smartphone Use and 'Screen Time'

Much of the concern around smartphones has been reflected in prominent debates on screen time. 'Screen time' commonly refers to the amount of time spent on a screen-based device, and many of the concerns about screen time are synonymous with smartphone addiction. Higher levels of screen time have been linked with similar adverse mental health outcomes to smartphone addiction, such as depression, anxiety, poor sleep, and attention deficits (Boers et al., 2019; Santos et al., 2023; Sohn et al., 2019). Both are linked with poorer psychosocial well-being, including greater sedentary behaviour and loneliness (Wang et al., 2019). Despite being acknowledged as problematic (Oswald et al., 2020; Schmidt et al., 2020), screen time is often synonymous with sedentary activity. One feature that distinguishes screen time from smartphone addiction is the intensive focus on the effects of screen time on young children across multiple devices (Byrne et al., 2021; McArthur et al., 2022). This focus has manifested into concerns about screen time impairing the development of executive function, impulse control, and other cognitive and psychological capacities (Manwell et al., 2022; Neophytou et al., 2021). In contrast, smartphone addiction tends to focus on adolescents and young adults (James et al., 2023; Yu & Sussman, 2020; Domoff et al., 2025).

However, there is fundamental disagreement between scholars on the conclusions that can be drawn from this research and its implications for policymakers and broader society. At one extreme, it has been proposed that smartphones are the primary cause driving a cohort effect of mental health problems among adolescents and young adults that has been described as an epidemic (Twenge et al., 2018; Haidt, 2024). The evidence proposed for this is heterogeneous, including evidence from national mental health statistics, neuroimaging, and observational studies (e.g. Twenge, 2017; Hutton et al., 2020). However, the core claim here is that while other technologies (e.g. gaming consoles, TVs) may have associated harms, the specific combination of unique features makes smartphones qualitatively distinct from other forms of behaviour. On the other hand, researchers have highlighted critical issues with the methodology and interpretation of findings from many screen time studies (Kaye et al., 2020). Beyond the most basic features, there is little consensus on what defines screen time and its operationalisation in research. At its broadest, screen time may encompass smartphones, tablets, computers, TV, video games, e-readers (e.g. Kindle), and other forms of screen-based technology. Distinctions may also not be made around ownership, such as whether the device is owned by a parent or the child, how such screens are accessed (e.g. at school, at home) and whether factors related to digital poverty are considered. There is also debate on what kind of activities are of interest. For instance, devices can become the focus of attention or instead be used passively in the background, for example, to listen to the radio, podcasts, or music. There is little consensus on whether passive and active use should be considered equivalent or on the relationship between passive use and engagement in other activities, especially if it is with another device. Other studies exclude certain forms of screen time, such as exercise games. When used in research, substantial variation exists in how screen time is elicited. Most research uses self-reported data (i.e. people estimating how long they spend on their phone or certain apps). Within that, screen time has been operationalised by asking multiple questions for different devices, a single-item question about several activities, which vary in their coverage, or a question about time spent on a single device or platform. It has been argued that the problems with the research in this field are so severe that it renders it impossible to draw substantiative, evidence-based conclusions that can lead to meaningful policy recommendations (Kaye et al., 2020; James & Hitcham, 2023). At the same time, both camps agree on the need for a more nuanced approach, with attention to specific activities, motivations, or patterns of use that may or may not be harmful.

Many of the debates and issues are similar between these concepts, and the two are correlated (Olson et al., 2022; Hitcham et al., 2023). However, the exact relationship between screen time and smartphone addiction is unclear. It is plausible that screen time might lead to smartphone addiction via exposure to addictive content. For example, excessive exposure to screen use has been linked to increases in impulsivity (due to executive dysfunction) that become a risk factor for addictive behaviour (Lissak, 2018; Marciano et al., 2021). Conversely, links between screen time and mental health difficulties could be mediated by smartphone addiction (Hitcham et al., 2023; Elhai & Contractor, 2018). Rather than a population-wide effect, distress is instead disproportionately located in a subset of the population experiencing dependence-related problems. For example, one account of problematic use has focused on motivations such as coping. If this explanation is correct, the relationship between screen time and mental health should be absent when smartphone addiction is accounted for. Other possible explanations include reverse causation or confounding. Psychological distress may exert causal effects on levels of screen use and perceived smartphone addiction. Alternatively, these might be manifestations of the same construct. The lack of conceptual clarity, as explored with screen time, might mean that these are capturing the same phenomenon. These issues are discussed further in Chap. 4.

Public Policy and Intervention

Concerns about the impact of smartphones have motivated pressure for policymakers to act (James & Hitcham, 2025). Several types of intervention have been proposed. For instance, the UK Government has considered a phone ban for children (under 13) in schools (see Chap. 5), while other proposals have included banning purchases of smartphones for those under 16 years old. Other ideas include limits on screen time, restricting access to social media platforms behind photographic ID verification, and increased content controls for children and adolescents. For adults, the 'right to disconnect' debate has implications for work-based smartphone use outside of contracted hours (e.g. Domoff et al., 2025). Internationally, countries have proposed time limits on smartphone use (e.g. China), requiring parental monitoring software to be installed on children's phones (e.g. South Korea), or banning young people from social media platforms altogether (e.g. Conroy, 2024). This has led to a recently implemented ban on social media for children in Australia. Concerns from a mixture of parents, educators, and pressure groups, alongside research on smartphone addiction, screen time and several popular books (Haidt, 2024), have created the conditions for policy change, with a focus on young adults at this time. However, such public policy and intervention efforts often exclude the views of children and young people despite them having the right to be consulted on matters that affect them and have their views be heard and taken seriously (United Nations Convention on the Rights of the Child, 1989).

How does smartphone addiction contribute to this? In isolation, concerns about the addictive potential of smartphones are unlikely to lead to significant policy change. Even if smartphone addiction were to be recognised by psychiatrists as a disorder, the impact is likely to be circumstantial or secondary. An accumulation of examples from other addictive disorders demonstrates that recognition of a substance or behaviour's addictive propensity has limited direct influence on policymaking. Instead, most policy change with addictive disorders is driven by evidence of harm. Harm is often conflated with addiction because the most severe harms tend to occur at the highest levels of addiction severity. However, it is also distinguishable from addiction because the distribution of harms is greater than simply those at risk of dependence (Browne et al., 2020), and harm is not isolated to the individual but extends to their network of contexts and society at large (Wardle et al., 2019).

The most relevant evidence comes from gambling and gaming, which were classified as addictive disorders in 2013 and 2019, respectively. In gambling, Ukhova et al. (2024) critically analysed the framing of 25 recent pieces of international gambling legislation, with gambling harms featured in nearly every bill. The framing of gambling harms was narrow, though, focusing on individual harms and addiction, with few exceptions. This framing could be interpreted as evidence of the value of diagnostic recognition. However, most of the legislation reviewed was concerned with reducing barriers to gambling; 23 of the 25 acts focused on liberalising gambling regulation. The overarching purpose of legislation in this period was to legalise online gambling. Given the policy aims, the focus on addiction is as much aimed at mitigating new harms due to policy change as addressing existing problems. Long et al. (2022)

compared international responses to the adoption of Gaming Disorder in the ICD-11. Their analysis highlighted areas of progress but otherwise evidenced limited policy change in the immediate aftermath of this recognition, hampered by a lack of capacity. One benefit noted by Hofmarcher et al. (2020) was that classifying gambling as an addictive disorder raised awareness and began to change attitudes in healthcare policymakers. Indirect mechanisms, such as attention from public health bodies, are more plausible drivers of change.

Public health policy for most addictive behaviours focuses on a mixture of primary population-level intervention (e.g. product, content and advertising restrictions), secondary preventative targeting of at-risk groups (e.g. brief interventions), and tertiary prevention in the form of treatment provision for those experiencing addiction disorders (e.g. Clune et al., 2024; Martineau et al., 2013). In some cases, the policy focus is balanced more towards one side than the other. For instance, one of the critiques of responsible gambling policies has been that they frequently place minimal emphasis on population-wide intervention and instead focus attention on a pathological minority, with most resources going towards clinical treatment, and information and awareness campaigns (Wardle et al., 2019). Instead, most primary and public health policies are motivated by the need to react to compelling evidence of harm. Increasing awareness of this with gambling has been a major motivating factor towards change in some jurisdictions. Positive evidence that smartphones facilitate harm is a more salient motivator for change. The current evidence suggests lawmakers are already considering these risks, though, and a change in diagnostic status may only lead to incremental impact.

Conclusion

The rapid spread of smartphones has led to concern about potential negative impacts, including smartphone addiction. However, these concerns have been subject to considerable scrutiny. This chapter focuses on the need to critically analyse both concepts of smartphone addiction and how they are employed in research. As a proposed psychiatric disorder, the implications of treating smartphone use as an addiction are substantial on their own. Separate from this debate, the narrative and framing of smartphone addiction is a useful medium for understanding our relationship with technology and its general effects on society. The issues around smartphone addiction feed into a broader set of debates around screen time and its proposed impacts. The final section of the chapter explored the policy implications concerning smartphone use and harm. Several regulations have been proposed to restrict smartphone use and ownership, especially among children and adolescents. However, the contribution of smartphone addiction here is mixed. Although its addictive potential is used as a piece of evidence to support these regulations, examples from addiction disorders suggest that the impact of smartphone addiction is likely to be limited.

References

American Psychiatric Association. (1980). *Diagnostic and statistical manual of mental disorders* (3rd ed.). American Psychiatric Association.

American Psychiatric Association. (1987). *Diagnostic and statistical manual of mental disorders* (3rd ed., Revised). American Psychiatric Association.

American Psychiatric Association. (2013). *Diagnostic and statistical manual of mental disorders, (DSM-5®).* American Psychiatric Publishing.

Augner, C., Vlasak, T., Aichhorn, W., & Barth, A. (2023). The association between problematic smartphone use and symptoms of anxiety and depression—A meta-analysis. *Journal of Public Health, 45*(1), 193–201. https://doi.org/10.1093/pubmed/fdab350

Berczik, K., Szabó, A., Griffiths, M. D., Kurimay, T., Kun, B., Urbán, R., & Demetrovics, Z. (2012). Exercise addiction: Symptoms, diagnosis, epidemiology, and etiology. *Substance Use & Misuse, 47*(4), 403–417. https://doi.org/10.3109/10826084.2011.639120

Billieux, J., Stein, D. J., Castro-Calvo, J., Higushi, S., & King, D. L. (2021). Rationale for and usefulness of the inclusion of gaming disorder in the ICD-11. *World Psychiatry, 20*(2), 198–199. https://doi.org/10.1002/wps.20848

Boers, E., Afzali, M. H., Newton, N., & Conrod, P. (2019). Association of screen time and depression in adolescence. *JAMA Pediatrics, 173*(9), 853–859. https://doi.org/10.1001/jamapediatrics.2019.1759

Browne, M., Volberg, R., Rockloff, M., & Salonen, A. H. (2020). The prevention paradox applies to some but not all gambling harms: Results from a Finnish population-representative survey. *Journal of Behavioral Addictions, 9*(2), 371–382. https://doi.org/10.1556/2006.2020.00018

Byrne, R., Terranova, C. O., & Trost, S. G. (2021). Measurement of screen time among young children aged 0–6 years: A systematic review. *Obesity Reviews, 22*(8), e13260. https://doi.org/10.1111/obr.13260

Campbell, M., Edwards, E. J., Pennell, D., Poed, S., Lister, V., Gillett-Swan, J., Kelly, A., Zec, D., & Nguyen, T.-A. (2024). Evidence for and against banning mobile phones in schools: A scoping review. *Journal of Psychologists and Counsellors in Schools, 34*(3), 242–265. https://doi.org/10.1177/20556365241270394

Carnes, P. (2001). *Out of the shadows: Understanding sexual addiction* (3rd ed.). Hazelden Foundation.

Carter, B., Rees, P., Hale, L., Bhattacharjee, D., & Paradkar, M. S. (2016). Association between portable screen-based media device access or use and sleep outcomes: A systematic review and meta-analysis. *JAMA Pediatrics, 170*(12), 1202–1208. https://doi.org/10.1001/jamapediatrics.2016.2341

Cassidy, R., Loussouarn, C., & Pisac, A. (2013). *Fair game: Producing gambling research*. European Research Council.

Chotpitayasunondh, V., & Douglas, K. M. (2016). How "phubbing" becomes the norm: The antecedents and consequences of snubbing via smartphone. *Computers in Human Behavior, 63*, 9–18. https://doi.org/10.1016/j.chb.2016.05.018

Chu, Y., Oh, Y., Gwon, M., Hwang, S., Jeong, H., Kim, H.-W., Kim, K., & Kim, Y. H. (2023). Dose-response analysis of smartphone usage and self-reported sleep quality: A systematic review and meta-analysis of observational studies. *Journal of Clinical Sleep Medicine, 19*(3), 621–630. https://doi.org/10.5664/jcsm.10392

Clune, S., Ratnaike, D., White, V., Donaldson, A., Randle, E., O'Halloran, P., & Lewis, V. (2024). What is known about population level programs designed to address gambling-related harm: Rapid review of the evidence. *Harm Reduction Journal, 21*(1), 118. https://doi.org/10.1186/s12954-024-01032-8

Conroy, G. (2024). Governments are banning kids from social media: Will that protect them from harm? *Nature*. https://www.nature.com/articles/d41586-024-03955-5

Davidson, B. I., Shaw, H., & Ellis, D. A. (2022). Fuzzy constructs in technology usage scales. *Computers in Human Behavior*, 107206. https://doi.org/10.1016/j.chb.2022.107206

De Coverley Veale, D. M. W. (1987). Exercise Dependence. *British Journal of Addiction, 82*(7), 735–740. https://doi.org/10.1111/j.1360-0443.1987.tb01539.x

Demirci, K., Akgönül, M., & Akpinar, A. (2015). Relationship of smartphone use severity with sleep quality, depression, and anxiety in university students. *Journal of Behavioral Addictions, 4*(2), 85–92. https://doi.org/10.1556/2006.4.2015.010

Domoff, S. E., Elhai, J. D., Long, J., Lopez-Fernandez, O., Montag, C., Starcevic, V., Szabo, A., Vanden Abeele, M. M. P., Demetrovics, Z., & Billieux, J. (2025). Dysregulated use of Mobile/smartphone. In D. A. Christakis & L. Hale (Eds.), *Handbook of children and screens: Digital media, development, and well-being from birth through adolescence*. Springer.

Eichenberg, C., Schott, M., & Schroiff, A. (2021). Problematic smartphone use—Comparison of students with and without problematic smartphone use in light of personality. *Frontiers in Psychiatry, 11*, 599241. https://doi.org/10.3389/fpsyt.2020.599241

Elhai, J. D., & Contractor, A. A. (2018). Examining latent classes of smartphone users: Relations with psychopathology and problematic smartphone use. *Computers in Human Behavior, 82*, 159–166. https://doi.org/10.1016/j.chb.2018.01.010

Ellis, D. A., Davidson, B. I., Shaw, H., & Geyer, K. (2019). Do smartphone usage scales predict behavior? *International Journal of Human-Computer Studies, 130*, 86–92. https://doi.org/10.1016/j.ijhcs.2019.05.004

Everitt, B. J., Belin, D., Economidou, D., Pelloux, Y., Dalley, J. W., & Robbins, T. W. (2008). Neural mechanisms underlying the vulnerability to develop compulsive drug-seeking habits and addiction. *Philosophical Transactions of the Royal Society B: Biological Sciences, 363*(1507), 3125–3135. https://doi.org/10.1098/rstb.2008.0089

Fortunati, L. (2023). The smartphone between the present and the future: Five changes. *Mobile Media & Communication, 11*(1), 19–24. https://doi.org/10.1177/20501579221131223

Gearhardt, A. N., Bueno, N. B., DiFeliceantonio, A. G., Roberto, C. A., Jiménez-Murcia, S., & Fernandez-Aranda, F. (2023). Social, clinical, and policy implications of ultra-processed food addiction. *BMJ, 383*, e075354. https://doi.org/10.1136/bmj-2023-075354

Gearhardt, A. N., Corbin, W. R., & Brownell, K. D. (2009). Food addiction: An examination of the diagnostic criteria for dependence. *Journal of Addiction Medicine, 3*(1) https://journals.lww.com/journaladdictionmedicine/fulltext/2009/03000/food_addiction__an_examination_of_the_diagnostic.1.aspx

Gold, S. N., & Heffner, C. L. (1998). Sexual addiction: Many conceptions, minimal data. *Clinical Psychology Review, 18*(3), 367–381. https://doi.org/10.1016/S0272-7358(97)00051-2

González-Bailón, S., Lazer, D., Barberá, P., Zhang, M., Allcott, H., Brown, T., Crespo-Tenorio, A., Freelon, D., Gentzkow, M., Guess, A. M., Iyengar, S., Kim, Y. M., Malhotra, N., Moehler, D., Nyhan, B., Pan, J., Rivera, C. V., Settle, J., Thorson, E., et al. (2023). Asymmetric ideological segregation in exposure to political news on Facebook. *Science, 381*(6656), 392–398. https://doi.org/10.1126/science.ade7138

Guess, A. M., Malhotra, N., Pan, J., Barberá, P., Allcott, H., Brown, T., Crespo-Tenorio, A., Dimmery, D., Freelon, D., Gentzkow, M., González-Bailón, S., Kennedy, E., Kim, Y. M., Lazer, D., Moehler, D., Nyhan, B., Rivera, C. V., Settle, J., Thomas, D. R., et al. (2023a). How do social media feed algorithms affect attitudes and behavior in an election campaign? *Science, 381*(6656), 398–404. https://doi.org/10.1126/science.abp9364

Guess, A. M., Malhotra, N., Pan, J., Barberá, P., Allcott, H., Brown, T., Crespo-Tenorio, A., Dimmery, D., Freelon, D., Gentzkow, M., González-Bailón, S., Kennedy, E., Kim, Y. M., Lazer, D., Moehler, D., Nyhan, B., Rivera, C. V., Settle, J., Thomas, D. R., et al. (2023b). Reshares on social media amplify political news but do not detectably affect beliefs or opinions. *Science, 381*(6656), 404–408. https://doi.org/10.1126/science.add8424

Haidt, J. (2024). *The anxious generation: How the great rewiring of childhood is causing an epidemic of mental illness*. Random House.

Han, X., Zhou, E., & Liu, D. (2024). Electronic media use and sleep quality: Updated systematic review and meta-analysis. *Journal of Medical Internet Research, 26*, e48356. https://doi.org/10.2196/48356

Harmon, E., & Mazmanian, M. (2013). Stories of the Smartphone in everyday discourse: Conflict, tension & instability. In *Proceedings of the SIGCHI con-*

ference on Human Factors in Computing Systems. https://doi.org/10.1145/2470654.2466134.

Hitcham, L., Jackson, H., & James, R. J. E. (2023). The relationship between smartphone use and smartphone addiction: An examination of logged and self-reported behavior in a pre-registered, two-wave sample. *Computers in Human Behavior*, 107822. https://doi.org/10.1016/j.chb.2023.107822

Hofmarcher, T., Romild, U., Spångberg, J., Persson, U., & Håkansson, A. (2020). The societal costs of problem gambling in Sweden. *BMC Public Health, 20*(1), 1921. https://doi.org/10.1186/s12889-020-10008-9

Hu, B., Mao, Y., & Kim, K. J. (2023). How social anxiety leads to problematic use of conversational AI: The roles of loneliness, rumination, and mind perception. *Computers in Human Behavior, 145*, 107760. https://doi.org/10.1016/j.chb.2023.107760

Huang, S., Lai, X., Ke, L., Li, Y., Wang, H., Zhao, X., Dai, X., & Wang, Y. (2024). AI technology panic—Is AI dependence bad for mental health? A cross-lagged panel model and the mediating roles of motivations for AI use among adolescents. *Psychology Research and Behavior Management, 17*, 1087–1102. https://doi.org/10.2147/PRBM.S440889

Hussain, Z., Griffiths, M. D., & Sheffield, D. (2017). An investigation into problematic smartphone use: The role of narcissism, anxiety, and personality factors. *Journal of Behavioral Addictions, 6*(3), 378–386. https://doi.org/10.1556/2006.6.2017.052

Hutton, J. S., Dudley, J., Horowitz-Kraus, T., DeWitt, T., & Holland, S. K. (2020). Associations between screen-based media use and brain white matter integrity in preschool-aged children. *JAMA Pediatrics, 174*(1), e193869–e193869. https://doi.org/10.1001/jamapediatrics.2019.3869

IDC. (2024). *Worldwide smartphone market forecast to grow 6.2% in 2024, fueled by robust growth for android in emerging markets and China, according to IDC*. Retrieved December 24, 2024, from https://www.idc.com/getdoc.jsp?containerId=prUS52757624#:~:text=NEEDHAM%2C%20Mass.%2C%20November%2026,Worldwide%20Quarterly%20Mobile%20Phone%20Tracker

Irvine, J. M. (1995). Reinventing perversion: Sex addiction and cultural anxieties. *Journal of the History of Sexuality, 5*(3), 429–450. http://www.jstor.org/stable/4617181

James, R. J. E., Dixon, G., Dragomir, M.-G., Thirlwell, E., & Hitcham, L. (2023). Understanding the construction of 'behavior' in smartphone addiction: A scoping review. *Addictive Behaviors*, 107503. https://doi.org/10.1016/j.addbeh.2022.107503

James, R. J. E., & Hitcham, L. (2023). *DESC evidence call response on screen time*. Retrieved December 29, 2024, from https://osf.io/3tmub

James, R. J. E., & Hitcham, L. (2025). Commentary on Sun & Tang: Measurement assessment and validity in problematic smartphone use. *Addiction*, in press. https://doi.org/10.1111/add.16764.

Kaye, L. K., Orben, A., Ellis, D. A., Hunter, S. C., & Houghton, S. (2020). The conceptual and methodological mayhem of "screen time". *International Journal of Environmental Research and Public Health, 17*(10), 3661. https://doi.org/10.3390/ijerph17103661

King, A. L. S., Valenca, A.-M., Silva, A.-C. O., Baczynski, T., Carvalho, M. R., & Nardi, A. E. (2013). Nomophobia: Dependency on virtual environments or social phobia? *Computers in Human Behavior, 29*(1), 140–144. https://doi.org/10.1016/j.chb.2012.07.025

King, D. L., Radunz, M., Galanis, C. R., Quinney, B., & Wade, T. (2024). "Phones off while school's on": Evaluating problematic phone use and the social, wellbeing, and academic effects of banning phones in schools. *Journal of Behavioral Addictions*. https://doi.org/10.1556/2006.2024.00058

Langham, E., Thorne, H., Browne, M., Donaldson, P., Rose, J., & Rockloff, M. (2016). Understanding gambling related harm: A proposed definition, conceptual framework, and taxonomy of harms. *BMC Public Health, 16*(1), 80. https://doi.org/10.1186/s12889-016-2747-0

Lee, J. H., & Seo, K. C. (2014). The comparison of cervical repositioning errors according to smartphone addiction grades. *Journal of Physical Therapy Science, 26*(4), 595–598. https://doi.org/10.1589/jpts.26.595

Lesieur, H. R. (1988). Altering the DSM-III criteria for pathological gambling. *Journal of Gambling Behavior, 4*(1), 38–47. https://doi.org/10.1007/BF01043527

Lin, Y.-H., Lin, Y.-C., Lee, Y.-H., Lin, P.-H., Lin, S.-H., Chang, L.-R., Tseng, H.-W., Yen, L.-Y., Yang, C. C., & Kuo, T. B. (2015). Time distortion associated with smartphone addiction: Identifying smartphone addiction via a mobile application (app). *Journal of Psychiatric Research, 65*, 139–145. https://doi.org/10.1016/j.jpsychires.2015.04.003

Lissak, G. (2018). Adverse physiological and psychological effects of screen time on children and adolescents: Literature review and case study. *Environmental Research, 164*, 149–157. https://doi.org/10.1016/j.envres.2018.01.015

Livingstone, S., Orben, A., & Odgers, C. (2023). Debate: Should academics collaborate with digital companies to improve young people's mental health? *Child and Adolescent Mental Health, 28*(1), 150–152. https://doi.org/10.1111/camh.12630

Long, J., Bhad, R., Potenza, M. N., Orsolini, L., Phan, V., Kanabar, M., & Achab, S. (2022). Public health approaches and policy changes after the inclusion of gaming disorder in ICD-11: Global needs. *BJPsych International, 19*(3), 63–66. https://doi.org/10.1192/bji.2021.57

Lu, X., An, X., & Chen, S. (2024). Trends and influencing factors in problematic smartphone use prevalence (2012–2022): A systematic review and meta-analysis. *Cyberpsychology, Behavior, and Social Networking, 27*(9), 616–634. https://doi.org/10.1089/cyber.2023.0548

Manwell, L. A., Tadros, M., Ciccarelli, T. M., & Eikelboom, R. (2022). Digital dementia in the internet generation: Excessive screen time during brain development will increase the risk of Alzheimer's disease and related dementias in adulthood. *JIN, 21*(1), 10.31083/j.jin2101028.

Marciano, L., Camerini, A.-L., & Morese, R. (2021). The developing brain in the digital era: A scoping review of structural and functional correlates of screen time in adolescence. *Frontiers in Psychology, 12*, 671817. https://doi.org/10.3389/fpsyg.2021.671817

Martineau, F., Tyner, E., Lorenc, T., Petticrew, M., & Lock, K. (2013). Population-level interventions to reduce alcohol-related harm: An overview of systematic reviews. *Preventive Medicine, 57*(4), 278–296. https://doi.org/10.1016/j.ypmed.2013.06.019

McArthur, B. A., Volkova, V., Tomopoulos, S., & Madigan, S. (2022). Global prevalence of meeting screen time guidelines among children 5 years and younger: A systematic review and meta-analysis. *JAMA Pediatrics, 176*(4), 373–383. https://doi.org/10.1001/jamapediatrics.2021.6386

Meng, S.-Q., Cheng, J.-L., Li, Y.-Y., Yang, X.-Q., Zheng, J.-W., Chang, X.-W., Shi, Y., Chen, Y., Lu, L., Sun, Y., Bao, Y.-P., & Shi, J. (2022). Global prevalence of digital addiction in general population: A systematic review and meta-analysis. *Clinical Psychology Review, 92*, 102128. https://doi.org/10.1016/j.cpr.2022.102128

Morgan, W. P. (1979). Negative addiction in runners. *The Physician and Sportsmedicine, 7*(2), 55–77. https://doi.org/10.1080/00913847.1979.11948436

Neophytou, E., Manwell, L. A., & Eikelboom, R. (2021). Effects of excessive screen time on neurodevelopment, learning, memory, mental health, and neurodegeneration: A scoping review. *International Journal of Mental Health and Addiction, 19*(3), 724–744. https://doi.org/10.1007/s11469-019-00182-2

Nyhan, B., Settle, J., Thorson, E., Wojcieszak, M., Barberá, P., Chen, A. Y., Allcott, H., Brown, T., Crespo-Tenorio, A., Dimmery, D., Freelon, D., Gentzkow, M., González-Bailón, S., Guess, A. M., Kennedy, E., Kim, Y. M., Lazer, D., Malhotra, N., Moehler, D., et al. (2023). Like-minded sources on Facebook are prevalent but not polarizing. *Nature, 620*(7972), 137–144. https://doi.org/10.1038/s41586-023-06297-w

Olson, J. A., Sandra, D. A., Colucci, É. S., Al Bikaii, A., Chmoulevitch, D., Nahas, J., Raz, A., & Veissière, S. P. L. (2022). Smartphone addiction is increasing across the world: A meta-analysis of 24 countries. *Computers in Human Behavior, 129*, 107138. https://doi.org/10.1016/j.chb.2021.107138

Olson, J. A., Sandra, D. A., Veissière, S. P., & Langer, E. J. (2023). Sex, age, and smartphone addiction across 41 countries. *International Journal of Mental Health and Addiction*, 1–9. https://doi.org/10.1007/s11469-023-01146-3

Orben, A. (2020). The Sisyphean cycle of technology panics. *Perspectives on Psychological Science, 15*(5), 1143–1157. https://doi.org/10.1177/1745691620919372

Orford, J. (2001). *Excessive appetites: A psychological view of addictions.* Wiley & Sons.

Osorio-Molina, C., Martos-Cabrera, M. B., Membrive-Jiménez, M. J., Vargas-Roman, K., Suleiman-Martos, N., Ortega-Campos, E., & Gómez-Urquiza, J. L. (2021). Smartphone addiction, risk factors and its adverse effects in nursing students: A systematic review and meta-analysis. *Nurse Education Today, 98*, 104741. https://doi.org/10.1016/j.nedt.2020.104741

Oswald, T. K., Rumbold, A. R., Kedzior, S. G. E., & Moore, V. M. (2020). Psychological impacts of "screen time" and "green time" for children and adolescents: A systematic scoping review. *PLoS One, 15*(9), e0237725. https://doi.org/10.1371/journal.pone.0237725

Panova, T., & Carbonell, X. (2018). Is smartphone addiction really an addiction? *Journal of Behavioral Addictions, 7*(2), 252–259. https://doi.org/10.1556/2006.7.2018.49

Reith, G. (2002). *The age of chance: Gambling in Western culture.* Psychology Press.

Rosenthal, R. J. (2020). Inclusion of pathological gambling in DSM-III, its classification as a disorder of impulse control, and the role of Robert Custer. *International Gambling Studies, 20*(1), 151–170. https://doi.org/10.1080/14459795.2019.1638432

Salah, M., Abdelfattah, F., Alhalbusi, H., & Al Mukhaini, M. (2024). Me and my AI Bot: Exploring the 'AIholic' phenomenon and university students' dependency on generative AI Chatbots-Is this the new academic addiction? [pre-print] https://doi.org/10.21203/rs.3.rs-3508563/v2.

Santos, R. M. S., Mendes, C. G., Sen Bressani, G. Y., de Alcantara Ventura, S., de Almeida Nogueira, Y. J., de Miranda, D. M., & Romano-Silva, M. A. (2023). The associations between screen time and mental health in adolescents: A systematic review. *BMC Psychology, 11*(1), 127. https://doi.org/10.1186/s40359-023-01166-7

Schmidt, S. C. E., Anedda, B., Burchartz, A., Eichsteller, A., Kolb, S., Nigg, C., Niessner, C., Oriwol, D., Worth, A., & Woll, A. (2020). Physical activity and screen time of children and adolescents before and during the COVID-19 lockdown in Germany: A natural experiment. *Scientific Reports, 10*(1), 21780. https://doi.org/10.1038/s41598-020-78438-4

Settles, R. E., Fischer, S., Cyders, M. A., Combs, J. L., Gunn, R. L., & Smith, G. T. (2012). Negative urgency: A personality predictor of externalizing behavior characterized by neuroticism, low conscientiousness, and disagreeableness. *Journal of Abnormal Psychology, 121*(1), 160. https://doi.org/10.1037/a0024948

Sha, P., Sariyska, R., Riedl, R., Lachmann, B., & Montag, C. (2019). Linking internet communication and smartphone use disorder by taking a closer look at the Facebook and WhatsApp applications. *Addictive Behaviors Reports, 9*, 100148. https://doi.org/10.1016/j.abrep.2018.100148

Shaw, H., Ellis, D., Geyer, K., Davidson, B., Ziegler, F., & Smith, A. (2020). Quantifying smartphone "use": Choice of measurement impacts relationships between "usage" and health. *Technology, Mind, and Behavior, 1*(2) https://psycnet.apa.org/doi/10.1037/tmb0000022

Sohn, S. Y., Rees, P., Wildridge, B., Kalk, N. J., & Carter, B. (2019). Prevalence of problematic smartphone usage and associated mental health outcomes amongst children and young people: A systematic review, meta-analysis and GRADE of the evidence. *BMC Psychiatry, 19*(1), 356. https://doi.org/10.1186/s12888-019-2350-x

Su, S., Cousijn, J., Molenaar, D., Freichel, R., Larsen, H., & Wiers, R. W. (2024). From everyday life to measurable problematic smartphone use: The development and validation of the smartphone use problems identification questionnaire (SUPIQ). *Journal of Behavioral Addictions*. https://doi.org/10.1556/2006.2024.00010

Sun, Y., & Zhang, Y. (2021). A review of theories and models applied in studies of social media addiction and implications for future research. *Addictive Behaviors, 114*, 106699. https://doi.org/10.1016/j.addbeh.2020.106699

Thomée, S. (2018). Mobile phone use and mental health. A review of the research that takes a psychological perspective on exposure. *International Journal of Environmental Research and Public Health, 15*(12). https://doi.org/10.3390/ijerph15122692

Tsetsi, E., & Rains, S. A. (2017). Smartphone internet access and use: Extending the digital divide and usage gap. *Mobile Media & Communication, 5*(3), 239–255. https://doi.org/10.1177/2050157917708329

Twenge, J. M. (2017). *iGen: Why today's super-connected kids are growing up less rebellious, more tolerant, less happy--and completely unprepared for adulthood--and what that means for the rest of us*. Simon and Schuster.

Twenge, J. M., Joiner, T. E., Rogers, M. L., & Martin, G. N. (2018). Increases in depressive symptoms, suicide-related outcomes, and suicide rates among US adolescents after 2010 and links to increased new media screen time. *Clinical Psychological Science, 6*(1), 3–17. https://doi.org/10.1177/2167702617723376

Ukhova, D., Marionneau, V., Nikkinen, J., & Wardle, H. (2024). Public health approaches to gambling: A global review of legislative trends. *The Lancet Public Health, 9*(1), e57–e67. https://doi.org/10.1016/S2468-2667(23)00221-9

United Nations (1989). Convention on the Rights of the Child. https://www.unicef.org.au/united-nations-convention-on-the-rights-of-the-child

Wang, J., Li, M., Zhu, D., & Cao, Y. (2020). Smartphone overuse and visual impairment in children and young adults: Systematic review and meta-analysis. *Journal of Medical Internet Research, 22*(12), e21923. https://doi.org/10.2196/21923

Wang, X., Li, Y., & Fan, H. (2019). The associations between screen time-based sedentary behavior and depression: A systematic review and meta-analysis. *BMC Public Health, 19*(1), 1524. https://doi.org/10.1186/s12889-019-7904-9

Wardle, H., Reith, G., Langham, E., & Rogers, R. D. (2019). Gambling and public health: We need policy action to prevent harm. *BMJ, 365*. https://doi.org/10.1136/bmj.l1807

World Health Organisation. (2024). *ICD-11*. Retrieved December 24, 2024, from https://icd.who.int/en

Yildirim, C., & Correia, A.-P. (2015). Exploring the dimensions of nomophobia: Development and validation of a self-reported questionnaire. *Computers in Human Behavior, 49*, 130–137. https://doi.org/10.1016/j.chb.2015.02.059
Yu, S., & Sussman, S. (2020). Does smartphone addiction fall on a continuum of addictive behaviors? *International Journal of Environmental Research and Public Health, 17*(2). https://doi.org/10.3390/ijerph17020422
Yu, S.-C., Chen, H.-R., & Yang, Y.-W. (2024). Development and validation the problematic ChatGPT use scale: A preliminary report. *Current Psychology, 43*(31), 26080–26092. https://doi.org/10.1007/s12144-024-06259-z
Zhang, X., Wu, Y., & Liu, S. (2019). Exploring short-form video application addiction: Socio-technical and attachment perspectives. *Telematics and Informatics, 42*, 101243. https://doi.org/10.1016/j.tele.2019.101243

2

Conceptualisation

Abstract Despite plenty of research on the topic of smartphone addiction, or problematic smartphone use, there is considerable disagreement on how it is defined. This chapter explores the main issues concerning how smartphone addiction is conceptualised, specifically focusing on: (a) whether smartphone use meets accepted criteria for an addiction, (b) whether the device or the content on it is the focus of the proposed disorder, (c) the relationship between smartphone addiction and internet addiction, and (d) the relationship between smartphone addiction and other technology use constructs. Each issue raises implications for how smartphone addiction could be conceptualised. Alongside these issues, we introduce key theories used to explain smartphone addiction.

Keywords Smartphone addiction • Problematic smartphone use • Internet addiction • Nomophobia

R. James, L. Hitcham, *Critical Perspectives on Smartphone Addiction*, Palgrave Studies in Cyberpsychology, https://doi.org/10.1007/978-3-031-96188-5_2

Introduction

The idea that smartphone use could be addictive is a controversial topic. Even among researchers who consider it plausible, there is significant disagreement about the form this addiction would take (e.g. Montag et al., 2021; Starcevic et al., 2021; Wu et al., 2021; Griffiths, 2021; Rumpf et al., 2021; Ryding & Kaye, 2018; Nawaz, 2024). Smartphone addiction is not classified as a disorder in current diagnostic manuals, and the consensus is that changing this would be premature. Critiques of smartphone addiction have led other researchers to use alternative terms that include a broader set of negative impacts, such as 'problematic smartphone use' (PSU), excessive use (Larsen et al., 2023), or dysregulated use (Domoff et al., 2025). Consequently, many different terms exist to describe constructs inconsistently treated as distinct, related, overlapping, or synonymous. Figure 2.1 captures some of the idealised distinctions proposed in conceptualising smartphone constructs.

The purpose of this chapter is to review the problems that plague how our relationship with smartphones is described and conceptualised. This chapter is structured around four issues that shed light on these problems, specifically:

(1) Does smartphone use meet recognised criteria for an addictive disorder?
(2) What is the proposed focus of the addictive behaviour, and specifically, is it the device or the activities engaged in on the phone?
(3) Should smartphone use be considered a distinct disorder from other proposed behavioural addictions, especially internet addiction?
(4) How does this proposed addiction relate to other phone use constructs (e.g. phubbing, nomophobia)?

Exploring these is necessary because it clarifies problems surrounding the existence and composition of addictive smartphone use. Such an analysis can also suggest alternative ways of thinking about the relationship between technology use and proposed harms. In addition to discussing these challenges, the chapter will introduce prominent theoretical accounts that explain addictive smartphone behaviours.

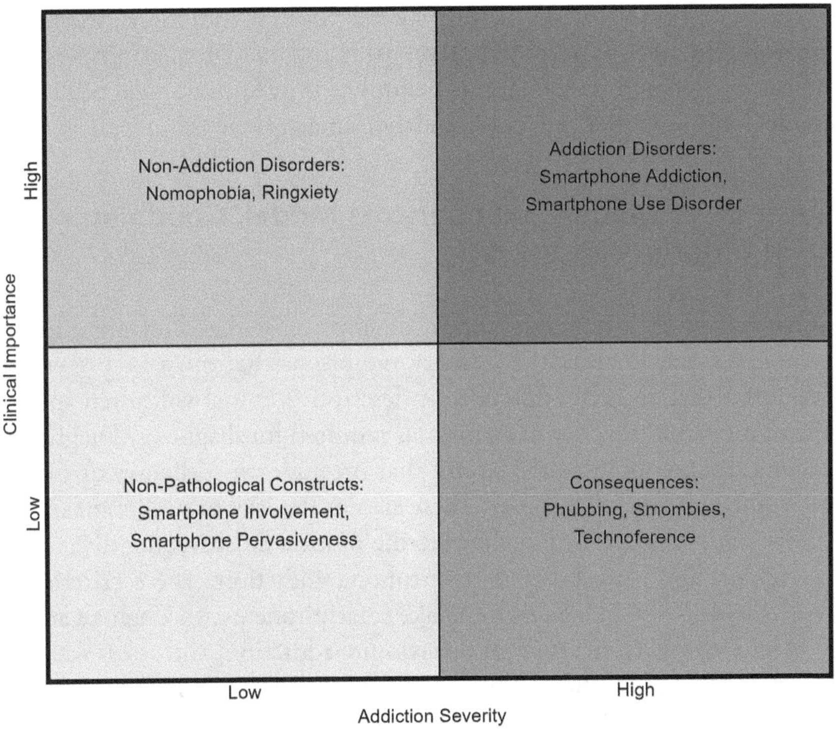

Fig. 2.1 Diagram of different smartphone use constructs. The entire box corresponds to the conceptual space occupied by problematic, dysregulated, and excessive smartphone use. The bottom left quadrant represents non-addictive or clinical constructs. The top left quadrant describes proposed disorders that are not addiction constructs. The bottom right quadrant represents constructs characterised by addictive tendencies but not explicitly addiction disorders (e.g. consequences of addiction). The top right quadrant covers smartphone addiction disorders

Does Smartphone Use Meet Recognised Criteria for an Addictive Disorder?

The first hurdle is to determine whether smartphone use meets established criteria for being classified as an addiction disorder. The existence of smartphone addiction remains controversial despite thousands of papers on the topic (e.g. Panova & Carbonell, 2018; Aagaard, 2021; Hogan et al., 2024; Baggio et al., 2022). This controversy arises because there are important flaws in the way behavioural addictions, including smartphone use, are proposed, developed, and validated. To understand why this approach is flawed, it is helpful to introduce popular addiction models and how they are used to analyse smartphone use.

Descriptive Models: Components Model, Goodman, DSM Criteria, and the ICD

What makes each of these models 'descriptive' is that they are a list of symptoms that identify the primary symptoms that must be present to support a diagnosis of addiction. A descriptive model will often specify the number and severity of symptoms required for diagnosis. Diagnostic criteria frequently include features that preclude an addiction or distinguish it from another disorder. These are not theories or models of smartphone addiction *per se*, but they are the models most frequently applied to support the plausibility of smartphone addiction. These criteria are widely used to analyse behaviours like smartphone use through an addiction lens, to create measures of behavioural addiction, and assess whether the findings support the definition of a new construct.

Four models are frequently cited for analysing potentially addictive behaviours. The first two attempt to define what an addiction is. These models were explicitly developed for both substance-based disorders (e.g. alcohol, opiates) and behaviours such as gambling. The third and fourth models abstract how addictions are defined in clinical manuals, specifically the ICD-11 (World Health Organisation, 2024). and DSM-5 (American Psychiatric Association [APA], 2013). When applied to behaviours such as smartphone use, diagnostic criteria are commonly adapted from existing behavioural addictions, namely Gambling Disorder or Gaming Disorder (e.g. Montag et al., 2021). Gambling Disorder heavily influenced the development of criteria for Gaming Disorder and many candidate behavioural addictions. Both gambling and gaming draw on diagnostic models originating in alcohol and substance abuse. These models are similar in scope and application. All of them have been used to extrapolate from existing addiction disorders to novel behaviours.

The first is the components model of addiction (CMA) (Brown, 1993; Griffiths, 2005). The CMA is a context-general model that proposes six

Table 2.1 Components model of addiction (CMA) (Brown, 1993; Griffiths, 2005)

Component	Description
Salience	The behaviour acquires aberrant cognitive and behavioural attention, manifested in symptoms such as preoccupation, craving, and impaired social behaviour
Mood modification	The behaviour is used to achieve a desired state (e.g. positive or negative reinforcement). It is often motivated by coping or self-medication
Tolerance	There is a process of psychological adaptation to the behaviour. If the behaviour fails to provide adequate reinforcement, more extensive/intensive engagement is needed to achieve the desired outcome
Withdrawal	Abstinence from the behaviour causes unpleasant or intolerable physical and psychological distress only alleviated by the behaviour
Conflict	The behaviour causes problems in relationships among close contacts and social obligations, such as family, friends, work, or education. Conflict also refers to internal distress, that is, a perceived loss of control caused by engaging in the behaviour despite a desire to stop
Relapse	Recurrence and reuptake of the addictive behaviour, often despite long-term abstinence or control

necessary features of all addictions: *salience, mood modification, tolerance, withdrawal, conflict, and relapse* (Table 2.1). The CMA characterises the psychological states that comprise addiction. It does not attempt to explain the factors that cause someone to become addicted to something, how these symptoms progress, or how a component is defined as present. The model assumes that addiction emerges from a mixture of biological, psychological, and social processes (Griffiths, 2005). It is influential in the development of assessments to measure severity across a wide range of candidate addictive behaviours, including smartphone use (Csibi et al., 2016, 2018), exercise (Terry et al., 2004), internet gaming (Charlton & Danforth, 2007), and social media (Andreassen et al., 2012).

The second framework was proposed by Goodman (1990) (Table 2.2), based on the DSM-III-R (APA, 1987) criteria for substance abuse, pathological gambling, and other impulse control disorders. The model can be summarised into two overarching features for defining an addiction disorder: a loss of control over interactions with the object of addiction and persistence despite significant negative consequences. These criteria, as well as being straightforward, concisely represent the current

Table 2.2 Goodman's addiction disorder criteria (1990)

	Criteria
1.	Inability to resist impulses to engage in the addictive behaviour
2.	Increasing psychological tension in the build up toward initiating the behaviour
3.	Pleasure or relief from released tension by engaging in the behaviour
4.	Impaired sense of control during the behaviour
5.	Endorsement of five of the following: – Preoccupation – Frequent engagement and at greater extent/intensity than planned – Attempting to stop/reduce the behaviour – Excessive time spent preparing/doing/recovering from the behaviour – Interference with major obligations – Continued engagement despite awareness of harm – Tolerance – Restlessness/irritability if unable to perform the behaviour
6.	Symptoms are persistent for over one month or intermittent over a longer period

consensus on the primary aspects of addiction disorders (APA, 2013). That is, it is not simply the presence of impaired control or a dependence syndrome; there also needs to be clear evidence of harm. Some cases might be excluded based on this model, including 'positive addictions', for example, exercise addiction, that may not clearly show harm.

The third and fourth frameworks derive from diagnostic criteria used in other addiction disorders (APA, 1987; 1994; 2013; World Health Organization, 2024). Diagnostic criteria for gambling disorder have served as a basis for developing criteria for many potential behavioural addictions, such as social media (van den Eijnden et al., 2016), television watching (Sussman & Moran, 2013), and exercise (Downs et al., 2004). However, the most prominent examples where concepts from gambling have been applied to novel behavioural addictions are proposed addictions to the internet (Young, 1998) and gaming (see Karhulahti et al., 2021, for a review). Of these, gaming has been the most successful, meriting further examination in the DSM-5 with the tentative label of Internet Gaming Disorder, and then classified as an addiction disorder in the ICD-11 as Gaming Disorder. The two manuals differ slightly in their prescriptiveness but converge on common phenomena for both: the DSM currently outlines nine criteria, four of which must be met to consider a diagnosis of gambling disorder (Table 2.3). The ICD has three

Table 2.3 Representations of behavioural addiction in the Diagnostic and Statistical Manual of Mental Disorders (DSM)

Symptom	DSM-III-R PG (1987)	DSM-IV PG (1994)	DSM-5 GD (2013)	DSM-5 IGD (2013)
Preoccupation	x	x	x	x
Engaging behaviour for longer or at a higher intensity than intended	x			
Tolerance	x	x	x	x
Repeated, unsuccessful attempts to reduce, stop or control	x	x	x	x
Withdrawal	x	x	x	x
Engages in behaviour to escape dysphoric mood (i.e. when upset)		x	x	x
Loss of interest in other hobbies				x
'Chasing' losses - returning with intent to make up losses	x	x	x	
Continued engagement despite awareness of problems or harm				x
Continued engagement when expected to meet obligations	x			
Lying to conceal the extent of behaviour		x	x	x
Committed crime to fund engagement in behaviour		x		

(continued)

Table 2.3 (continued)

Symptom	DSM-III-R PG (1987)	DSM-IV PG (1994)	DSM-5 GD (2013)	DSM-5 IGD (2013)
Lost or jeopardised significant commitment or opportunity	x	x	x	x
Others provide money to resolve financial stress		x	x	
Continued use despite debts, major problems made worse by gambling	x			
Cutoff	4+	5+	4+	5+
Period	12 months			
Exclusions	None	Manic episode	Manic episode	None
Modifiers	Differential diagnosis for manic, hypomanic, and antisocial personality disorders	None	Episodic vs. persistent time frame Early vs. sustained remission	None

PG = Pathological Gambling. GD = Gambling Disorder. IGD = Internet Gaming Disorder.

criteria, all of which must be met, and includes clinical features that overlap considerably with the DSM (Table 2.4). Both specify that this must manifest over an extended period. Additionally, both necessitate significant impairment or distress stemming from the behaviour and state that the symptoms of the disorder cannot be explained by another psychiatric disorder (i.e. a manic episode).

Symptom Models and Smartphone Addiction

Descriptive models support the claim that smartphone use is an addiction by identifying symptomatic behaviours and developing scales based on one of these frameworks (Csibi et al., 2018; Lin et al., 2015). Although

Table 2.4 International Classification of Diseases, 11th Revision (ICD-11) criteria for behavioural addictions: gambling and gaming

Domain	Criteria
Symptoms	All of the following criteria: (a) Impaired control (b) Precedence over other activities (c) Persistence or escalation despite negative consequences
Additional Features	Other related phenomena may be characterised by: – Repeated, failed efforts to abstain – Tolerance – Urges and cravings – Impact on health and health behaviours – Deceiving others – Engaging to escape or cope
Timeframe	– Whether continuous or intermittent, the pattern of disordered engagement persists over an extended period – Diagnosis may be made in a shorter timeframe if symptoms are severe
Exclusions	– Diagnosis only when the behaviour cannot be explained by manic episodes or acute bipolar disorder – When found in comorbidity with substance addictions and/or antisocial personality disorder, diagnosis of both is feasible
Modifiers:	– Predominantly online versus predominantly offline categorisation – Another disorder or medication does not account for the behaviour – Behaviour produces significant distress or functional impairment – Diagnosis excluded for persistent engagement in social, professional, or routine gambling/gaming. Specific examples include habitual purchasing of lottery tickets, increased gaming to acquire skills, or e-sports – Problems without meeting criteria fall into hazardous use

most studies note the lack of current classification in diagnostic manuals (e.g. Ryding & Kuss, 2020; Marengo et al., 2020), the existence and severity of the addiction symptoms that constitute these disorders are frequently stressed (Marciano et al., 2021). The inclusion of behavioural addictions such as gaming disorder in diagnostic manuals is also used to promote the feasibility of smartphone addiction (Elhai et al., 2021). Several case reports propose that some instances meet these criteria for smartphone addiction (e.g. Körmendi et al., 2016; Jameel et al., 2019).

These models have also been used to critically reflect on whether smartphone use should be considered an addiction (Panova & Carbonell, 2018).

However, this approach to identifying addictive behaviours has come under extensive criticism. This methodology evaluates candidate disorders without considering the unique characteristics, features, and contexts of the behaviour and risks over-pathologising everyday activities (James & Tunney, 2017; Flayelle et al., 2022, 2023). This risk increases when flawed research practices lower the burden of proof. Billieux et al. (2015b) critiqued this process, outlining how standard practices in behavioural addiction research produce problematic findings. First, researchers identify a potentially addictive behaviour, source relevant data (e.g. case studies, statistics on popularity), evaluate it using existing diagnostic frameworks and addiction criteria, and determine whether an addiction perspective is plausible. Then, a scale will be developed to measure 'addiction' to the novel behaviour, often from these same frameworks, and attempt to estimate the prevalence of the putative addiction (see Chap. 3). Finally, scores on the new scale will be correlated against other behavioural addictions, personality traits, and psychological distress to establish validity. This approach implicitly assumes in advance that addictive behaviour exists. Because this paradigm is atheoretical and domain-general, it does not rigorously assess whether these criteria are appropriate for the behaviour.

Consequently, there is a low bar to pass in justifying support for a new potential behavioural addiction. The flexibility of these models means that they can apply to any behaviour, and these criteria cannot distinguish plausible from implausible suggestions. These approaches have been used to justify a range of activities, such as Argentine tango dancing (Targhetta et al., 2013), fortune telling (Grall-Bronnec et al., 2015), and milk (bubble) tea drinking (Qu et al., 2023), as potentially addictive behaviours. This methodology has also been applied parodically to 'offline' social interaction to demonstrate the limits of this approach (Satchell et al., 2021). Thus, these components and criteria may be necessary, but they are insufficient for discriminating whether a behaviour should be considered an addiction. This problem occurs across all the models discussed so far, especially when symptoms or criteria are the main unit of analysis.

This methodology is generally flawed, but it has specific issues when applied to smartphone use. Panova and Carbonell (2018) critically evaluated whether smartphone addiction meets accepted standards for an addictive disorder. The first stage of their analysis considered whether addiction symptoms—specifically salience, tolerance, withdrawal, loss of control, and relapse—could be found in smartphone use. On each count, they argue that the research literature fails to support the assertion that these criteria exist. Even when symptoms like preoccupation were identified, they were insufficiently severe to be clinically significant or could be explained by the context in which smartphone use occurs. The lack of emergent, clinically severe symptoms is especially notable given the high prevalence of smartphone addiction that has been identified using existing measures (Meng et al., 2022). This discordance suggests that responses to many assessment items fail to distinguish between high engagement/involvement and clinically significant dysfunction.

The possibility that purported symptoms inappropriately attribute everyday phone use to an addiction is particularly important. Panova & Carbonell highlight how smartphones have become a mediator for many social and societal obligations. It is inappropriate to attribute increasing amounts of time (see Chap. 1 on '*Screen Time*') or importance to phone use as a symptom of addiction without due consideration of other factors, for example, motivated use due to an increase in social or professional obligations. This point has been made elsewhere, with Kardefelt-Winther (2014) noting that symptoms of internet addiction appear to measure normative shifts in behaviour that are inappropriately framed as pathological. Some addiction criteria seem particularly ill-suited for translation to smartphone use and other technologies, such as tolerance and preoccupation, in part because they are operationalised using questions that probe the volume of use without regard to context (Razum et al., 2023; Kardefelt-Winther, 2015; Billieux et al., 2019).

Problems with the criteria aside, Carbonell and Panova's critique identifies that many investigations focus on symptoms at the expense of other features of these models. Most assessment instruments ask about addiction symptoms' relevance, presence, or frequency, but do not query exclusionary criteria such as a lack of functional impairment or alternative causes. Evidence of attributable functional and physical impairment is especially limited. Although smartphone addiction is extensively linked with harm, most of these studies use cross-sectional designs (see Chap. 4). In many cases, it is plausible that these proposed impairments predate smartphone engagement, and the problematic features of phone use have served as adaptations or coping mechanisms. For example, certain smartphone behaviours (e.g. excessive checking) could occur because of psychological distress, such as anxiety and obsessive-compulsive traits. Alternatively, both could share a common cause. In addition, even if smartphone use contributes to these, as some longitudinal studies have implied, it is not just the presence of a link but the size of the relationship that is important. Even if a relationship is established, the effect sizes are typically insufficient to demonstrate functional impairment.

Alternative Frameworks and Motivational Models of Smartphone Use

Given these problems, Kardefelt-Winther et al. (2017) proposed a new set of criteria for behavioural addiction that included four exclusionary criteria: (1) that the individual's behaviour is better explained by another disorder (e.g. depression, impulsivity), (2) that functional impairment arises from a wilfully chosen behaviour, (3) that engagement may involve significant time focus but does not create substantial functional impairment or distress, and (4) the behaviour serves as a coping strategy. The use of this framework in smartphone addiction research has tended to focus on the indeterminate nature of the proposed disorder rather than evaluating it against the criteria (e.g. Jameel et al., 2019). Nonetheless, Carbonell & Panova's (2018) critical analysis evaluated some of these factors, concluding that many potential exclusionary criteria apply against addictive phone use. Ultimately, this highlights how discussions of behavioural addiction criteria are still premature and demonstrates the problems associated with using symptom models alone as a basis for claiming that smartphone use is an addiction.

A theoretical model originating from internet use that is relevant here is the compensatory use model (Kardefelt-Winther, 2014a, 2014b). The compensatory use model proposes that online behaviour is driven by specific motivations to engage with online content. Examples of these motivations include fulfilling unmet needs (e.g. social interactions), coping mechanisms (e.g. escapism), and adaptations to distress. Although coping is a motivation common to many addictions (Griffiths, 2017), the point the compensatory use model makes is that there is not a direct relationship between prior vulnerability and problematic use; rather, this is expressed through certain motivations that manifest in specific patterns of behaviour used as coping mechanisms (Fig. 2.2). Critically, the volume or intensity of engagement in online behaviours is insufficient to evidence disorder. This model also emphasises that the same behaviour can be harmful or unproblematic in different contexts. Whilst this model is agnostic on the existence of internet addiction and argues against treating problematic online behaviour as disordered by default, it is widely used as a model for internet and smartphone addictions (e.g. Cheng & Meng,

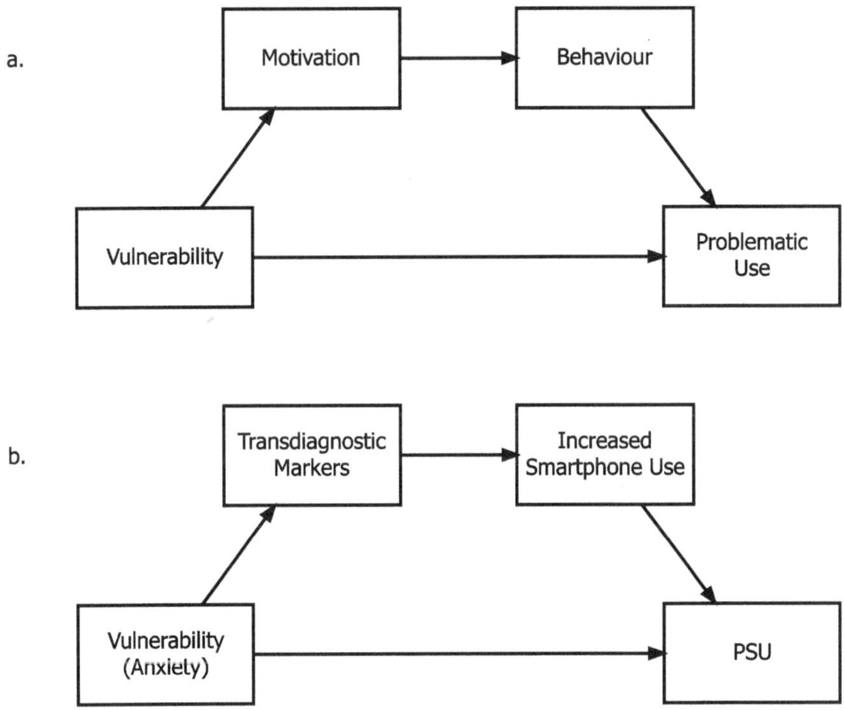

Fig. 2.2 Compensatory use models of problematic smartphone use. Panel (a) is based on Kardefelt-Winther (2014), and panel (b) is based on Elhai et al. (2017)

2021; Vujic & Szabo, 2022). Elhai et al. (2017) proposed a variant of the model that focuses on the relationship between anxiety and PSU. This modification focuses on transdiagnostic manifestations of anxiety (e.g. fear of missing out, rumination) instead of motivations, although these act as motivations for increased smartphone use. The idea that there are motivational differences in smartphone use has also been explored elsewhere. Much of this ties in with the idea that people use different types of content for various purposes, applying theories such as the Uses and Gratifications model (e.g. Lee & Lee, 2017; Wei et al., 2024). However, most of these make broad distinctions, such as social versus process use (e.g. Elhai et al., 2020) or active versus passive use (e.g. Noe et al., 2019). In practice, these tend to operationalise motivations using the frequency or preferred type of behaviour, which may not be sufficiently nuanced (e.g. Kaye et al., 2024).

What Is the Proposed Focus of Addictive Behaviour?

The next issue is identifying what people classified as having a smartphone addiction are thought to be addicted to: is it the device itself? Is it the specific content on phones? Is it the way we use them? Or is it a generalised disorder that emerges from using multiple types of potentially harmful content?

There is a lack of clarity regarding the role of the device and the content in the aetiology, reinforcement, and maintenance of smartphone addiction. The smartphone is a device with specific functionalities and a platform for many different types of online content (Lin et al., 2025). Most popular smartphone content types (e.g. social media, the internet) have been proposed as separate addictive behaviours (Baggio et al., 2022). Some (i.e. gambling, gaming) are already classified as behavioural addictions in diagnostic manuals. While disordered behaviour may occur through the smartphone, it is unclear whether there is anything remarkable about the device.

The case of mobile gambling is informative for thinking through these issues. Should someone experiencing impairment because of mobile gambling be considered at risk of gambling disorder, smartphone addiction, or a specific mobile gambling disorder? Specific mobile gaming (Pan et al., 2019) and social media (Xu et al., 2023) addictions have been proposed and measured, implying that the interaction between device and content is uniquely problematic. Mobile gambling is a potential risk factor for gambling harm (e.g. James et al., 2017; Hing et al., 2023). Like other forms of online gambling, gambling on mobile phones is readily available and accessible. Mobile gambling enables gambling wherever there is mobile internet, such as on public transport or in the workplace. It allows further integration with watching sports, which may encourage riskier gambling. Mobile gambling has been frequently promoted alongside more harmful forms of activity, such as in-play betting (Gray et al., 2012; Vieira et al., 2023). The affordances of phones also allow apps to engage with users in novel ways and can reduce barriers to gambling engagement. Although phone use has now saturated, the highest level of use still tends to be among adolescents and younger adults, who are at greater risk of experiencing gambling harm (Dellosa & Browne, 2024).

The example of mobile gambling is particularly instructive because the literature does not typically treat mobile gambling as a discrete 'mobile gambling disorder' or addiction in the way that it is proposed for some smartphone behaviours, nor as specially related to smartphone addiction at all. The locus of harm is attributed to gambling, and the smartphone is a means of accessing gambling content. The smartphone might act as a moderator for gambling problems, either because smartphone use is more intensive among demographic groups that are at greater risk of harm, the affordances of the device promote harmful gambling behaviours, or because the products that are characteristic of mobile gambling are more harmful. In either case, we would anticipate that, if asked, most people experiencing harms related to mobile gambling would principally attribute this to gambling, not the smartphone. The example of mobile gambling situates the harm in the content rather than the device. The phone may contribute to an increased risk of harm, but its role is indirect. It is not clear whether this applies to other forms of potentially addictive behaviour.

Problematic or addictive smartphone use measurements rely on items that query general phone use. This framing implies a role for the device, or it uses the device as a proxy for multiple behaviours. This role could take the form of people being literally addicted to their phones. However, this is highly unlikely. Although people tend to develop an attachment and a relationship to their smartphones (Fullwood et al., 2017), this relationship depends on the activities enabled by the phone. Even before the smartphone as we know it was developed, earlier conceptualisations of cell or mobile phone addiction focused on activities like texting and calling. A literal definition of smartphone addiction does not accurately represent the concept's application in research usage either. In reviewing the literature, Yu and Sussman (2020) found little common support for the idea of the device being the object of addiction. The phone could acquire salience through conditioned reinforcement from online content and its reward schedule (O'Donnell & Epstein, 2019). The reinforcing features of these behaviours might instrumentally associate the phone with them and elicit behaviour. There is a rationale for this; it is commonly noted that phone use is habitual and sequentially triggered (Oulasvirta et al., 2012). For example, people's daily routines might include looking at a social media app, followed by a news app, and then playing a game. Activities that have addictive properties are likely to be more reinforcing and encourage conditioned reinforcement. However, very few studies have addressed this hypothesis. Instead, the tendency has been to treat smartphone addiction as a generalised construct comprising multiple online activities. This conceptualisation reflects the distinction previously made of being addicted *through* a device instead of being addicted *to* a device (e.g. Griffiths, 2021). However, as the next section will explore, generalised constructs pose another set of difficulties.

Should Smartphone Use Be Considered a Distinct Disorder?

Even if treating smartphone addiction as a generalised construct overcomes concerns about the source of the proposed addictive behaviour, it immediately runs into another major obstacle. If this account is accurate, it would question the need for a smartphone addiction disorder. Specifically, smartphone addiction would be redundant because these characteristics already feature in another candidate disorder, namely Internet Addiction. Indeed, Panova and Carbonell (2018) highlight that the smartphone's unique features require internet functionality, which ought to be the focus instead of creating a new disorder. There is a strong rationale for this consideration. The way smartphone addiction is often conceptualised, particularly as a general disorder, is remarkable in its similarity to internet addiction.

A Unified Taxonomy of Internet-Related Disorders (Montag et al., 2021)

This similarity and the other conceptual problems discussed so far have led to proposals for new models. For example, Montag et al. (2021) proposed a taxonomy of internet-related disorders that distinguished between specific and generalised internet use and between mobile and non-mobile internet usage. In this model, smartphone and internet addiction would unify into an internet use disorder qualified by the means of access. They capture the same fundamental phenomenon, as many smartphone activities of concern are online, but the smartphone might act as a moderator. In this model, internet use disorder is a higher-order construct above specific behaviours, namely gaming, gambling, buying-shopping, pornography, social media, and other uses. There are merits to this approach: it is theoretically consistent with the overall conceptualisation of internet addiction, which has been the basis for most research in the field. The ability to distinguish separate behaviours and unique characteristics of each modality also allows for important distinctions if there is evidence that certain types of content are more harmful on mobile phones than on other devices.

At the same time, it is worth questioning the basis for this rationale. As noted in the commentaries on the proposal (e.g. Starcevic et al., 2021), it assumes there is a generalised internet addiction. The distinction between 'specific' and 'generalised' internet addiction was proposed by Davis (2001). However, the meaning of 'specific' addiction is ambiguous and not clearly defined in comparison to offline problematic engagement with a behaviour. In Davis' formulation, the mixture of internet behaviour, prior psychopathological risk factors, and reinforcement contributes to maladaptive cognitions. These lead to problematic use of a specific activity or generalised problematic use when accompanied by poor social support. The symptoms of internet addiction then exacerbate these cognitive biases further. In this model, generalised PIU (Problematic Internet Use) is conceptualised as being more severe and harmful than specific PIU, characterised by uniquely online behaviours.

There are reasons to take this account with caution. Both Montag and Davis' models make a distinction between specific PIU and people who may have a generalised (online and offline) addiction to a behaviour. However, the evidence evaluating this distinction is not encouraging. The literature on online gambling has tended to treat internet gambling as a high-risk, harmful activity (e.g. Papineau et al., 2018) whilst identifying that a specific online gambling PIU is atypical (e.g. Wardle et al., 2011; Hing et al., 2022; Richardson et al., 2024). The risk associated with internet gambling appears to be more consistent with gambling disorder than a specific PIU. Indeed, the basis for distinguishing between online and offline or mobile and non-mobile engagement does not make sense for all activities and may change over time. Additionally, most internet and smartphone addiction studies have used assessment batteries that measure generalised PIU. These considerations qualify the merits of conceptualising specific disorders within this framework.

The meaning of 'generalised' internet addiction is also open to question. Davis (2001) defines this as a distinct condition characterised by extensive engagement with internet-unique activities and overall dysfunction. In other formulations, generalised internet addiction is an 'umbrella' construct that serves as a common causal determinant of a multitude of potentially addictive behaviours (e.g. Young et al., 2009) (Fig. 2.3a). Evidence for either is inconclusive. Montag et al. (2015) conducted a study to examine the merits of measuring specific and generalised PIU, ultimately supporting the need to measure both. All the specific online behaviours studied (gaming, social media, pornography, shopping) were moderately correlated with PIU, suggesting they overlapped, but the particular behaviours measured unique variance. The potential exception was social media use, which was substantially more correlated with internet addiction than the other behaviours. Although ostensibly supportive of a general-specific distinction, this highlights a major concern. The cognitive-behavioural model proposes that the danger of generalised PIU is most serious for activities that would not be possible without the internet (or smartphones). The examples cited by Davis (2001) were activities that are precursors to social media (e.g. chat rooms, internet forums). It is reasonable to suggest that 'generalised' internet addiction is an early formulation of concerns about social media use that, over time, has been subsumed into its own category of behaviour. The same point has been made regarding social media and smartphone addiction (Kuss & Griffiths, 2017; Griffiths, 2021) because most usage occurs on social media.

A related but critical line of thinking has been to use approaches such as network analysis to examine whether internet and smartphone addictions are best thought of as either a reflective or 'umbrella' construct that is expressed through a multitude of online activities (Fig. 2.3a) or a 'spectrum' of related but distinct problematic behaviours (Fig. 2.3b). If the spectrum hypothesis is correct, then both internet and smartphone addiction are a composite of separate online behaviours. In contrast, the standard internet and smartphone addiction account describes a generalised disorder that causally determines individual activities. The findings from this line of research have tended to support the spectrum hypothesis, with internet addiction representing a formative construct that imprecisely captures a variety of distinct problematic online behaviours (Baggio et al., 2018). The evidence is more convincing for internet addiction than smartphone addiction, but the main point is that neither appropriately measures online behaviour (Lin et al., 2025; Baggio et al., 2022, 2024). The logic of the spectrum approach mandates measuring specific behaviours rather than a generalised addiction. Ultimately, this approach suggests that debating whether smartphone use should be considered a subset of internet addiction is uninformative, as both ultimately lead to inadequate constructs.

Interaction of Person-Affect-Cognitive-Execution (I-PACE)

The I-PACE model is a prominent account of behavioural addictions (Brand et al., 2016, 2019). I-PACE was originally developed as a theoretical model of internet addiction, but focuses on specific addictive

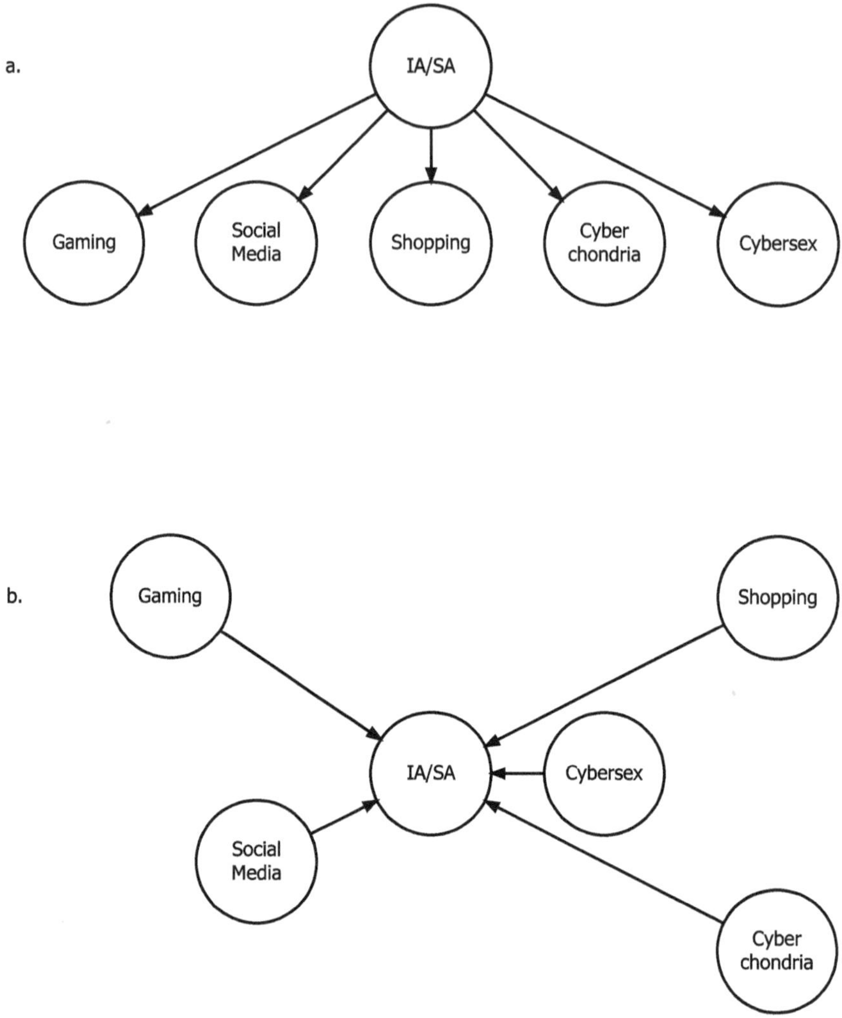

Fig. 2.3 Competing models of internet/smartphone addiction. Panel (a) represents the umbrella model; panel (b) represents a spectrum model

behaviours rather than generalised IA/SA. The model highlights the role of four different processes that contribute to the initiation, development, and maintenance of addictive behaviour. The first are (1) 'person' factors or core characteristics. These are circumstances or psychological traits that predispose someone towards engaging in addictive behaviours or increase tendencies towards motivations and patterns of use that are harmful. The remaining three are (2) 'affect', (3) 'cognition', and (4) 'execution'. The core point of I-PACE is the interaction between personal factors and triggers, both internal (e.g. mood) and external (e.g. stimuli, cues), which leads to emotional and cognitive responses that drive actions. These actions, when executed, reinforce impulsive behaviours, increasing their salience and the expectancy of reward. Over time, these become habituated, producing cravings and impaired behavioural control that is characteristic of addictive behaviour.

The I-PACE model is well elaborated, but there are some qualifications with the existing evidence base. First, a lot of research utilising the I-PACE model focuses on a small number of processes, which tend to be 'person' related factors. Constructs such as depression, early childhood experiences, personality traits, and other individual differences are extensively used when citing the I-PACE (e.g. Jhone et al., 2021). In contrast, the other three components are not as widely tested. Second, most of the research is cross-sectional and does not test the dynamic nature of the model. The behavioural and neurobiological processes that underpin I-PACE unfold over time, and this is explicitly reflected in the model, with differences between earlier and later stages of addiction psychopathology. Nonetheless, I-PACE is a comprehensive model that can be applied to a spectrum approach, where smartphone use mediates or exacerbates problematic online behaviours.

How Does This Proposed Addiction Relate to Other Phone Use Constructs?

For clarity, most of this chapter has used smartphone addiction as a generic term. However, researchers, practitioners, and the public use many terms that refer to similar behaviours and ideas. Table 2.5 gives a summary of the addiction-related and addiction-adjacent terms associated with smartphone use. Although 'smartphone addiction' is the most obvious of these, other terms are widely used as well, such as compulsive

Table 2.5 Examples of concepts and terms related to smartphone usage

Term	Common definition
	Devices
Smartphone	Mobile phones with personal computing capacity and internet connectivity. Features include larger displays, touchscreen interactions, and a wider array of sensors for interacting and detecting behaviour
Mobile Phone	Generic term for portable phone, more common in British English. Once used to distinguish older (feature) phones from smartphones
Cell Phone	Another term for 'mobile phone' that is more common in American contexts
	Constructs
Addiction	Class of psychiatric disorders characterised by impaired control over interactions with the object of addiction, leading to a state of psychological dependence. Engagement is persistent despite intentions to regulate or cease behaviour and despite (functional) impairment to well-being and personal and social obligations
Problematic use	Intended to encompass a broader spectrum of harm than addiction (e.g. use in inappropriate or dangerous situations). Includes non-addictive and potentially addictive smartphone use
Dependence	Inconsistently used. Some studies have treated dependence as a separate phenomenon from addiction (i.e. absence of harm, feelings of anxiety when unable to use or access the phone). Others have used dependence as a synonym for smartphone addiction, similar to the older use of dependence as a synonym for addictive disorders
Excessive use	Excessive use ostensibly refers to a volume of smartphone use or engagement beyond reasonable limits. In practice, however, it is largely treated as synonymous with problematic use, overlaps with addiction, and is measured using PSU/SA scales, occasionally operationalised using the amount of phone use
Involvement	Intended to capture elevated psychological attachment to a behaviour, rather than problematic or addictive use. Based on Brown's components of addiction
Disorder	Primarily used as a synonym of 'addiction' and intended to mirror the use of gambling and gaming disorder in the DSM and ICD

(*continued*)

Table 2.5 (continued)

Term	Common definition
Nomophobia	Portmanteau of 'NO MObile PHOne PhoBIA'. Nomophobia was independently defined in the USA as anxiety-centric and in Brazil as a phobia. Has become enmeshed with PSU and SA in its application
Dysregulated	Recently proposed as an alternative term for excessive or addictive smartphone use
Phubbing	Portmanteau of phone snubbing. Ignoring others (e.g. family, friends) in favour of one's phone. Popular conceptualisations of phubbing propose it may be a consequence of smartphone addiction
Smombies	Portmanteau of smartphone zombies. Refers to potentially harmful behaviour where people focus on their smartphone while walking, with potentially harmful consequences (e.g. walking into others, ignoring traffic, falling down stairs)
Ringxiety	Originally coined to refer to 'phantom ringing', where people attributed other people's phone ringing to their own. It has been generalised to cover phantom vibrations (i.e. texts, notifications)
Pervasiveness	Pervasiveness focuses on the interaction between the frequency and volume of engagement and contexts and situations in which use could become problematic
	Umbrella constructs
Internet	Smartphone use is frequently conceptualised as part of a broad internet addiction because most phone engagements occur online
Social media	Construct has similar symptoms and scope to smartphone and internet addiction. Some studies have incorporated smartphone use
(Information) Technology	Used to refer to a wide range of computer-based behaviours
Device	Variously used to refer specifically to smartphones, or an umbrella of smartphone use, tablets, computers, TV, games consoles, and the Internet
Gadget	Used in some contexts as a synonym for screen-based devices
Digital	Increasingly used as a higher-level umbrella construct to include smartphone, internet, social media, gaming, and other technology-based addictive behaviours
Screen	Encompasses multiple screen-based digital devices, that is, smartphones, tablets, computers, and (sometimes) television
Media	'Media' covers a wide range of interactive content. Some conceptualisations evolved from the idea of television addiction to include the internet and digital media

smartphone use, problematic smartphone use, smartphone overuse, and excessive smartphone use. Translating these into theoretical statements about our relationship with our phones is tricky because terminology, when utilised, is often imprecise. There is little consensus on the boundaries between different constructs and how they are related. In other words, these are *fuzzy constructs*, a term that Davidson et al. (2022) used to highlight the pervasive issues with technology use research.

These problems begin with the device of interest. Over the past 20 years, studies have used different terms to refer to distinct types of devices. The meaning of these terms has changed over time, and their continued use creates inherent ambiguity. For example, there are clusters of studies on cell phone, mobile phone, and smartphone addictions. The literature on the addictive use of cell phones and text messaging predates the smartphone (e.g. Carbonell et al., 2009; Leung, 2008; Park, 2005). Cellular or mobile phones were distinguished from smartphones because they had fewer capabilities, with some exceptions (e.g. Japan) where a clearer continuum exists between mobile phones and smartphones (Akematsu et al., 2012). Consequently, initial studies on smartphone addiction sought to differentiate smartphone use from internet use and older mobile phones (Kim et al., 2014). As smartphones supplanted less sophisticated phones as the default purchase option, terms like 'mobile phone' and 'cell phone' became generic, increasingly referring to smartphones. Many contemporary studies describe mobile phone ownership and addiction, but they actually refer to smartphone use (e.g. Tian & Wang, 2023). Fewer studies continue to refer to cell phone addiction, but these also reflect smartphone usage (e.g. Hong et al., 2024; Hu et al., 2024). Thus, the distinction between these constructs becomes fuzzy. Older studies used these terms to refer to distinct devices, but more recent studies treat them as synonymous with the smartphone. It also entrenches uncertainty about the role of the device as the source of addictive behaviour because device terms are not consistent over time. Similarly, many umbrella terms are employed, such as 'device', 'screen', 'IT', 'technology', or 'media' addictions. These often act as synonyms for smartphone addiction or represent a concept of internet/technology addiction that specifically includes smartphones within its scope.

These problems multiply when other clinical terms are used. While some terms are commonly defined outside the parameters of an addiction disorder, these ideas frequently become interwoven because they contribute to the symptoms of addiction. This confusion is seen with terms such as 'excessive', 'compulsive', or 'dependence'. Each of these can be a criterion for addictive behaviour, but, on their own, do not characterise addiction. Take compulsion, for example. Addiction is characterised by a compulsion to engage with the substance or behaviour that is the object of the disorder (Dalley et al., 2011). Nonetheless, compulsions occur for many other reasons, and there is a family of obsessive-compulsive disorders (OCD) in psychiatry that are distinct from addictive behaviours. Dependence is another example, where its adoption in addiction psychiatry in the 1980s inadvertently led to conflation between addiction-relevant dependence and physiological dependence and withdrawal that may be unrelated to substance abuse (i.e. certain medications) (Szalavitz, 2024). Dependence is also frequently conflated with emotional attachment and coping. Because these overlap with addictive phenomena, they often become synonyms for an addiction construct when used.

Other terms may ostensibly be separate from addiction-related concepts but have become synonymous over time. Smartphone addiction overlaps with proposed clinical disorders, situational behaviours, and individual differences that may be harmful but not addictive. Constructs such as 'nomophobia' and 'phubbing' fall into this group (also see Chap. 3). Nomophobia was proposed as a dependence conceptualised in terms of anxiety and phobia (King et al., 2013; Yildirim & Correia, 2015). In practice, it is often applied as another synonym of SA, and popular scales include subscales that represent this. The same occurs with phubbing, where the most common measures to assess phubbing propensity or perpetration have subscales of smartphone addiction/dependence despite being thought of as a situational and interpersonal phenomenon (Chotpitayasunondh & Douglas, 2016; Karadağ et al., 2015). Like phubbing, other constructs such as phantom ringing, 'smombies', or 'ringxiety' are not addiction-specific but have become associated as proposed consequences of smartphone addiction.

The consequence is that many smartphone and technology use constructs have emerged. It is unclear whether they are meaningfully distinct from one another. Some terms (e.g. problematic, excessive, or dependent) overlap significantly with smartphone addiction in theory and practice, employing identical concepts and measurements in empirical research. The differences between these concepts become the most appropriate term for describing the same underlying phenomenon rather than distinguishing one construct from another. Alternatively, problematic use or involvement concepts have frequently been intended to encompass a broader continuum of behaviour than disordered use. Although their usage may stem from concerns about applying an addiction model, these terms tend to be open to the possibility of addiction-like phenomena in extreme cases (Elhai et al., 2021). Other terms have conveyed differences in functionality that have become vestigial, such as mobile/cell phone addiction. Others still are not addiction-specific but have been treated at various junctures as being either synonymous with smartphone addiction, a component of smartphone addiction, a precursor or consequence of smartphone addiction, or even a higher-level construct that encompasses addictive smartphone use. There is fundamental disagreement and confusion about how these concepts relate to one another and the circumstances in which they are distinct or synonymous.

Even if these terms intend to measure different constructs, there is increasing evidence that they don't when applied in practice. Davidson et al. (2022, Study 1) conducted a principal components analysis of 10 different smartphone use scales that ostensibly measure distinct properties such as smartphone addiction (e.g. Smartphone Addiction Scale (SAS; Kwon et al., 2013), Smartphone Application Based Addiction Scale (SABAS; Csibi et al., 2018), smartphone use (e.g. Media Technology Usage and Attitudes Scale [MTUAS]; Rosen et al., 2013), nomophobia (i.e. Nomophobia Scale (NMP-Q; Yildirim & Correia, 2015) and problematic smartphone use (e.g. Mobile Phone Problem Use Scale (MPPUS; Bianchi & Phillips, 2005)). The analysis demonstrated that scores from each measure fitted onto a single principal component, suggesting they all measure very similar things. The second study then used the same approach to look at the SAS, the most commonly used measure of smartphone addiction, and whether it was distinguishable from psychological distress and general smartphone use. This analysis identified two components, distress and phone use, and that smartphone addiction scores were interposed between the two.

From this, Davidson and colleagues (2022) ultimately concluded that these measures capture the same fundamental variation in behaviour related to technology use rather than a series of related but distinct constructs. Thus, even if concepts such as nomophobia focus on specific behaviours, these are insufficiently distinguishable from other scales measuring other constructs when developed into questionnaires. Similarly, in our work (Hitcham et al., 2023), we found very high levels of correspondence between smartphone addiction scales and other behavioural addictions, most notably internet addiction. The implications are that even if these constructs are theoretically separate, they are measured using instruments that have not been appropriately developed, which makes distinguishing them impossible. This is especially true of concepts considered adjacent to smartphone addiction, such as nomophobia and phubbing. The next chapter on measurement will focus on these implications.

What Does This Mean for Smartphone Use?

Two types of solutions have been proposed. These solutions are not mutually exclusive either. The first is to focus on specific behaviours rather than 'smartphone addiction'. The 'spectrum' approach argues that addictive behaviours should be represented as individual behaviours. Terms like internet or smartphone addiction represent a central tendency across online activities rather than a discrete entity separate from those behaviours. However, moving to individual behaviours isn't without its problems. Davidson et al. (2022) conducted a third analysis, using the same approach described above, that included multiple behavioural addictions. The same issues were observed in addictive smartphone use, binge-watching, internet gaming, and social media as with smartphone use alone. However, this finding was not replicated in subsequent item-level analyses. Instead, these supported separate factors with specific items cross-loading across behavioural addictions, and between behavioural addictions and wellbeing. Nonetheless, this highlights how measuring individual problematic behaviours instead of generalised smartphone addiction is not a complete solution. Measurement issues are common in specific behaviours, as with technology use in general.

The second is to move away from conceptualising phone use in terms of addiction. The clearest proposal here has been to promote problematic smartphone or mobile phone use as a term instead of smartphone addiction (see Chap. 6). This alternative proposes encompassing a wider range of harms associated with phone use (e.g. dangerous use, negative habits) that do not meet clinical severity or are coping mechanisms. It has also been proposed as a replacement if the addiction model is not appropriate. It includes behaviours that are specifically not within an addiction framework. Similarly, smartphone pervasiveness (Gerosa et al., 2022) has been proposed for interactions in specific contexts that are problematic or harmful rather than a generalised disorder. Consequently, this differs in terms of its breadth of coverage of different engagements and ostensibly in the range of severity. Such an approach is not contingent on a possible smartphone addiction either. However, doing so would require changing how we think about the smartphone. Rather than treating phones or their content as inherently problematic, PSU might represent a composite or formative construct of potentially harmful behaviours that are situation specific. Ideas about problematic or dysfunctional use may persist, but would instead be best viewed as flawed instruments for understanding our relationship with technology.

Pathways Model of Problematic Smartphone Use

The final model of interest is the Pathways Model of problematic mobile/smartphone use (Billieux, 2012; Billieux et al., 2015a). The Pathways Model was explicitly designed with critiques of the behavioural addiction model in mind and to account for heterogeneity in both antecedents and outcomes of problematic phone use. The model proposes three distinct causal pathways to problematic use, manifesting in three different types of problematic smartphone use. Each pathway is characterised by prior individual risk factors, specifically *excessive reassurance* (disordered mood, poor self-esteem), *impulsivity* (urgency, lack of premeditation and self-control), and *extraversion* (social connection, sensation-seeking). In turn, these can lead to *addictive/dependent*, *antisocial/prohibited* (i.e. when not supposed to), and *risky/dangerous* (e.g. use whilst driving, inappropriate sexting) patterns of use. Some pathways are more characteristic of specific PSUs than others. The excessive reassurance pathway is primarily linked with dependent use, whilst impulsivity and extraversion are linked with all three. The model also does not treat antecedents as mutually exclusive, but does not specify how these interact, either. This is important as some major risk factors for PSU, such as negative urgency (Hitcham et al., 2023), are characterised by an admixture of neuroticism and impulsivity. The Pathways Model has empirical support, with several papers using path models to support the hypothesised mechanisms (e.g. Pivetta et al., 2019; Dey et al., 2019; Canale et al., 2021).

Conclusion

This chapter reviewed different conceptual accounts of problematic and addictive smartphone use. There are reasons for scepticism regarding smartphone use meeting the criteria for an addiction disorder. The process of defining behavioural addictions has notable flaws; other factors can potentially explain the behaviours attributed to addictive smartphone use, and there is limited evidence of widespread functional impairment. Most published research explicitly or implicitly adopts a generalised conceptual model of smartphone addiction. This model also has extensive issues, including whether a separate smartphone addiction construct would be redundant. The consequence of these is the existence of dozens of fuzzy constructs inconsistently treated as equivalent or distinct entities, which is reflected in practice when these are measured as well.

References

Aagaard, J. (2021). Beyond the rhetoric of tech addiction: Why we should be discussing tech habits instead (and how). *Phenomenology and the Cognitive Sciences, 20*, 559–572. https://doi.org/10.1007/s11097-020-09669-z

Akematsu, Y., Shinohara, S., & Tsuji, M. (2012). Empirical analysis of factors promoting the Japanese 3G mobile phone. *Telecommunications Policy, 36*(3), 175–186. https://doi.org/10.1016/j.telpol.2011.11.027

American Psychiatric Association. (1987). Diagnostic and statistical manual of mental disorders (*DSM-III-R*). American Psychiatric Association.

American Psychiatric Association. (1994). *Diagnostic and statistical manual of mental disorders (DSM-IV)*. American Psychiatric Association.

American Psychiatric Association. (2013). *Diagnostic and statistical manual of mental disorders, (DSM-5®)*. American Psychiatric Publishing.

Andreassen, C. S., Torsheim, T., Brunborg, G. S., & Pallesen, S. (2012). Development of a Facebook addiction scale. *Psychological Reports, 110*(2), 501–517. https://doi.org/10.2466/02.09.18.PR0.110.2.501-517

Baggio, S., Bosson, M., Berle, D., Starcevic, V., Simon, O., & Billieux, J. (2024). Problematic online behaviors constitute related yet distinct conditions: A cross-sectional study. *Computers in Human Behavior, 160*, 108358. https://doi.org/10.1016/j.chb.2024.108358

Baggio, S., Starcevic, V., Billieux, J., King, D. L., Gainsbury, S. M., Eslick, G. D., & Berle, D. (2022). Testing the spectrum hypothesis of problematic online behaviors: A network analysis approach. *Addictive Behaviors, 135*, 107451. https://doi.org/10.1016/j.addbeh.2022.107451

Baggio, S., Starcevic, V., Studer, J., Simon, O., Gainsbury, S. M., Gmel, G., & Billieux, J. (2018). Technology-mediated addictive behaviors constitute a spectrum of related yet distinct conditions: A network perspective. *Psychology of Addictive Behaviors, 32*(5), 564. https://doi.org/10.1037/adb0000379

Bianchi, A., & Phillips, J. G. (2005). Psychological predictors of problem mobile phone use. *Cyberpsychology & Behavior, 8*(1), 39–51. https://doi.org/10.1089/cpb.2005.8.39

Billieux, J. (2012). Problematic use of the mobile phone: A literature review and a pathways model. *Current Psychiatry Reviews, 8*(4), 299–307. https://doi.org/10.2174/157340012803520522

Billieux, J., Flayelle, M., Rumpf, H.-J., & Stein, D. J. (2019). High involvement versus pathological involvement in video games: A crucial distinction for

ensuring the validity and utility of gaming disorder. *Current Addiction Reports, 6*, 323–330. https://doi.org/10.1007/s40429-019-00259-x
Billieux, J., Maurage, P., Lopez-Fernandez, O., Kuss, D. J., & Griffiths, M. D. (2015). Can disordered Mobile phone use be considered a behavioral addiction? An update on current evidence and a comprehensive model for future research. *Current Addiction Reports, 2*(2), 156–162. https://doi.org/10.1007/s40429-015-0054-y
Billieux, J., Schimmenti, A., Khazaal, Y., Maurage, P., & Heeren, A. (2015). Are we overpathologizing everyday life? A tenable blueprint for behavioral addiction research. *Journal of Behavioral Addictions, 4*(3), 119–123. https://doi.org/10.1556/2006.4.2015.009
Brand, M., Wegmann, E., Stark, R., Müller, A., Wölfling, K., Robbins, T. W., & Potenza, M. N. (2019). The interaction of person-affect-cognition-execution (I-PACE) model for addictive behaviors: Update, generalization to addictive behaviors beyond internet-use disorders, and specification of the process character of addictive behaviors. *Neuroscience & Biobehavioral Reviews, 104*, 1–10. https://doi.org/10.1016/j.neubiorev.2019.06.032
Brand, M., Young, K. S., Laier, C., Wölfling, K., & Potenza, M. N. (2016). Integrating psychological and neurobiological considerations regarding the development and maintenance of specific internet-use disorders: An interaction of person-affect-cognition-execution (I-PACE) model. *Neuroscience & Biobehavioral Reviews, 71*, 252–266. https://doi.org/10.1016/j.neubiorev.2016.08.033
Brown, R. I. F. (1993). Some contributions of the study of gambling to the study of other addictions. *Gambling Behavior and Problem Gambling, 1*, 241–272.
Canale, N., Moretta, T., Pancani, L., Buodo, G., Vieno, A., Dalmaso, M., & Billieux, J. (2021). A test of the pathway model of problematic smartphone use. *Journal of Behavioral Addictions, 10*(1), 181–193. https://doi.org/10.1556/2006.2020.00103
Carbonell, X., Guardiola, E., Beranuy, M., & Bellés, A. (2009). A bibliometric analysis of the scientific literature on internet, video games, and cell phone addiction. *Journal of the Medical Library Association, 97*(2), 102–107. https://doi.org/10.3163/1536-5050.97.2.006
Charlton, J. P., & Danforth, I. D. W. (2007). Distinguishing addiction and high engagement in the context of online game playing. *Computers in Human Behavior, 23*(3), 1531–1548. https://doi.org/10.1016/j.chb.2005.07.002

Cheng, Y., & Meng, J. (2021). The association between depression and problematic smartphone behaviors through smartphone use in a clinical sample. *Human Behavior and Emerging Technologies, 3*(3), 441–453. https://doi.org/10.1002/hbe2.258

Chotpitayasunondh, V., & Douglas, K. M. (2016). How "phubbing" becomes the norm: The antecedents and consequences of snubbing via smartphone. *Computers in Human Behavior, 63*, 9–18. https://doi.org/10.1016/j.chb.2016.05.018

Csibi, S., Demetrovics, Z., & Szabo, A. (2016). Hungarian adaptation and psychometric characteristics of brief addiction to smartphone scale (BASS). *Psychiatria Hungarica, 31*(1), 71–77.

Csibi, S., Griffiths, M. D., Cook, B., Demetrovics, Z., & Szabo, A. (2018). The psychometric properties of the smartphone application-based addiction scale (SABAS). *International Journal of Mental Health and Addiction, 16*(2), 393–403. https://doi.org/10.1007/s11469-017-9787-2

Dalley, J. W., Everitt, B. J., & Robbins, T. W. (2011). Impulsivity, compulsivity, and top-down cognitive control. *Neuron, 69*(4), 680–694. https://doi.org/10.1016/j.neuron.2011.01.020

Davidson, B. I., Shaw, H., & Ellis, D. A. (2022). Fuzzy constructs in technology usage scales. *Computers in Human Behavior, 107206*. https://doi.org/10.1016/j.chb.2022.107206

Davis, R. A. (2001). A cognitive-behavioral model of pathological internet use. *Computers in Human Behavior, 17*(2), 187–195. https://doi.org/10.1016/S0747-5632(00)00041-8

Dellosa, G., & Browne, M. (2024). The influence of age on gambling problems worldwide: A systematic review and meta-analysis of risk among younger, middle-aged, and older adults. *Journal of Behavioral Addictions, 13*(3), 702–715. https://doi.org/10.1556/2006.2024.00051

Dey, M., Studer, J., Schaub, M. P., Gmel, G., Ebert, D. D., Lee, J. Y.-C., & Haug, S. (2019). Problematic smartphone use in young Swiss men: Its association with problematic substance use and risk factors derived from the pathway model. *Journal of Behavioral Addictions, 8*(2), 326–334. https://doi.org/10.1556/2006.8.2019.17

Domoff, S. E., Elhai, J. D., Long, J., Lopez-Fernandez, O., Montag, C., Starcevic, V., Szabo, A., Vanden Abeele, M. M., Demetrovics, Z. and Billieux, J., 2025. Dysregulated use of mobile/smartphone. Handbook of Children and Screens, pp.195-201. Springer

Downs, D. S., Hausenblas, H. A., & Nigg, C. R. (2004). Factorial validity and psychometric examination of the exercise dependence scale-revised. *Measurement in Physical Education and Exercise Science, 8*(4), 183–201. https://doi.org/10.1207/s15327841mpee0804_1

Elhai, J. D., Yang, H., & Levine, J. C. (2021). Applying fairness in labeling various types of internet use disorders: commentary on how to overcome taxonomical problems in the study of internet use disorders and what to do with "smartphone addiction"?. Journal of Behavioral Addictions, 9(4), 924–927. https://doi.org/10.1556/2006.2020.00071

Flayelle, M., Brevers, D., King, D. L., Maurage, P., Perales, J. C., & Billieux, J. (2023). A taxonomy of technology design features that promote potentially addictive online behaviours. *Nature Reviews Psychology, 2*(3), 136–150. https://doi.org/10.1038/s44159-023-00153-4

Flayelle, M., Schimmenti, A., Starcevic, V., & Billieux, J. (2022). The pitfalls of recycling substance-use disorder criteria to diagnose behavioral addictions. In *Evaluating the brain disease model of addiction* (pp. 339–349). Routledge.

Fullwood, C., Quinn, S., Kaye, L. K., & Redding, C. (2017). My virtual friend: A qualitative analysis of the attitudes and experiences of smartphone users: Implications for smartphone attachment. *Computers in Human Behavior, 75*, 347–355. https://doi.org/10.1016/j.chb.2017.05.029

Gerosa, T., Gui, M., & Büchi, M. (2022). Smartphone use and academic performance: A pervasiveness approach beyond addiction. *Social Science Computer Review, 40*(6), 1542–1561. https://doi.org/10.1177/08944393211018969

Goodman, A. (1990). Addiction: Definition and implications. *British Journal of Addiction, 85*(11), 1403–1408. https://doi.org/10.1111/j.1360-0443.1990.tb01620.x

Grall-Bronnec, M., Bulteau, S., Victorri-Vigneau, C., Bouju, G., & Sauvaget, A. (2015). Fortune telling addiction: Unfortunately a serious topic about a case report. *Journal of Behavioral Addictions, 4*(1), 27–31. https://doi.org/10.1556/jba.4.2015.1.7

Gray, H. M., LaPlante, D. A., & Shaffer, H. J. (2012). Behavioral characteristics of internet gamblers who trigger corporate responsible gambling interventions. *Psychology of Addictive Behaviors, 26*(3), 527–535. https://doi.org/10.1037/a0028545

Griffiths, M. D. (2005). A 'components' model of addiction within a biopsychosocial framework. *Journal of Substance Use, 10*(4), 191–197. https://doi.org/10.1080/14659890500114359

Griffiths, M. D. (2017). Behavioural addiction and substance addiction should be defined by their similarities not their dissimilarities. *Addiction, 112*(10), 1718–1720. https://doi.org/10.1111/add.13828

Griffiths, M. D. (2021). Internet use disorders: What's new and what's not? Commentary on: How to overcome taxonomical problems in the study of internet use disorders and what to do with "smartphone addiction"? (Montag et al., 2019). *Journal of Behavioral Addictions, 9*(4), 934–937. https://doi.org/10.1556/2006.2020.00072

Hing, N., Browne, M., Rockloff, M., Russell, A. M., Tulloch, C., Lole, L., Thorne, H., & Newall, P. (2023). Situational features of smartphone betting are linked to sports betting harm: An ecological momentary assessment study. *Journal of Behavioral Addictions, 12*(4), 1006–1018. https://doi.org/10.1556/2006.2023.00065

Hing, N., Russell, A. M., Black, A., Rockloff, M., Browne, M., Rawat, V., Greer, N., Stevens, M., Dowling, N. A., & Merkouris, S. (2022). Gambling prevalence and gambling problems amongst land-based-only, online-only and mixed-mode gamblers in Australia: A national study. *Computers in Human Behavior, 132*, 107269. https://doi.org/10.1016/j.chb.2022.107269

Hitcham, L., Jackson, H., & James, R. J. E. (2023). The relationship between smartphone use and smartphone addiction: An examination of logged and self-reported behavior in a pre-registered, two-wave sample. *Computers in Human Behavior, 107822*. https://doi.org/10.1016/j.chb.2023.107822

Hogan, J. N., Heyman, R. E., & Smith Slep, A. M. (2024). A meta-review of screening and treatment of electronic "addictions". *Clinical Psychology Review, 113*, 102468. https://doi.org/10.1016/j.cpr.2024.102468

Hong, Y., Rong, X., & Liu, W. (2024). Construction of influencing factor segmentation and intelligent prediction model of college students' cell phone addiction model based on machine learning algorithm. *Heliyon, 10*(8). https://doi.org/10.1016/j.heliyon.2024.e29245

Hu, B., Wu, Q., Xie, Y., Guo, L., & Yin, D. (2024). Cell phone addiction and sleep disturbance among medical students in Jiangsu Province, China: The mediating role of psychological resilience and the moderating role of gender. *Frontiers in Psychiatry, 15*, 1405139. https://doi.org/10.3389/fpsyt.2024.1405139

Jameel, S., Shahnawaz, M. G., & Griffiths, M. D. (2019). Smartphone addiction in students: A qualitative examination of the components model of addiction using face-to-face interviews. *Journal of Behavioral Addictions, 8*(4), 780–793. https://doi.org/10.1556/2006.8.2019.57

James, R. J. E., O'Malley, C., & Tunney, R. J. (2017). Understanding the psychology of mobile gambling: A behavioural synthesis. *British Journal of Psychology, 108*(3), 608–625. https://doi.org/10.1111/bjop.12226

James, R. J. E., & Tunney, R. J. (2017). The need for a behavioural analysis of behavioural addictions. *Clinical Psychology Review, 52*, 69–76. https://doi.org/10.1016/j.cpr.2016.11.010

Jhone, J. H., Song, I. H., Lee, M. S., Yoon, J. Y., & Bhang, S. Y. (2021). Is the I-PACE (interaction of person-affect-cognition-execution) model valid in South Korea? The effects of adverse childhood experiences (ACEs) on internet gaming disorder and the mediating effect of stress on adolescents. *Journal of Behavioral Addictions, 10*(4), 967–982. https://doi.org/10.1556/2006.2021.00081

Karadağ, E., Tosuntaş, Ş. B., Erzen, E., Duru, P., Bostan, N., Şahin, B. M., Çulha, İ., & Babadağ, B. (2015). Determinants of phubbing, which is the sum of many virtual addictions: A structural equation model. *Journal of Behavioral Addictions, 4*(2), 60–74. https://doi.org/10.1556/2006.4.2015.005

Kardefelt-Winther, D. (2014a). A conceptual and methodological critique of internet addiction research: Towards a model of compensatory internet use. *Computers in Human Behavior, 31*, 351–354. https://doi.org/10.1016/j.chb.2013.10.059

Kardefelt-Winther, D. (2014b). The moderating role of psychosocial well-being on the relationship between escapism and excessive online gaming. Computers in Human Behavior, 38, 68–74. https://doi.org/10.1016/j.chb.2014.05.020

Kardefelt-Winther, D. (2015). A critical account of DSM-5 criteria for internet gaming disorder. *Addiction Research & Theory, 23*(2), 93–98. https://doi.org/10.3109/16066359.2014.935350

Kardefelt-Winther, D., Heeren, A., Schimmenti, A., Van Rooij, A., Maurage, P., Carras, M., Edman, J., Blaszczynski, A., Khazaal, Y., & Billieux, J. (2017). How can we conceptualize behavioural addiction without pathologizing common behaviours? *Addiction, 112*(10), 1709–1715. https://doi.org/10.1111/add.13763

Karhulahti, V.-M., Martončik, M., & Adamkovič, M. (2021). Measuring internet gaming disorder and gaming disorder: A qualitative content validity analysis of validated scales. *Assessment, 30*(2), 402–413. https://doi.org/10.1177/10731911211055435

Kaye, L. K., Egan, I. M., Rowe, B., & Taylor, J. (2024). A qualitative study exploring behaviors which underpin different types of social media use.

Psychology of Popular Media, 14(2), 264–275. https://psycnet.apa.org/doi/10.1037/ppm0000533

Kim, D., Lee, Y., Lee, J., Nam, J. K., & Chung, Y. (2014). Development of Korean smartphone addiction proneness scale for youth. *PLoS One, 9*(5), e97920. https://doi.org/10.1371/journal.pone.0097920

King, A. L. S., Valenca, A.-M., Silva, A.-C. O., Baczynski, T., Carvalho, M. R., & Nardi, A. E. (2013). Nomophobia: Dependency on virtual environments or social phobia? *Computers in Human Behavior, 29*(1), 140–144. https://doi.org/10.1016/j.chb.2012.07.025

Körmendi, A., Brutoczki, Z., Vegh, B. P., & Szekely, R. (2016). Smartphone use can be addictive? A case report. *Journal of Behavioral Addictions, 5*(3), 548–552. https://doi.org/10.1556/2006.5.2016.033

Kuss, D. J., & Griffiths, M. D. (2017). Social networking sites and addiction: Ten lessons learned. *International Journal of Environmental Research and Public Health, 14*(3), 311. https://doi.org/10.3390/ijerph14030311

Kwon, M., Lee, J.-Y., Won, W.-Y., Park, J.-W., Min, J.-A., Hahn, C., Gu, X., Choi, J.-H., & Kim, D.-J. (2013). Development and validation of a smartphone addiction scale (SAS). *PLoS One, 8*(2), e56936. https://doi.org/10.1371/journal.pone.0056936

Larsen, H., Wiers, R. W., Su, S., & Cousijn, J. (2023). Excessive smartphone use and addiction: When harms start outweighing benefits. *Addiction, 118*(4), 586–588. https://doi.org/10.1111/add.16060

Lee, C., & Lee, S. J. (2017). Prevalence and predictors of smartphone addiction proneness among Korean adolescents. Children and Youth Services Review, 77, 10–17. https://doi.org/10.1016/j.childyouth.2017.04.002

Leung, L. (2008). Leisure boredom, sensation seeking, self-esteem, and addiction: Symptoms and patterns of cell phone use. In *Mediated interpersonal communication* (pp. 373–396). Routledge.

Lin, H., He, G., Zheng, H., & Ai, J. (2025). What makes Chinese adolescents glued to their smartphones? Using network analysis and three-wave longitudinal analysis to assess how adverse childhood experiences influence smartphone addiction. *Computers in Human Behavior, 163*, 108484. https://doi.org/10.1016/j.chb.2024.108484

Lin, Y.-H., Lin, Y.-C., Lee, Y.-H., Lin, P.-H., Lin, S.-H., Chang, L.-R., Tseng, H.-W., Yen, L.-Y., Yang, C. C., & Kuo, T. B. (2015). Time distortion associated with smartphone addiction: Identifying smartphone addiction via a mobile application (app). *Journal of Psychiatric Research, 65*, 139–145. https://doi.org/10.1016/j.jpsychires.2015.04.003

Marciano, L., Schulz, P. J., & Camerini, A. L. (2021). How smartphone use becomes problematic: Application of the ALT-SR model to study the predicting role of personality traits. *Computers in Human Behavior, 119*, 106731. https://doi.org/10.1016/j.chb.2021.106731

Marengo, D., Sindermann, C., Häckel, D., Settanni, M., Elhai, J. D., & Montag, C. (2020). The association between the big five personality traits and smartphone use disorder: A meta-analysis. *Journal of Behavioral Addictions, 9*(3), 534–550. https://doi.org/10.1556/2006.2020.00069

Mehmood, A., Bu, T., Zhao, E., Zelenina, V., Alexander, N., Wang, W., Siddiqi, S. M., Qiu, X., Yang, X., Qiao, Z., & Zhou, J. (2021). Exploration of psychological mechanism of smartphone addiction among international students of China by selecting the framework of the I-PACE model. *Frontiers in Psychology, 12*, 758610. https://doi.org/10.3389/fpsyg.2021.758610

Meng, S.-Q., Cheng, J.-L., Li, Y.-Y., Yang, X.-Q., Zheng, J.-W., Chang, X.-W., Shi, Y., Chen, Y., Lu, L., Sun, Y., Bao, Y.-P., & Shi, J. (2022). Global prevalence of digital addiction in general population: A systematic review and meta-analysis. *Clinical Psychology Review, 92*, 102128. https://doi.org/10.1016/j.cpr.2022.102128

Montag, C., Bey, K., Sha, P., Li, M., Chen, Y.-F., Liu, W.-Y., Zhu, Y.-K., Li, C.-B., Markett, S., Keiper, J., & Reuter, M. (2015). Is it meaningful to distinguish between generalized and specific internet addiction? Evidence from a cross-cultural study from Germany, Sweden, Taiwan and China. *Asia-Pacific Psychiatry, 7*(1), 20–26. https://doi.org/10.1111/appy.12122

Montag, C., Wegmann, E., Sariyska, R., Demetrovics, Z., & Brand, M. (2021). How to overcome taxonomical problems in the study of internet use disorders and what to do with "smartphone addiction"? *Journal of Behavioral Addictions, 9*(4), 908–914. https://doi.org/10.1556/2006.8.2019.59

Nawaz, S. (2024). Distinguishing between effectual, ineffectual, and problematic smartphone use: A comprehensive review and conceptual pathways model for future research. *Computers in Human Behavior Reports, 14*, 100424. https://doi.org/10.1016/j.chbr.2024.100424

Noë, B., Turner, L. D., Linden, D. E., Allen, S. M., Winkens, B., & Whitaker, R. M. (2019). Identifying indicators of smartphone addiction through user-app interaction. Computers in Human Behavior, 99, 56–65. https://doi.org/10.1016/j.chb.2019.04.023

O'Donnell, S., & Epstein, L. H. (2019). Smartphones are more reinforcing than food for students. Addictive behaviors, 90, 124–133. https://doi.org/10.1016/j.addbeh.2018.10.018

Oulasvirta, A., Rattenbury, T., Ma, L., & Raita, E. (2012). Habits make smartphone use more pervasive. Personal and Ubiquitous Computing, 16(1), 105–114. https://doi.org/10.1007/s00779-011-0412-2

Pan, Y.-C., Chiu, Y.-C., & Lin, Y.-H. (2019). Development of the problematic mobile gaming questionnaire and prevalence of mobile gaming addiction among adolescents in Taiwan. *Cyberpsychology, Behavior, and Social Networking, 22*(10), 662–669. https://doi.org/10.1089/cyber.2019.0085

Panova, T., & Carbonell, X. (2018). Is smartphone addiction really an addiction? *Journal of Behavioral Addictions, 7*(2), 252–259. https://doi.org/10.1556/2006.7.2018.49

Papineau, E., Lacroix, G., Sevigny, S., Biron, J.-F., Corneau-Tremblay, N., & Lemétayer, F. (2018). Assessing the differential impacts of online, mixed, and offline gambling. *International Gambling Studies, 18*(1), 69–91. https://doi.org/10.1080/14459795.2017.1378362

Park, W. K. (2005). Mobile phone addiction. In *Mobile communications: Re-negotiation of the social sphere* (pp. 253–272). Springer.

Pivetta, E., Harkin, L., Billieux, J., Kanjo, E., & Kuss, D. J. (2019). Problematic smartphone use: An empirically validated model. *Computers in Human Behavior, 100*, 105–117. https://doi.org/10.1016/j.chb.2019.06.013

Qu, D., Zhang, X., Wang, J., Liu, B., Wen, X., Feng, Y., & Chen, R. (2023). New form of addiction: An emerging hazardous addiction problem of milk tea among youths. *Journal of Affective Disorders, 341*, 26–34. https://doi.org/10.1016/j.jad.2023.08.102

Razum, J., Baumgartner, B., & Glavak-Tkalić, R. (2023). Psychometric validity and the appropriateness of tolerance as a criterion for internet gaming disorder: A systematic review. *Clinical Psychology Review, 101*, 102256. https://doi.org/10.1016/j.cpr.2023.102256

Richardson, A. C., Flack, M., & Caudwell, K. M. (2024). Two for the GOES: Exploring gambling outcome expectancies scores across mixed and offline-only gamblers in relation to problem gambling risk status. *Journal of Gambling Studies, 40*(2), 571–585. https://doi.org/10.1007/s10899-023-10234-x

Rosen, L. D., Whaling, K., Carrier, L. M., Cheever, N. A., & Rokkum, J. (2013). The media and technology usage and attitudes scale: An empirical investigation. *Computers in Human Behavior, 29*(6), 2501–2511. https://doi.org/10.1016/j.chb.2013.06.006

Rumpf, H.-J., Browne, D., Brandt, D., & Rehbein, F. (2021). Addressing taxonomic challenges for internet use disorders in light of changing technologies and diagnostic classifications: Commentary on: "How to overcome taxonomical problems in the study of internet use disorders and what to do with "smartphone addiction"?"(Montag et al., 2020). *Journal of Behavioral Addictions, 9*(4), 942–944. https://doi.org/10.1556/2006.2020.00094

Ryding, F. C., & Kaye, L. K. (2018). "Internet addiction": A conceptual minefield. *International Journal of Mental Health and Addiction, 16*, 225–232. https://doi.org/10.1007/s11469-017-9811-6

Ryding, F. C., & Kuss, D. J. (2020). Passive objective measures in the assessment of problematic smartphone use: A systematic review. *Addictive Behaviors Reports, 11*, 100257. https://doi.org/10.1016/j.abrep.2020.100257

Satchell, L. P., Fido, D., Harper, C. A., Shaw, H., Davidson, B., Ellis, D. A., Hart, C. M., Jalil, R., Bartoli, A. J., & Kaye, L. K. (2021). Development of an offline-friend addiction questionnaire (O-FAQ): Are most people really social addicts? *Behavior Research Methods, 53*(3), 1097–1106. https://doi.org/10.3758/s13428-020-01462-9

Starcevic, V., King, D. L., Delfabbro, P. H., Schimmenti, A., Castro-Calvo, J., Giardina, A., & Billieux, J. (2021). "Diagnostic inflation" will not resolve taxonomical problems in the study of addictive online behaviours. Commentary on: How to overcome taxonomical problems in the study of internet use disorders and what to do with "smartphone addiction"? (Montag et al., 2020). *Journal of Behavioral Addictions, 9*(4), 915–919. https://doi.org/10.1556/2006.2020.00083

Sussman, S., & Moran, M. B. (2013). Hidden addiction: Television. *Journal of Behavioral Addictions, 2*(3), 125–132. https://doi.org/10.1556/JBA.2.2013.008

Szalavitz, M. (2024). Addiction: Where framing can be a matter of life and death: Response to Flusberg et al. *Psychological Science in the Public Interest, 25*(3), 101–104. https://doi.org/10.1177/15291006241299319

Targhetta, R., Nalpas, B., & Perney, P. (2013). Argentine tango: Another behavioral addiction? *Journal of Behavioral Addictions, 2*(3), 179–186. https://doi.org/10.1556/JBA.2.2013.007

Terry, A., Szabo, A., & Griffiths, M. (2004). The exercise addiction inventory: A new brief screening tool. *Addiction Research & Theory, 12*(5), 489–499. https://doi.org/10.1080/16066350310001637363

Tian, H., & Wang, Y. (2023). Mobile phone addiction and sleep quality among older people: The mediating roles of depression and loneliness. *Behavioral Sciences, 13*(2), 153. https://doi.org/10.3390/bs13020153

van den Eijnden, R. J. J. M., Lemmens, J. S., & Valkenburg, P. M. (2016). The social media disorder scale. *Computers in Human Behavior, 61*, 478–487. https://doi.org/10.1016/j.chb.2016.03.038

Vieira, J. L., Coelho, S. G., Snaychuk, L. A., Parmar, P. K., Keough, M. T., & Kim, H. S. (2023). Who makes in-play bets? Investigating the demographics, psychological characteristics, and gambling-related harms of in-play sports bettors. *Journal of Behavioral Addictions, 12*(2), 547–556. https://doi.org/10.1556/2006.2023.00030

Vujić, A., & Szabo, A. (2022). Hedonic use, stress, and life satisfaction as predictors of smartphone addiction. Addictive Behaviors Reports, 15, 100411. https://doi.org/10.1016/j.abrep.2022.100411

Wardle, H., Moody, A., Griffiths, M. D., Orford, J., & Volberg, R. (2011). Defining the online gambler and patterns of behaviour integration: Evidence from the British gambling prevalence survey 2010. *International Gambling Studies, 11*(3), 339–356. https://doi.org/10.1080/14459795.2011.628684

Wei, D., Chan, L. S., Du, N., Hu, X., & Huang, Y. T. (2024). Gratification and its associations with problematic internet use: A systematic review and meta-analysis using Use and Gratification theory. Addictive Behaviors, 155, 108044. https://doi.org/10.1016/j.addbeh.2024.108044

World Health Organisation. (2024). *ICD-11*. Retrieved December 24, 2024, from https://icd.who.int/en

Wu, Y.-L., Lin, S.-H., & Lin, Y.-H. (2021). Two-dimensional taxonomy of internet addiction and assessment of smartphone addiction with diagnostic criteria and mobile apps. *Journal of Behavioral Addictions, 9*(4), 928–933. https://doi.org/10.1556/2006.2020.00074

Xu, X., Han, W., & Liu, Q. (2023). Peer pressure and adolescent mobile social media addiction: Moderation analysis of self-esteem and self-concept clarity. *Frontiers in Public Health, 11*, 1115661. https://doi.org/10.3389/fpubh.2023.1115661

Yildirim, C., & Correia, A.-P. (2015). Exploring the dimensions of nomophobia: Development and validation of a self-reported questionnaire. *Computers in Human Behavior, 49*, 130–137. https://doi.org/10.1016/j.chb.2015.02.059

Young, K. S. (1998). Internet addiction: The emergence of a new clinical disorder. *Cyberpsychology & Behavior, 1*(3), 237–244. https://doi.org/10.1089/cpb.1998.1.237

Young, K. (2009). Internet addiction: diagnosis and treatment considerations. Journal of Contemporary Psychotherapy, 39(4), 241–246. https://doi.org/10.1007/s10879-009-9120-x

Yu, S., & Sussman, S. (2020). Does smartphone addiction fall on a continuum of addictive behaviors? *International Journal of Environmental Research and Public Health, 17*(2). https://doi.org/10.3390/ijerph17020422

3

Measurement

Abstract This chapter focuses on measuring smartphone addiction (or problematic use). In light of the conceptual issues discussed in Chap. 2, it is unsurprising that difficulties emerge with translating these into measurement scales. As a result, nearly one hundred questionnaires have been developed to measure problematic or addictive phone use. In addition, a significant minority of studies develop ad-hoc scales or adjustments. Despite, or perhaps because of the volume of scale development research, there are substantial gaps in instrument validity, especially when comparing between different groups. These flaws place significant doubts on attempts to use these scales to classify people as meeting criteria for smartphone addiction, especially when these classify large sections of the population as at-risk. Finally, these issues crystallise when smartphone addiction scales are used in statistical modelling. A combination of poor practices and flexible modelling creates a substantial risk of bias. These measurement issues represent the most substantive threat to the validity of empirical research on smartphone addiction.

Keywords Measurement • Assessment • Instrument validity • Factor analysis • Measurement invariance • Content validity • Smartphone addiction • Problematic smartphone use

R. James, L. Hitcham, *Critical Perspectives on Smartphone Addiction*, Palgrave Studies in Cyberpsychology, https://doi.org/10.1007/978-3-031-96188-5_3

Introduction

This chapter focuses on the issues that permeate the measurement of smartphone addiction. Accurate and reliable measurement is a fundamental component of valid quantitative research. Smartphone addiction (SA) research relies heavily on self-report questionnaires and scales to determine the prevalence and severity of addictive behaviour. Inadequate measurement practices impair goals such as assessing risk factors, understanding mechanisms of problematic behaviour, and diagnosing potential disorders. Unfortunately, measurement difficulties represent the most serious methodological issue in SA research. Furthermore, these issues cannot be ignored because they apply regardless of the conceptual model adopted for addictive or problematic smartphone use. Measurement problems are pervasive in specific problematic online behaviours as well as in generalised smartphone addiction instruments.

The problems with measurement mirror concerns about replicability and reproducibility that have damaged the credibility of psychological research over the past fifteen years (Open Science Collaborative, 2015). These have motivated attempts to reform practice by improving rigour and transparency in the research process (e.g. Pennington et al., 2021). Although these concerns originated with methodological problems in experimental psychology, Flake and Fried (2020) explained how *questionable measurement practices* (QMPs) frequently threaten validity in questionnaire studies. The problems with research on technology use and its effects, including smartphone addiction, have been singled out for particularly concerning practices. Davidson et al. (2022) highlight how many of the conceptual problems explored in the previous chapter (see Chap. 2) go together with poor measurement and validation practices. Using Carpenter's (2018) guidelines for scale development, Davidson et al. (2022) critically analysed the development process of twelve technology use scales, highlighting considerable gaps in best practice with most measures. The lack of theoretical development occurs because constructs are often taken from general addiction models or other behavioural addictions, which the previous chapter highlighted as flawed. These issues with conceptualisation and assessment, alongside an absence of other measures of technology use such as objective logs, frequently lead to obscured associations with other factors of interest such as mental and physical health (Shaw et al., 2020).

However, a focus on scale development alone substantially underestimates the severity of measurement problems in the area. The guidelines used in the Davidson et al. (2022) analysis only cover the theoretical development and initial empirical assessment during scale development. Wider issues with scale validation, usage, and statistical modelling are potentially more serious and equally pervasive. This chapter focuses on four core issues: the variety of measures employed, determining scale validity, assessing smartphone addiction prevalence, and using these scales for statistical modelling.

Scale Variety

Fundamental disagreement on the appropriate tools to measure addictive/problematic smartphone use plagues the field. This disagreement is partly because of the variety of proposed constructs we explored in the previous chapter. To illustrate the scale of this problem, a systematic review by Harris et al. (2020) identified 78 distinct problematic smartphone use (PSU) measures developed between 2004 and 2019. Since this review was published in 2020, more than a dozen studies have been published describing the validation of new scales (e.g. Ranjan et al., 2024; Donjdee et al., 2024; Su et al., 2024; Geçer et al., 2024; Bradish et al., 2023; Berntsen et al., 2023; Park & Oh, 2024; Manara et al., 2024; Pressey et al., 2024; Luque-Reca et al., 2024; Park & Kim, 2021; Roberts & David, 2022). Even as the number of scales measuring negative smartphone effects approaches one hundred, researchers continue to conclude that there is a need for novel measurements (Harris et al., 2020; Nawaz, 2023). This is also true for smartphone use more generally, which continues to rely heavily on self-report scales as opposed to more objective measures (Ellis et al., 2019) (see Chap. 4). The volume of scales developed to measure similar or identical constructs is remarkable and illuminates the depth of disagreement and concern.

This variety creates numerous problems. It creates redundancy because much of the published research literature seeks to validate these instruments in different contexts and identify possible risk factors or consequences. Because of the variety of scales in use, this leads to a growing body of studies that look at associations between problematic/addictive phone use and well-established correlates (e.g. depression, anxiety), where the main distinction is the scale used. In some ways, this is not a problem. A crucial part of scientific endeavour is building a body of reliable, replicable evidence. However, it can become a barrier in this case because doubts about measurement inhibit further theoretical, methodological and analytic development. The volume of scales also means that more substantial validation of these instruments does not occur, as effort is spread between the many scales available. Major studies have refined existing scales (e.g. Sun & Tang, 2025; Bian & Leung, 2015), but significant efforts continue to focus on creating novel instruments. It also increases the risk of QMPs because it increases the array of instruments to choose from, and evidence to justify the use of specific measures is sparse. A lack of clarity in mapping constructs onto measures, with scales such as the Smartphone Addiction Scale (SAS) (Kwon et al., 2013a, 2013b) being used to measure PSU, increases this further.

The sheer variety of scales makes comparing across cultures and studies extremely difficult. Notwithstanding statistical concerns about comparability (discussed in the section on 'Adaptation and Bias'), different scales have become preferred in specific countries or settings due to factors such as the availability of translations or researcher preference. It further becomes a problem when conducting reviews and meta-analyses, as instrument-specific effects may bias results (see Chap. 4). This is particularly relevant when comparing across cultures and determining whether there are genuine differences in the rate or severity of SA, or instead, there are cultural and instrument-specific effects that bias those differences.

The situation is clearer with the scales used in empirical research. Kwon et al.'s (2013a) Smartphone Addiction Scale (SAS), and particularly its abbreviated Short Version (SAS-SV) (Kwon et al., 2013b), is the most popular measure and is used in a significant portion (around 30%) of studies (James et al., 2023). The SAS, developed in the early 2010s and validated in a Korean adolescent sample, has continued gaining traction as the field's most popular measure. Other measures, such as Yildirim and Correia's (2015) Nomophobia Questionnaire (NMP-Q) and the

Smartphone Addiction Proneness Scale (SAPS) (Kim et al., 2014), are also popular and are used in around 10% of studies. After that, a small number of measures (e.g. SABAS, MPAI, SPAI, SAS-C) were used in between 3% and 5% of the studies, respectively. The SAPS enjoys further use in secondary analysis beyond this estimate because it has been administered in national surveys in South Korea. It is also extensively used in studies published in Korean-language journals.

This filtering is both a positive and a negative. It reduces the scale of the problem because many developed scales are used only once or twice, which mirrors practice elsewhere in psychology (Elson et al., 2023). At the same time, it highlights that the selection pressures influencing scale adoption may not be sensitive to measurement quality. Many of the most popular instruments have been highlighted as lacking robust scale development (Davidson et al., 2022). Their prominence may result from being among the first scales developed or from using a popular conceptual model rather than scale quality. Because many were adapted from existing models or instruments, the ability to produce these at speed comes at the cost of a deeper examination of the conceptual and empirical issues present with these scales (Flayelle et al., 2023). In other words, better measures may already exist but have not proliferated. Equally, calls for scale refinement of the development of new scales could be interpreted as a judgement on the perceived validity of many novel measures (Harris et al., 2020).

Bespoke Scales

The sheer choice of validated scales is only the first layer of this problem. A notableminority, around 5% of studies, created a bespoke measure. This bespoke measure is either a new scale developed by the authors or constructed out of parts of other measures. There are two types of bespoke scales. The first is a scale created or combined *ad hoc* for the reported study. These measures tend only to be used for a single study, sometimes consisting of a single item or two. Scale validation is minimal, usually limited to reporting internal consistency (Flake et al., 2017). Flake and Fried (2020) highlight this practice as a specific QMP. These are especially problematic because it is frequently unclear whether the items meaningfully combine to measure a smartphone use-related construct.

The second cluster primarily consists of adaptations from existing instruments to reduce the number of items or adapt the content to the construct of interest. This cluster is also characterised by disciplinary differences, with many of these studies coming from fields such as information systems (IS) with different methodological traditions and assessment practices. These are distinguishable from other bespoke scales because scale validation is typically thorough and more appropriate formative models are applied (e.g. Partial Least Squares—Structural Equation Modeling (PLS-SEM)). In this sense, these bespoke measures are substantially better validated and modelled than the first cluster. However, these tend to use items from existing scales rather than completely novel measures. Consequently, many of these bespoke measures rely on the validity of the original sourced scales. As the rest of the chapter will explore, this reliance is the main weakness of these instruments.

Inconsistency

Even when validated scales are applied, they are not always used as designed. In our work scoping the smartphone addiction literature (James et al., 2023, we found that around 15% of studies used an existing scale differently from the originally reported measure. This practice is another of Flake and Fried's (2020) QMPs. These adaptations occur when items have been added or removed, the timescale changed, or the response options have been altered, for example, from a 5-point to a 7-point Likert scale or different labels for the ordered categories. These types of adaptation are rarely validated and sometimes appear to be made by mistake. Sometimes, the reporting of a change is mistaken, too. We found examples where the methods seemed to report using a modified scale, only for the results to confirm that the scale was used as intended (and many more *vice versa*). Occasionally, these amendments occur because of poor psychometric model fit. For example, researchers often remove items because there is evidence (e.g. lower loadings in factor analyses) that they behave differently from other questions on the scale, or relax poor-fitting structural models to allow correlated residuals between items. Nevertheless, non-standard instrument use is often accidental, and the data are interpreted in the same manner as the original scale. This estimate of 15% is likely to be conservative because it relies upon correct reporting of the instrument and procedures. This estimate is also separate from scales that have been changed substantially and validated during adaptation to different languages and cultures (see the section on *Adaptation*).

Sometimes, these changes do not make a large difference, depending on how the scale is used. However, there are cases where it can completely change the interpretation and meaning of a study—for example, going from an even to an odd number of response options can bias responses. Many odd-numbered Likert scales will include an anchor at the median response for 'neutral' or 'neither agree nor disagree'. The presence of a neutral answer might shift responses towards the median because the item is applicable in specific contexts or its meaning is unclear (Kulas & Stachowski, 2013). In these circumstances, adding or removing neutral items could have a similar effect across cultures and demographic groups. Such changes create challenges for statistical analysis. The presence of a neutral answer assumes that a neutral response is somewhere in the middle of a positive or negative evaluation of the question. This assumption is not guaranteed. If the change increases the number of response options, this will also inflate scores. These modifications become especially problematic if the purpose of the study is to classify respondents, and cutoffs are not scaled as well. Similarly, the choice of response anchors may affect how participants endorse items (e.g. changing from the degree of agreement to the level of frequency). Each of these may affect the response to a scale entirely or to specific items. Potential biases like this are especially problematic when employing cutoffs to classify people as 'addicted' and 'not addicted'. If the scale changes, particularly to increase the number of options and biases responding, this will affect the sample proportion that exceeds the intended cutoff, especially if it is not amended.

Item Validity

From the first stages of scale design and development, concerns with questionnaire item creation create further problems. The first development step involves theoretical justification for the proposed construct and its conceptualisation. Chapter 2 explored the many issues that occur when conceptualising smartphone addiction. However, it is important to explore how these affect scale development. Table 3.1 outlines the influences of some of the most popular smartphone addiction measurements. As Davidson et al. (2023) note, many instruments do not provide detailed

Table 3.1 Most popular smartphone addiction scales

Scale	Development process
Smartphone Addiction Scale (Kwon et al., 2013a)	The initial 48-item pool was developed from the K-Scale, created from the IAT. During the item development process, two items were removed, one amended, and ten more added
Smartphone Addiction Scale—Short Version (Kwon et al., 2013b))	The ten-item SAS-SV was selected using expert judgement from the 33-item SAS (Kwon et al., 2013a)
Smartphone Addiction Proneness Scale (SAPS) (Kim et al., 2014)	Developed out of the Internet Addiction Proneness Scale, a shortened version of the K-Scale. Added items to reflect unique features of smartphone use and ensured items reflected Young's and Greenfield's diagnostic criteria for internet addiction
Smartphone Application-Based Addiction Scale (SABAS) (Csibi et al., 2016, 2018)	Developed based on the Exercise Addiction Inventory (Terry et al., 2004). The SABAS and the EAI are derived from the Components Model
Smartphone Addiction Inventory (SPAI) (Lin et al., 2014)	Developed by amending the Chen Internet Addiction Scale for smartphone addiction
Mobile Phone Addiction Inventory (MPAI) (Leung, 2008), Smartphone Addiction Index (Bian & Leung, 2015)	Adapted out of IAT, MPPUS, DSM criteria, and Television Addiction Scale. The MPAI and SPAI are distinct but have a common set of items. These are commonly used across both for determining addiction, based on Young's diagnostic criteria for internet addiction
Problematic Mobile Phone Use Questionnaire (PMPUQ) (Billieux et al., 2008)	Novel measure based on theoretical model and constructs of impulsivity
MPPUS (Bianchi & Phillips, 2005)	Questions based on the addiction literature
NMP-Q (Yildirim & Correia, 2015)	Novel measure, with theoretical and empirical development of the construct before scale construction (Yildirim & Correia, 2015b)

theoretical justification for the assessed construct. One reason is that many popular smartphone addiction questionnaires were not created *de novo*. For example, the Smartphone Application-Based Addiction Scale (SABAS) (Csibi et al., 2018) is adapted from another instrument using the same model to measure exercise addiction (Terry et al., 2004). Most of the item generation process for these scales involves adaptation from other behavioural addiction scales. Few are created without adapting from an existing measure or construct. Sometimes, the scale is adapted entirely from another context and applied to smartphone use.

Even when this is not the case, the validation process can become circular. Consider the Smartphone Addiction Scale (SAS) and its short version (SAS-SV). The SAS was developed from a pool of 48 items, including 38 items from the K-Scale (Kim et al., 2002), a measure of internet addiction partially developed out of the Internet Addiction Test (IAT) (Young, 1998), and ten novel items to capture the distinctiveness of smartphone use. The subscales of the final 33-item scale were validated against the K-Scale and an adaptation of the IAT, with internet-specific content replaced by smartphone-focused terms. One measure, the IAT, indirectly contributes to the item pool and to the concurrent validity of the SAS. The SAS-SV, in turn, was also validated against the SAPS (developed from the K-Scale) and an abbreviated version of the K-Scale, which, as noted, was partly developed out of the IAT.

As these examples highlight, a lot of the development process involves translation from addiction models or other behavioural addictions. When smartphones started gaining popularity, initial investigations into problematic smartphone use adapted items and questionnaires from internet addiction measures (i.e. IAT). Others adapted measures from earlier cell phone and mobile phone addiction scales, which often used internet addiction concepts as well. A clear concern is whether these adaptations are appropriate in the first place. In the case of questions adapted from internet addiction, regardless of the proposed conceptual model, these will bias the scale towards measuring a generalised construct. As noted in the previous chapter, this approach to conceptualising internet and smartphone addiction is deeply problematic.

Many internet addiction items were originally adapted from other addictive disorders, especially pathological gambling. The translation from gambling to the internet and other behavioural addictions is even more questionable than the translation from internet to smartphone addiction. It is easy to see how the same items applied to smartphone use and gambling or substance misuse produce substantially different responses. The threshold for endorsing behaviours such as preoccupation and excessive use in gambling and substance use is high, with a minority of gamblers endorsing individual items assessing disordered gambling criteria (James et al., 2024). However, with smartphones and the internet, endorsement is relatively common. It is quite possible that equating the two is fundamentally inappropriate. Most people would consider spending excessive amounts of time on gambling or alcohol consumption as a sign of a potential disorder. This judgement is not as straightforward for phones because of the variety of functions the smartphone serves (Panova & Carbonell, 2018). Further, this variety makes it difficult to determine which activities respondents evaluate when considering their smartphone use, that is, whether it includes necessary work and communication with wilful recreational activity. Someone who feels compelled to use their phone at night to respond to work messages might well be experiencing technology-facilitated harm from their job. However, it does not appear necessary or appropriate to attribute this to a smartphone addiction.

As noted in the previous chapter, one concern with using broad questions to assess PSU is that a wide range of contextual motivations of phone use are misattributed to addictive behaviour. Consequently, many measures include items that appear insufficiently sensitive to clinical severity and risk, specifically conflating adaptive and maladaptive use. For example, questions about excessive use or use when feeling sad or upset potentially capture mundane behaviour and attribute it to an addictive disorder. The content of these items has not been updated as phones have become necessary for our everyday lives. Questions about certain engagement patterns may fail to capture changes in societal norms and instead assign them to disordered behaviour. This concern was raised about internet addiction nearly a decade ago (Kardefelt-Winther, 2014) and has largely been ignored. Like internet addiction, many smartphone addiction items were developed in the early stages of smartphone adoption. For example, using preferences for online or phone interaction as an indicator of addiction is less sustainable as our relationships with people become increasingly multimodal. This is especially so in unusual circumstances, such as during a pandemic. Many studies were conducted during the COVID-19 pandemic to test whether social isolation increased 'screen time' and smartphone addiction (Serra et al., 2021). Many of these changes are likely attributable to contextual factors, that is, health anxiety or changing behaviours, rather than addiction severity. Several reviews have highlighted potential risks of bias (Masaeli & Farhadi, 2021; Alimoradi et al., 2022) in interpreting the findings from these studies. Consequently, these items increasingly risk measuring changes in societal norms in technology use and inappropriately attribute them to a psychological disorder, potentially leading to the 'over-pathologising' of everyday life and use (Billieux et al., 2015).

These processes lead to the creation of scales that are fundamentally flawed. Satchell et al. (2021) applied practices from social media addiction, which are essentially identical to smartphone addiction, to develop the Offline Friends Addiction Questionnaire (O-FAQ) as a parody and critique of this process. Of particular note, the O-FAQ items were adapted from existing measures of behavioural addiction and correlated with relevant domains of risk-taking and impulsivity. The result was a scale that met and frequently exceeded the standard of evidence used to create addiction scales, whilst being obviously inappropriate. Like many of these instruments' conceptual models, these practices fail to discriminate between plausible and absurd candidate behavioural addictions.

Scale Validity

So far, the problems encountered cover the choice and content of measurement scales. This section focuses on whether these scales are statistically valid. Researchers do not typically treat each questionnaire item as unique. Instead, they assume these items contribute towards measuring one or more underlying (or latent) constructs. For example, the ten items of the SAS-SV intend to measure a single latent construct of smartphone addiction. Other measures, such as the full SAS, measure several latent subscales (i.e. daily-life disturbance, positive anticipation, withdrawal, cyberspace-oriented relationship, overuse, and tolerance). As part of validating a scale, researchers typically collect data and subject the measurement to statistical analysis to model these latent constructs using techniques such as principal components (PCA) or exploratory factor analysis (EFA). These techniques can determine which items fit a latent construct and how strongly each item fits (or loads) onto a factor. The results are frequently used to refine the measure, often by removing items that do not fit the construct of interest. Some studies may further validate this model in a different sample using confirmatory factor analysis (CFA), where the structure is pre-specified, and the analysis tests how well this structure fits the data. Despite, or perhaps because there are so many scales, many of them have not been tested to the highest level of structural validity. There are also problems with applying these validation procedures in smartphone addiction research. The problems of inconsistency and poor criterion validity are pervasive, whereas issues concerning the structural validity of each questionnaire vary a lot. This means there are some measures where we know a lot about their structural validity, but there are common gaps across the existing empirical literature.

Factor analysis is a powerful and flexible technique for assessing structural validity. But this flexibility can be a double-edged sword. Many different analytic choices can be made with factor analysis, influencing the outcome and, ultimately, the scale that emerges from the development process. One of the first analytical choices is whether to model the questionnaire items as continuous or ordinal. Almost every smartphone addiction questionnaire uses ordinal scales. For example, the SAS-SV asks respondents to rate each item on a 6-point scale. The six points are labelled 'strongly disagree' (1), 'disagree' (2), 'weakly (or slightly) disagree' (3), 'weakly agree' (4), 'agree' (5), and 'strongly agree' (6). It is often taken for granted that this data can be treated as continuous, and in most cases, the impact of doing so is small (Rhemtulla et al., 2012). However, there are cases where this choice can completely change the results. Suppose the items are scored on a small number of categories, the responses are skewed, or the thresholds between points on a scale are not roughly similar; treating the data as continuous will systematically bias the results in these cases. Often, this will lead to items loading on each factor to a smaller degree, potentially removing adequate items unnecessarily. It also may produce spurious factors.

Another significant source of bias is in the criteria used to guide decisions about a questionnaire's underlying structure, such as the number of factors to retain when using exploratory factor analysis.. Many criteria have been proposed to decide this, and normative practice has preferred some of the worst-performing measures. In exploratory factor analysis, some popular statistical programmes continue to use the heuristic of retaining eigenvalues greater than 1 (Kaiser, 1960) despite decades of research highlighting that this procedure is frequently unreliable (Yeomans & Golder, 1982). Few validation studies apply more empirically robust methods, such as parallel analysis (Horn, 1965). Otherwise, many metrics used to assess how well a model fits the data are inappropriately used in exploratory and confirmatory factor analysis. These practices are especially complicated when treating the data as categorical. Many confirmatory factor analyses that model items as ordinal use guidelines developed for continuous data (Hu & Bentler, 1999). Often, these are not appropriate and end up being biased.

It is common to rotate the factors to aid their interpretability. These rotations can be *orthogonal* (uncorrelated) or *oblique* (correlated). Some smartphone scales (i.e. NMP-Q) have used orthogonal rotation during development, whereas others have used oblique rotations (i.e. SAS). An orthogonal rotation will produce separable factors, but if multiple factors are correlated or the items are complex, these factors may not be meaningful or interpretable (Abdi, 2003). In most psychological domains, latent factors are likely to be correlated, and there is no detriment to using an oblique rotation (Reise et al., 2000; Preacher & MacCallum, 2003). Oblique rotations will accurately capture these dependencies, but in the case of highly correlated factors, these rotations may not clearly distinguish whether they are distinct. Conversely, items loading onto multiple factors may show poor fit in confirmatory analyses when they are typically expected to fit onto a single factor. Because these are often used to justify the retention and removal of items, this is worth bearing in mind because it can lead to excluding theoretically meaningful or important behaviours.

Often, scale development studies will conduct factor analyses to determine whether the questionnaire measures multiple subscales but fail to distinguish whether these subscales are meaningful or whether a single score is appropriate. Suppose a scale has been validated with an orthogonally rotated factor matrix, and the clusters of items are genuinely uncorrelated. Treating those scales as a composite score makes little sense. Measures of personality traits, like the Big Five, treat these subscales as separate scores. It is not standard practice to combine them into a single score of how much personality someone has. Other times, a single score is acceptable or preferable, especially when the factors are highly correlated. A single score will be more sensitive than its constituent subscales, and if the scales are highly correlated, the additional information gained from using subscales is minimal (e.g. Widaman & Revelle, 2023; Sijtsma et al., 2024). Most validation studies only test the first-order factor structure without demonstrating whether a single score is suitable using an appropriate method such as a hierarchical or bifactor model (Reise et al., 2010). The lack of guidance creates flexibility in analytic choices that can lead to biased conclusions.

The range of choices across exploratory and confirmatory analyses creates a mixture of inconsistencies and ambiguities in these validation studies. One of the main problems with these structural analyses is that inappropriate guidelines often determine the final model. When inappropriately applied, these lead to exaggerated claims of scale validity, inadvisable selection/removal of items, or the creation of spurious subscales.

External Validity

Once a scale has been structurally tested, it is common to validate it further by comparing it against other measurements to see if it correlates with constructs that are supposed to (i.e. convergent/concurrent validity) and does not correlate with constructs it should not. Often, this compares whether the scale is better than older scales. However, as explored earlier in the section on item validity, many questionnaires source items from existing assessments. Aside from these problems, these measures commonly validate the new measure by testing whether they are substantially correlated with existing scales. The scale development processes of the SAS and SAS-SV are instructive because of the influence of one measure, the Internet Addiction Test, in developing the questionnaire items and then being used as a benchmark of external validity. This example highlights some of the circularity that is common in the field. One measure becomes the basis and benchmark of a range of popular scales. Consequently, many of these measures are very highly correlated with each other. It is also problematic because it makes it difficult to determine whether this correlation is because they are equivalent constructs or because they use synonymous items to measure different behaviours, which is a source of methodological bias. It further biases scale development towards picking items that measure a generalised construct. The consequence is that many measures of SA/PSU are substantially correlated with each other, and with other behavioural addictions (i.e. internet addiction, social media addiction). For example, in our research, we observed a correlation between a smartphone addiction measure (SABAS) and an internet addiction scale (a shortened version of the IAT) in the region of $r = 0.7$ (Hitcham et al., 2023).

Adaptation and Bias

This problem compounds when a scale is used (or translated) in different populations from the one for which it was developed. Very few studies have tested whether the properties of a scale are comparable between groups, both in general (Hussey & Hughes, 2020) and specifically in smartphone use research. Although there is disagreement on whether this property, known as differential item functioning or measurement invariance, is a necessary precondition for comparing across groups (e.g. Welzel et al., 2021; Robitzsch & Lüdtke, 2023), it is an informative method to diagnose and interpret potential sources of bias.

Consider these questions: Do differences on a smartphone addiction scale represent meaningful gender or cultural differences on SA as a whole? Alternatively, are they driven by systematically different interpretations of one or two items? For example, the SAS-SV has a question that asks about whether the respondent is "feeling pain in the wrists or at the back of the neck while using a smartphone". It is plausible to hypothesise this may not perform equivalently across age groups. The average score for this item (the intercept) is likely to be higher in older adults as the baseline level of musculoskeletal-related distress is higher (Briggs et al., 2018), which has little to do with smartphone use. Because these issues are rarely explored, this problem compounds when researchers try to make claims of certain groups being at higher or lower risk of addiction. One example is the large, inconsistent literature on the relationship between gender and PSU (Busch & McCarthy, 2021). These effects could be because of a genuine difference, but it could depend on the scale used, item-specific biases, or contextual factors not captured by these scales.

One of the problems here is that these validation studies often try to do many things simultaneously. It is not unusual to find psychometric validation studies that translate an existing scale into a different language or culture, apply the scale to a distinct population group from the original measure (e.g. adolescents), administer the questionnaire in a different mode (e.g. online), or deploy scales with amended items or alternative response options. Often, several of these changes are happening at the same time. This makes it difficult to determine what is happening with these adaptations, especially if amendments are made due to poor fit. Consequently, most adaptation studies are limited to surface-level tests of validity. These will report the adequacy of the translation, whether the scale's factor structure is comparable, and its internal consistency. There might be a comparison of item and scale means to the original measure or the performance of the cutoffs. Beyond that, validation practices are haphazard and, in most cases, do not include direct evidence of comparability.

Separate from this, some existing questionnaires have been changed substantially during validation. For example, the Brazilian adaptation of the Smartphone Addiction Inventory (Khoury et al., 2017) changes the response options from ordinal (4 options) to dichotomous yes/no scoring to reduce administration time. Like the original scale, this has been widely adopted, and so despite the same name, these largely represent different measures. Other times, an item might be removed because it makes less sense when translated. All of these potential changes and adaptations result in different biases being introduced or different constructs being measured, often unintentionally.

Assessing the Prevalence of Smartphone Addiction

One particularly controversial use of instruments is to classify people into smartphone addiction risk categories, including whether they might have a smartphone addiction or not. It is unclear whether the scales can reliably distinguish between people with or without a clinically diagnosed disorder (Ting & Chen, 2020). It is worth bearing in mind that not all addiction and problematic use scales classify people in this manner. Some explicitly intended to measure a continuum of risk and severity (e.g. SABAS). In addition, more studies than not tend to use these measures as continuous scores to model the risk or severity of smartphone problems.

Nevertheless, many popular measures include cutoffs designed to classify people. Several studies have tried to estimate the prevalence of smartphone addiction and similar constructs by synthesising estimates from many studies (e.g. Humood et al., 2021; Jahrami et al., 2022). Smartphone addiction measures typically classify large proportions of empirical samples as being addicted to their smartphones, in the region of 25–30% (Meng et al., 2022). Although this estimate is biased by comparing non-representative samples and oversampling groups believed to be at higher risk of addiction disorders (i.e. adolescents), more representative samples concur with classifying a substantial minority of the population as being 'addicted' to their phones (Meng et al., 2023). This is most instructive from the research in South Korea, where measures of smartphone dependence have been routinely collected in representative samples for over a decade. These studies have typically estimated smartphone addiction prevalence in groups such as adolescents to be 20% or higher (e.g. Noh & Shim, 2024).

However, the probability that these estimates are plausible indicators of widespread psychosocial impairment is exceptionally low, even when the best sampling methods are used. For the estimates from these scales to be true, the prevalence of addictive or problematic smartphone use would eclipse every other established addictive behaviour, including alcohol, nicotine, gambling, and substance use disorders (McManus et al., 2016). Indeed, the number of people meeting the cutoff for smartphone addiction would be approximately the same as all of these *combined* (e.g. McManus et al., 2009, 2016). Smartphones could be associated with widespread, deleterious impacts on mental health, and this has not led to appropriate clinical and psychological support. However, the simplest explanation is that these estimates are fanciful. The thresholds used in smartphone addiction scales are almost certainly too low, and this classifies people experiencing negligible harm or impairment as having a smartphone addiction.

There is evidence to support this assertion. Rochat et al. (2024) recently compared rates of PSU using the SABAS in a representative American sample. Based on the scale alone, 13% met the criteria for potential smartphone addiction by affirming four or more components of addiction. However, when restricted to cases affirmatively endorsing the item assessing interpersonal conflict due to their phone use, this fell tenfold to 1.2%. An alternative classification, comprising the proportion meeting the criteria and endorsing a functional impairment item, was even lower, at 0.75%. Similarly, King et al. (2024) identified 2.6% of a sample of Australian secondary school students as having problematic use when using a polythetic cutoff alongside functional impairment. Together, these suggest that assessing functional impairment alongside SA/PSU reduces the estimated prevalence and implies that most such cases are likely to be false positives.

The final problem is considerable variation in how these cutoffs are developed and used. Although several scales have developed benchmarks against external outcomes (e.g. clinical interviews) (Kwon et al., 2013a; Lin et al., 2015), attempts to categorise scale scores are speculative in most cases. The starkest demonstration of this is the NMP-Q (range = 20–140), which proposed categories of 20 = no nomophobia, 21–59 = mild nomophobia, 60–99 = moderate nomophobia, and 100–140 = severe nomophobia. The choice of labels here has led to claims that over 90% of the population experience nomophobia (e.g. Vagka et al., 2023; Aldhahir et al., 2023). These can also become problematic when applied in research. Scales with multiple cutoffs, such as the NMP-Q or the IAT, are inconsistently combined to classify people into interpretative groups. For example, one study might classify nomophobia vs. no-nomophobia based on classification to the 'severe nomophobia' grouping. Another study might instead define 'nomophobia' to mean both 'severe' and 'moderate' nomophobia groups. This inconsistency represents a potential threat to validity when combined for a meta-analysis.

Fuzzy Constructs and Fuzzy Measurements

A recurring theme in this chapter and Chap. 2 is that smartphone and technology use constructs are fuzzy. This fuzziness can be deconstructed into fuzziness inherent to the measured construct and fuzziness created when a construct is turned into a measurement instrument. Both are important causes of uncertainty among problematic smartphone use constructs. This section explores this idea using nomophobia and phubbing as two contrasting examples.

Nomophobia

Nomophobia is an excellent example of a fuzzy measurement. A British delivery company originally coined nomophobia as a portmanteau of 'NO MObile PHOBIA'. Since then, approximately 700 articles have been published on this topic. A couple of strands of work are especially influential in developing nomophobia. The first, by King and colleagues in Brazil, sought to understand the clinical characteristics of this proposed construct as a phobia (King et al., 2013). The second, by Yildirim in the United States and Turkey, sought to understand the different aspects of nomophobia and develop a questionnaire to measure it, conceptualised as situational anxiety (Yildirim & Correia, 2015b). Importantly, neither conceptualises nomophobia as being an addiction or part of smartphone addiction. However, most of the research on nomophobia is quite atheoretical, often being ambiguous on whether it should be treated as a phobia, situational anxiety, or something else, including addiction. Many studies into nomophobia either explicitly or implicitly conceptualise it as an addiction. For example, it is common to see addiction ideas incorporated into discussions of nomophobia through concepts such as dependence or withdrawal. However, it is ambiguous whether it refers to emotional dependence (i.e. attachment) or psychological dependence (i.e. addiction).

This ambiguity becomes more pronounced when applied using psychometric scales. Measures of nomophobia are highly correlated with measures of smartphone addiction, often to the order of $r = 0.7$ (e.g. Galhardo et al., 2020; Coenen & Gorlich, 2022). The reason for this becomes clear when looking at the original validation of the Nomophobia Questionnaire (Yildirim & Correia, 2015). Compared to many other measures (i.e. Davidson et al., 2022, Table 7), the scale development process was comprehensive, including a qualitative study to understand possible features of nomophobia and guide scale development and detailed reporting of the validation analyses. However, the final scale tested construct validity against the Mobile Phone Involvement Questionnaire (MPIQ) (Walsh et al., 2010). Although 'mobile/smartphone involvement' intends to capture broader sub-clinical engagement, the MPIQ is based on the Components Model (see Chap. 2). The validation analysis also supposes a multidimensional construct but uses an orthogonal rotation. Combined with item content that overlaps with addiction-relevant features (e.g. dependence), it is not surprising to see that this correlates with problematic smartphone use.

Phubbing

Phubbing is an exemplar of a fuzzy construct and fuzzy measurement. Ostensibly, phubbing refers to a situational behaviour in which someone snubs someone else in a social situation (e.g. during a conversation) in favour of using their phone. This could happen for many reasons: the relationship with the person being phubbed, the specific use of the phone, or the mood of the person phubbing the other. A general tendency towards phubbing could be a consequence of addiction-related deficits such as impaired control over interactions with the phone, increased salience, or urges to look at the phone. When turned into measurement scales, phubbing becomes particularly fuzzy because the degree of overlap with problematic, addictive smartphone measures depends on the measure used. The phubbing literature is split between measures that assess the degree of being phubbed by someone else (i.e., parents, friends, colleagues) and the degree someone engages in phubbing themselves (Roberts & David, 2016). The General Scale of Phubbing (Chotpitayasunondh & Douglas, 2018) has been used in many studies to assess phubbing. This has proposed factors of nomophobia and interpersonal conflict that exemplify the fuzziness of these constructs. In some studies, this nomophobia subscale is instead named smartphone dependence or addiction. The GSP was tested for construct validity against the SAS-SV and the IAT, demonstrating substantial correlations ($r = 0.80$ for SAS-SV and $r = 0.75$ for a shortened IAT (Pawilowski et al., 2013)). Similarly, Karadag et al.'s (2015) ten-item Phubbing Scale has 'phubbing' and 'phone obsession' factors. It is correlated with addiction scales to a substantial degree and was validated against mobile phone addiction. Scales that focus on the action of phubbing and being phubbed (e.g. Roberts & David, 2016) are still correlated but may show greater differences with phone use constructs ($r = 0.3 - 0.5$; e.g. Akbağ et al., 2025; Niu et al., 2020). Contrasted against nomophobia, the fuzziness with problematic use constructs occurs much earlier, right at the beginning of the scale development process.

These examples highlight how issues with conceptualisation, scale development, and scale validation create fuzzy constructs that frustrate the intended aims of the original research. The example of the Nomophobia Questionnaire is striking because many of the best scale development practices were applied. The scale underwent substantial theoretical and conceptual development before creating the questionnaire. The issues with the NMP-Q appear to be related to the statistical validation of the scale. The choice of factor rotation, measures used for criterion validity and the selection of interpretative categories all occur at the end of the scale development process to create ambiguity. In contrast, the case of phubbing demonstrates how problems can be found at each point in the process, leading to a series of scales that measure fundamentally different properties.

Fuzzy Modelling: Use of Assessments in Empirical Research

These issues come together when scales are used in empirical research to test the relationships between smartphone addiction and other behaviours or psychological constructs. This is especially important when analyses are undertaken to model more complex mechanisms underlying problematic smartphone use. Many studies use techniques such as conditional process analysis, path analysis, and structural equation modelling to test mechanistic effects, such as mediation and moderation, across sequences of constructs. A popular example is to test whether fear of missing out (FOMO) mediates the relationship between anxiety and PSU (e.g. Elhai et al., 2020). We return to this in the next chapter (see Chap. 4).

These methods build on concepts from correlation, regression, and factor analysis to test these hypotheses. Unsurprisingly, they are highly flexible, and this flexibility can become a major drawback because the same data can be modelled in dozens of different ways. Even the simplest models can be subject to analytic flexibility that has the potential to bias the results (see https://osf.io/6e8n3/). Many of these decisions are the same ones encountered while validating a scale. The analyst is confronted with an array of possible options for modelling the data and must make a sequence of choices, which means a multiverse of possible specifications is available. If the analyst uses previous literature, they will typically find a lack of consensus on these choices, often starting with the original development of a scale. Consequently, many degrees of freedom in modelling smartphone addiction questionnaires are created by a mixture of flawed assessment practices and a high risk of specification bias.

Attributing this specification bias to questionable modelling practices can be tempting, and studies have explored this possibility (e.g. Crede & Harms, 2019). However, caution must be urged when drawing this conclusion too widely. One of the difficulties with critiquing these practices is that many of the decisions made are justifiable in isolation. The problems discussed in this chapter can emerge from a sequence of individually sound choices that, when taken together, are inappropriate. Most of these choices come with trade-offs; using a certain procedure is recommended under certain circumstances but it complicates another part of the analysis. For example, numerous papers have advised psychologists to model ordinal data appropriately (Bürkner & Vuorre, 2019; Liddell & Kruschke, 2018). This sound advice falls into difficulty when it interacts with choices for judging model fit or assessing measurement invariance (e.g. Sass et al., 2014). To complicate matters, the literature on how these choices interact has a greater tendency to be inconsistent or sparse. This absence then leaves prior research to fall back on, where there may be inconsistencies in practice. The researcher may not have explicitly specify these decisions, either. Many of the analytic problems discussed relate to default choices in popular statistical programmes. It is similarly difficult to fault researchers when there are differences in how metrics are calculated between software programmes (e.g. Savalei, 2018).

Nonetheless, the combination of poor measurement practices applied to a set of flexible statistical tools creates a chaotic situation, as seen in problematic smartphone use or smartphone addiction research. Although there are many reasons why this may occur, the field cannot ignore these problems. Approximately one-third of SA or PSU studies employ measurement or structural modelling, and many of these concerns are echoed in other behavioural addictions. The field can ill afford to neglect them.

Conclusion

Measuring problematic or addictive smartphone use is fraught with difficulties. Some of these are conceptual, with many of the most popular self-report scales adapted from other behavioural addictions (i.e. gambling disorder or internet addiction). Meanwhile, other problems that prevent substantive measurement occur during the scale development and validation process. Additionally, many existing scales have not been analysed to the strongest level of validation, especially when applied to new groups and contexts. These problems recur when these measures are used in empirical research. As a result of this, the field of problematic/addiction phone use is beset by a lack of consensus on how to measure and model smartphone addiction.

References

Abdi, H., 2003. Factor rotations in factor analyses. Encyclopedia for research methods for the social sciences, pp.792-795.

Akbağ, M., Aydoğdu, F. and Rizzo, A., 2025. Developing a novel parental phubbing scale of mother and father forms for adolescents in Türkiye: A validity and reliability study. Personality and Individual Differences, 235, p.112963.

Aldhahir, A. M., Bintalib, H. M., Siraj, R. A., Alqahtani, J. S., Alqarni, O. A., Alqarni, A. A., Alghamdi, H. S., Alyami, M. M., Naser, A. Y., & Fatani, A. I. (2023). Prevalence of nomophobia and its impact on academic performance among respiratory therapy students in Saudi Arabia. *Psychology Research and Behavior Management*, 877–884. https://doi.org/10.2147/prbm.s404898

Alimoradi, Z., Lotfi, A., Lin, C.-Y., Griffiths, M. D., & Pakpour, A. H. (2022). Estimation of behavioral addiction prevalence during COVID-19 pandemic: A systematic review and meta-analysis. *Current Addiction Reports, 9*(4), 486–517. https://doi.org/10.1007/s40429-022-00435-6

Berntsen, D., Hoyle, R. H., Munkholm Møller, D., & Rubin, D. C. (2023). Digital daydreaming: Introducing the spontaneous smartphone checking scale. *Applied Cognitive Psychology, 37*(1), 147–160. https://doi.org/10.1002/acp.4034

Bian, M., & Leung, L. (2015). Linking loneliness, shyness, smartphone addiction symptoms, and patterns of smartphone use to social capital. *Social Science Computer Review, 33*(1), 61–79. https://doi.org/10.1177/0894439314528779

Bianchi, A., & Phillips, J. G. (2005). Psychological predictors of problem Mobile phone use. *Cyberpsychology & Behavior, 8*(1), 39–51. https://doi.org/10.1089/cpb.2005.8.39

Billieux, J., Van der Linden, M., & Rochat, L. (2008). The role of impulsivity in actual and problematic use of the mobile phone. *Applied Cognitive Psychology: The Official Journal of the Society for Applied Research in Memory and Cognition, 22*(9), 1195–1210. https://doi.org/10.1002/acp.1429

Billieux, J., Schimmenti, A., Khazaal, Y., Maurage, P., and Heeren, A. (2015) Are we overpathologizing everyday life? A tenable blueprint for behavioral addiction research Journal of Behavioral Addictions 4(3) 119-123 10.1556/2006.4.2015.009

Bradish, T., Locker, L., Jr., Ryan, R. G., & Wilson, J. H. (2023). The smartphone addiction measure (SAM): Subscales, validity, and reliability. *Psychological Reports*, 00332941231219791. https://doi.org/10.1177/00332941231219791

Briggs, A. M., Woolf, A. D., Dreinhöfer, K., Homb, N., Hoy, D. G., Kopansky-Giles, D., Åkesson, K., & March, L. (2018). Reducing the global burden of musculoskeletal conditions. *Bulletin of the World Health Organization, 96*(5), 366–368. https://doi.org/10.2471/BLT.17.204891

Bürkner, P.-C., & Vuorre, M. (2019). Ordinal regression models in psychology: A tutorial. *Advances in Methods and Practices in Psychological Science, 2*(1), 77–101. https://doi.org/10.1177/2515245918823199

Busch, P. A., & McCarthy, S. (2021). Antecedents and consequences of problematic smartphone use: A systematic literature review of an emerging research area. *Computers in Human Behavior, 114*, 106414. https://doi.org/10.1016/j.chb.2020.106414

Carpenter, S. (2018). Ten steps in scale development and reporting: A guide for researchers. *Communication Methods and Measures, 12*(1), 25–44. https://doi.org/10.1080/19312458.2017.1396583

Coenen, M., & Görlich, Y. (2022). Exploring nomophobia with a German adaption of the nomophobia questionnaire (NMP-QD). *PLoS One, 17*(12), e0279379. https://doi.org/10.1371/journal.pone.0279379

Chotpitayasunondh, V., & Douglas, K. M. (2018). Measuring phone snubbing behavior: Development and validation of the Generic Scale of Phubbing (GSP) and the Generic Scale of Being Phubbed (GSBP). Computers in Human Behavior, 88, 5–17.

Crede, M., & Harms, P. (2019). Questionable research practices when using confirmatory factor analysis. *Journal of Managerial Psychology, 34*(1), 18–30. https://doi.org/10.1108/JMP-06-2018-0272

Csibi, S., Demetrovics, Z., & Szabo, A. (2016). Hungarian adaptation and psychometric characteristics of brief addiction to smartphone scale (BASS). *Psychiatria Hungarica, 31*(1), 71–77.

Csibi, S., Griffiths, M. D., Cook, B., Demetrovics, Z., & Szabo, A. (2018). The psychometric properties of the smartphone application-based addiction scale (SABAS). *International Journal of Mental Health and Addiction, 16*(2), 393–403. https://doi.org/10.1007/s11469-017-9787-2

Davidson, B. I., Shaw, H., & Ellis, D. A. (2022). Fuzzy constructs in technology usage scales. *Computers in Human Behavior, 107206*. https://doi.org/10.1016/j.chb.2022.107206

Donjdee, K., Poonpol, P., & Ruksee, N. (2024). Development and validation of the Thai version of the problematic smartphone use scale for school-age (PSU-SA) children. *Journal of Health Research, 38*(6), 3. https://doi.org/10.56808/2586-940X.1107

Elhai, J.D., Yang, H., Fang, J., Bai, X. and Hall, B.J., 2020. Depression and anxiety symptoms are related to problematic smartphone use severity in Chinese young adults: Fear of missing out as a mediator. Addictive Behaviors, 101, p.105962.

Ellis, D. A., Davidson, B. I., Shaw, H., & Geyer, K. (2019). Do smartphone usage scales predict behavior? *International Journal of Human-Computer Studies, 130*, 86–92. https://doi.org/10.1016/j.ijhcs.2019.05.004

Elson, M., Hussey, I., Alsalti, T., & Arslan, R. C. (2023). Psychological measures aren't toothbrushes. *Communications Psychology, 1*(1), 25. https://doi.org/10.1038/s44271-023-00026-9

Flake, J. K., & Fried, E. I. (2020). Measurement schmeasurement: Questionable measurement practices and how to avoid them. *Advances in Methods and Practices in Psychological Science, 3*(4), 456–465. https://doi.org/10.1177/2515245920952393

Flake, J. K., Pek, J., & Hehman, E. (2017). Construct validation in social and personality research: Current practice and recommendations. *Social Psychological and Personality Science, 8*(4), 370–378. https://doi.org/10.1177/1948550617693063

Flayelle, M., Brevers, D., King, D. L., Maurage, P., Perales, J. C., & Billieux, J. (2023). A taxonomy of technology design features that promote potentially addictive online behaviours. *Nature Reviews Psychology, 2*(3), 136–150. https://doi.org/10.1038/s44159-023-00153-4

Galhardo, A., Loureiro, D., Raimundo, E., Massano-Cardoso, I., & Cunha, M. (2020). Assessing nomophobia: Validation study of the European Portuguese version of the nomophobia questionnaire. *Community Mental Health Journal, 56*(8), 1521–1530. https://doi.org/10.1007/s10597-020-00600-z

Geçer, E., Yıldırım, M., Bağci, H., & Atar, C. (2024). Development and factor structure of problematic multidimensional smartphone use scale. *International Journal of Mental Health and Addiction.* https://doi.org/10.1007/s11469-024-01265-5

Harris, B., Regan, T., Schueler, J., & Fields, S. A. (2020). Problematic mobile phone and smartphone use scales: A systematic review. *Frontiers in Psychology, 11*, 672. https://doi.org/10.3389/fpsyg.2020.00672

Hitcham, L., Jackson, H., & James, R. J. E. (2023). The relationship between smartphone use and smartphone addiction: An examination of logged and self-reported behavior in a pre-registered, two-wave sample. Computers in Human Behavior, 146, 107822.

Horn, J. L. (1965). A rationale and test for the number of factors in factor analysis. *Psychometrika, 30*, 179–185. https://doi.org/10.1007/BF02289447

Hu, L. T., & Bentler, P. M. (1999). Cutoff criteria for fit indexes in covariance structure analysis: Conventional criteria versus new alternatives. *Structural Equation Modeling: A Multidisciplinary Journal, 6*(1), 1–55. https://doi.org/10.1080/10705519909540118

Humood, A., Altooq, N., Altamimi, A., Almoosawi, H., Alzafiri, M., Bragazzi, N. L., Husni, M., & Jahrami, H. (2021). The prevalence of nomophobia by population and by research tool: A systematic review, meta-analysis, and meta-regression. *Psych, 3*(2), 249–258. https://doi.org/10.3390/psych3020019

Hussey, I., & Hughes, S. (2020). Hidden invalidity among 15 commonly used measures in social and personality psychology. *Advances in Methods and Practices in Psychological Science, 3*(2), 166–184. https://doi.org/10.1177/2515245919882903

Jahrami, H., Trabelsi, K., Boukhris, O., Hussain, J. H., Alenezi, A. F., Humood, A., Saif, Z., Pandi-Perumal, S. R., & Seeman, M. V. (2022). The prevalence of mild, moderate, and severe nomophobia symptoms: A systematic review, meta-analysis, and meta-regression. *Behavioral Sciences, 13*(1), 35. https://doi.org/10.3390/bs13010035

James, R. J. E., Dixon, G., Dragomir, M.-G., Thirlwell, E., & Hitcham, L. (2023). Understanding the construction of 'behavior' in smartphone addiction: A scoping review. *Addictive Behaviors, 107503*. https://doi.org/10.1016/j.addbeh.2022.107503

James, R. J. E., Tillsley, J. E., Hitcham, L., Mou, C., Kim, H., & Tunney, R. J. (2024). Disordered gambling, or dependence and consequences: A bifactor exploratory structural equation model analysis of the problem gambling severity index. *Addiction Research & Theory, 1–12*. https://doi.org/10.1080/16066359.2024.2352094

Kaiser, H. F. (1960). The application of electronic computers to factor analysis. *Educational and Psychological Measurement, 20*(1), 141–151. https://doi.org/10.1177/001316446002000116

Karadağ, E., Tosuntaş, Ş. B., Erzen, E., Duru, P., Bostan, N., Şahin, B. M., Çulha, İ. and Babadağ, B. (2015) Determinants of phubbing which is the sum of many virtual addictions: A structural equation model. Journal of Behavioral Addictions 4(2) 60–74 https://doi.org/10.1556/2006.4.2015.005

Kardefelt-Winther, D. (2014). A conceptual and methodological critique of internet addiction research: Towards a model of compensatory internet use. *Computers in Human Behavior, 31*, 351–354. https://doi.org/10.1016/j.chb.2013.10.059

Khoury, J. M., de Freitas, A. A. C., Roque, M. A. V., Albuquerque, M. R., das Neves, M. D. C. L., & Garcia, F. D. (2017). Assessment of the accuracy of a new tool for the screening of smartphone addiction. *PLoS One, 12*(5), e0176924. https://doi.org/10.1371/journal.pone.0176924

Kim, C. T., Kim, D. I., Park, J. K., & Lee, S. J. (2002). *A study on internet addiction counseling and the development of prevention programs*. National IT Industrial Promotion Agency.

Kim, D., Lee, Y., Lee, J., Nam, J. K., & Chung, Y. (2014). Development of Korean smartphone addiction proneness scale for youth. *PLoS One, 9*(5), e97920. https://doi.org/10.1371/journal.pone.0097920

King, A. L. S., Valenca, A.-M., Silva, A.-C. O., Baczynski, T., Carvalho, M. R., & Nardi, A. E. (2013). Nomophobia: Dependency on virtual environments or social phobia? *Computers in Human Behavior, 29*(1), 140–144. https://doi.org/10.1016/j.chb.2012.07.025

King, D. L., Radunz, M., Galanis, C. R., Quinney, B., & Wade, T. (2024). "Phones off while school's on": Evaluating problematic phone use and the social, wellbeing, and academic effects of banning phones in schools. *Journal of Behavioral Addictions*. https://doi.org/10.1556/2006.2024.00058

Kulas, J. T., & Stachowski, A. A. (2013). Respondent rationale for neither agreeing nor disagreeing: Person and item contributors to middle category endorsement intent on Likert personality indicators. *Journal of Research in Personality, 47*(4), 254–262. https://doi.org/10.1016/j.jrp.2013.01.014

Kwon, M., Kim, D. J., Cho, H., & Yang, S. (2013b). The smartphone addiction scale: Development and validation of a short version for adolescents. *PLoS One, 8*(12), e83558. https://doi.org/10.1371/journal.pone.0083558

Kwon, M., Lee, J.-Y., Won, W.-Y., Park, J.-W., Min, J.-A., Hahn, C., Gu, X., Choi, J.-H., & Kim, D.-J. (2013a). Development and validation of a smartphone addiction scale (SAS). *PLoS One, 8*(2), e56936. https://doi.org/10.1371/journal.pone.0056936

Leung, L. (2008). Linking psychological attributes to addiction and improper use of the Mobile phone among adolescents in Hong Kong. *Journal of*

Children and Media, 2(2), 93–113. https://doi.org/10.1080/17482790802078565

Liddell, T. M., & Kruschke, J. K. (2018). Analyzing ordinal data with metric models: What could possibly go wrong? *Journal of Experimental Social Psychology, 79*, 328–348. https://doi.org/10.1016/j.jesp.2018.08.009

Lin, Y.-H., Chang, L.-R., Lee, Y.-H., Tseng, H.-W., Kuo, T. B., & Chen, S.-H. (2014). Development and validation of the smartphone addiction inventory (SPAI). *PLoS One, 9*(6), e98312. https://doi.org/10.1371/journal.pone.0098312

Lin, Y. H., Lin, Y. C., Lee, Y. H., Lin, P. H., Lin, S. H., Chang, L. R., Tseng, H. W., Yen, L. Y., Yang, C. C. and Kuo, T. B. (2015) Time distortion associated with smartphone addiction: Identifying smartphone addiction via a mobile application (App). Journal of Psychiatric Research 65139-145 10.1016/j.jpsychires.2015.04.003

Luque-Reca, O., Marchena-Giráldez, C., Carbonell-Colomer, M., Bewernick, C., & Bernabéu-Brotóns, E. (2024). Social aspects of problematic smartphone use: Development and validation of the PSSNUS and mental health implications for Spanish youth. *Psychology Research and Behavior Management, 17*, 3919–3942. https://doi.org/10.2147/PRBM.S466070

Manara, C. V., Mingolo, S., Grassi, M., Sors, F., Prpic, V., Agostini, T., & Murgia, M. (2024). The abstinence from smartphone scale (ABSS-10): Psychometric properties and practical utility. *Computers in Human Behavior Reports, 14*, 100428. https://doi.org/10.1016/j.chbr.2024.100428

Masaeli, N., & Farhadi, H. (2021). Prevalence of internet-based addictive behaviors during COVID-19 pandemic: A systematic review. *Journal of Addictive Diseases, 39*(4), 468–488. https://doi.org/10.1080/10550887.2021.1895962

McManus, S., Bebbington, P., Jenkins, R., & Brugha, T. (2016). *Mental health and wellbeing in England: Adult psychiatric morbidity survey 2014. A survey carried out for NHS digital by NatCen social research and the Department of Health Sciences*. University of Leicester.

McManus, S., Meltzer, H., Brugha, T., Bebbington, P., & Jenkins, R. (2009). *Adult psychiatric morbidity in England, 2007: Results of a household survey*. NHS Information Centre.

Meng, S.-Q., Cheng, J.-L., Li, Y.-Y., Yang, X.-Q., Zheng, J.-W., Chang, X.-W., Shi, Y., Chen, Y., Lu, L., Sun, Y., Bao, Y.-P., & Shi, J. (2022). Global prevalence of digital addiction in general population: A systematic review and meta-analysis. *Clinical Psychology Review, 92*, 102128. https://doi.org/10.1016/j.cpr.2022.102128

Nawaz, S. (2023). Rethinking classifications and metrics for problematic smartphone use and dependence: Addressing the call for reassessment. *Computers in Human Behavior Reports, 12*, 100327. https://doi.org/10.1016/j.chbr.2023.100327

Niu, G., Yao, L., Wu, L., Tian, Y., Xu, L. and Sun, X., 2020. Parental phubbing and adolescent problematic mobile phone use: The role of parent-child relationship and self-control. Children and Youth Services Review, 116, p.105247.

Noh, D., & Shim, M.-S. (2024). Factors influencing smartphone overdependence among adolescents. *Scientific Reports, 14*(1), 7725. https://doi.org/10.1038/s41598-024-58152-1

Open Science Collaboration. (2015). Estimating the reproducibility of psychological science. *Science, 349*(6251), 943. https://doi.org/10.1126/science.aac4716

Park, S., & Kim, B. (2021). Development and validation of a novel instrument to measure pedestrians' smartphone use: The Smombie scale. *Transportation Research Part F: Traffic Psychology and Behaviour, 82*, 440–449. https://doi.org/10.1016/j.trf.2021.09.004

Park, S., & Oh, S. (2024). Development and psychometric analysis of the smombie scale for adolescents. *Journal of Pediatric Nursing, 75*, 89–98. https://doi.org/10.1016/j.pedn.2023.11.028

Panova, T., & Carbonell, X. (2018). Is smartphone addiction really an addiction?. Journal of Behavioral Addictions, 7(2), 252–259. https://doi.org/10.1556/2006.7.2018.49

Pawlikowski, M., Altstötter-Gleich, C., & Brand, M. (2013). Validation and psychometric properties of a short version of Young's Internet Addiction Test. Computers in Human Behavior, 29(3), 1212–1223. https://doi.org/10.1016/j.chb.2012.10.014

Pennington, C. R., Jones, A., Bartlett, J. E., Copeland, A., & Shaw, D. J. (2021). Raising the bar: Improving methodological rigour in cognitive alcohol research. *Addiction, 116*(11), 3243–3251. https://doi.org/10.1111/add.15563

Preacher, K. J., & MacCallum, R. C. (2003). Repairing tom swift's electric factor analysis machine. *Understanding Statistics: Statistical Issues in Psychology, Education, and the Social Sciences, 2*(1), 13–43. https://doi.org/10.1207/S15328031US0201_02

Pressey, A., Houghton, D., & Istanbulluoglu, D. (2024). The problematic use of smartphones in public: The development and validation of a measure of smartphone "zombie" behaviour. *Information Technology & People, 37*(1), 479–501. https://doi.org/10.1108/ITP-06-2022-0472

Ranjan, R., Balhara, Y. P. S., Mishra, B. R., Ahmad, S., Sarkar, S., Bharti, A., Panigrahi, S., Sinha, M., Rajguru, A. J., Kumar, P., Mohapatra, D., Parmar, A., & Jain, M. (2025). Factor structure, reliability and validity of an Indian scale for assessment of nomophobia (ISAN) among college students: A multicentre Indian study. *Journal of Psychiatric Research*. https://doi.org/10.1016/j.jpsychires.2024.12.036

Reise, S. P., Moore, T. M., & Haviland, M. G. (2010). Bifactor models and rotations: Exploring the extent to which multidimensional data yield univocal scale scores. *Journal of Personality Assessment, 92*(6), 544–559. https://doi.org/10.1080/00223891.2010.496477

Reise, S. P., Waller, N. G., & Comrey, A. L. (2000). Factor analysis and scale revision. *Psychological Assessment, 12*(3), 287. https://doi.org/10.1037/1040-3590.12.3.287

Rhemtulla, M., Brosseau-Liard, P. É., & Savalei, V. (2012). When can categorical variables be treated as continuous? A comparison of robust continuous and categorical SEM estimation methods under suboptimal conditions. *Psychological Methods, 17*(3), 354. https://doi.org/10.1037/a0029315

Roberts, J. A., & David, M. E. (2022). Me, my smartphone, and I: Development of the smartphone orientation scale (SOS). *International Journal of Human–Computer Interaction*, 38(13), 1267–1275. https://doi.org/10.1080/10447318.2021.1990521.

Robitzsch, A., & Lüdtke, O. (2023). Why full, partial, or approximate measurement invariance are not a prerequisite for meaningful and valid group comparisons. *Structural Equation Modeling: A Multidisciplinary Journal, 30*(6), 859–870. https://doi.org/10.1080/10705511.2023.2191292

Rochat, L., Cruz, G. V., Aboujaoude, E., Courtois, R., Brahim, F. B., Khan, R., & Khazaal, Y. (2024). Problematic smartphone use in a representative sample of US adults: Prevalence and predictors. *Addictive Behaviors, 108228*. https://doi.org/10.1016/j.addbeh.2024.108228

Sass, D. A., Schmitt, T. A., & Marsh, H. W. (2014). Evaluating model fit with ordered categorical data within a measurement invariance framework: A comparison of estimators. *Structural Equation Modeling: A Multidisciplinary Journal, 21*(2), 167–180. https://doi.org/10.1080/10705511.2014.882658

Satchell, L.P., Fido, D., Harper, C.A., Shaw, H., Davidson, B., Ellis, D.A., Hart, C.M., Jalil, R., Bartoli, A.J., Kaye, L.K. and Lancaster, G.L., 2021. Development of an Offline-Friend Addiction Questionnaire (O-FAQ): Are most people really social addicts?. Behavior Research Methods, 53(3), pp.1097–1106.

Savalei, V. (2018). On the computation of the RMSEA and CFI from the mean-and-variance corrected test statistic with nonnormal data in SEM. *Multivariate Behavioral Research, 53*(3), 419–429. https://doi.org/10.1080/00273171.2018.1455142

Serra, G., Lo Scalzo, L., Giuffrè, M., Ferrara, P., & Corsello, G. (2021). Smartphone use and addiction during the coronavirus disease 2019 (COVID-19) pandemic: Cohort study on 184 Italian children and adolescents. *Italian Journal of Pediatrics, 47*(1), 150. https://doi.org/10.1186/s13052-021-01102-8

Shaw, H., Ellis, D., Geyer, K., Davidson, B., Ziegler, F., & Smith, A. (2020). Quantifying smartphone "use": Choice of measurement impacts relationships between "usage" and health. *Technology, Mind, and Behavior, 1*(2). https://doi.org/10.1037/tmb0000022

Sijtsma, K., Ellis, J. L., & Borsboom, D. (2024). Recognize the value of the sum score, psychometrics' greatest accomplishment. *Psychometrika, 89*(1), 84–117. https://doi.org/10.1007/s11336-024-09964-7

Su, S., Cousijn, J., Molenaar, D., Freichel, R., Larsen, H., & Wiers, R. W. (2024). From everyday life to measurable problematic smartphone use: The development and validation of the smartphone use problems identification questionnaire (SUPIQ). *Journal of Behavioral Addictions.* https://doi.org/10.1556/2006.2024.00010

Sun, H. and Tang, K., 2025. Psychometric evaluation and measurement invariance of the problematic smartphone use scale among college students: A national survey of 130 145 participants. Addiction, 120(4), pp.629-641.

Terry, A., Szabo, A., & Griffiths, M. (2004). The exercise addiction inventory: A new brief screening tool. Addiction Research & Theory, 12(5), 489–499.

Ting, C. H. & Chen. Y. Y. (2020). Smartphone addiction. In Adolescent Addiction (2nd Ed): Epidemiology, Assessment, and Treatment Practical Resources for the Mental Health Professional. Elsevier 215–240

Vagka, E., Gnardellis, C., Lagiou, A., & Notara, V. (2023). Prevalence and factors related to nomophobia: Arising issues among young adults. *European Journal of Investigation in Health, Psychology and Education, 13*(8), 1467–1476. https://doi.org/10.3390/ejihpe13080107

Walsh, S. P., White, K. M., & Young, R. M. (2010). Needing to connect: The effect of self and others on young people's involvement with their mobile phones. *Australian Journal of Psychology, 62*(4), 194–203. https://doi.org/10.1080/00049530903567229

Welzel, C., Brunkert, L., Kruse, S., & Inglehart, R. F. (2021). Non-invariance? An overstated problem with misconceived causes. *Sociological Methods & Research, 52*(3), 1368–1400. https://doi.org/10.1177/0049124121995521

Widaman, K. F., & Revelle, W. (2023). Thinking thrice about sum scores, and then some more about measurement and analysis. *Behavior Research Methods, 55*(2), 788–806. https://doi.org/10.3758/s13428-022-01849-w

Yeomans, K. A., & Golder, P. A. (1982). The Guttman-Kaiser criterion as a predictor of the number of common factors. *The Statistician, 221–229*. https://doi.org/10.2307/2987988

Yildirim, C., & Correia, A.-P. (2015). Exploring the dimensions of nomophobia: Development and validation of a self-reported questionnaire. *Computers in Human Behavior, 49*, 130–137. https://doi.org/10.1016/j.chb.2015.02.059

Yildirim, C., & Correia, A. P. (2015b). Understanding nomophobia: A modern age phobia among college students. In International Conference on Learning and Collaboration Technologies (pp. 724–735). Cham: Springer international publishing.

Young, K. S. (1998). Internet addiction: The emergence of a new clinical disorder. Cyberpsychology & Behavior, 1(3), 237–244.

4

Methodology

Abstract This chapter critically reflects on the prevalent research practices in smartphone addiction research. We focus on four issues that impede the study of addictive/problematic smartphone use. The first is a focus on cross-sectional research, which limits the conclusions that can be drawn about smartphone use. Combined with the prevalent use of mediation analysis, many of these mechanisms are biased. The second and third issues centre on who participates in smartphone addiction research. The field is internationally diverse but systematically undersamples certain groups: adults outside of the student population, especially older adults, and people seeking treatment for smartphone addiction. These create risks of measurement biases and impede the development of robust assessment tools. Finally, the field relies heavily on self-report measures of smartphone behaviour, which appear inaccurate and difficult to defend in light of the ease of collecting this data from phones.

Keywords Measurement bias • Sampling bias • Clinical samples • Cross-cultural • Cross-sectional

R. James, L. Hitcham, *Critical Perspectives on Smartphone Addiction*, Palgrave Studies in Cyberpsychology, https://doi.org/10.1007/978-3-031-96188-5_4

Introduction

The previous two chapters have explored some of the most serious concerns with smartphone addiction: a fundamental disagreement about the definition and conceptualisation of the proposed disorder and its measurement. This chapter focuses on problems that emerge when these concepts are applied in research studies. These problems intersect with those discussed thus far, but our primary focus is on distinct issues arising from the research designs used, the samples recruited, and other common methodological limitations found in the literature.

Cross-sectional Research

We first focus on the choice of research design (i.e. how the research is conducted) because it determines the type of research question being asked and what conclusions can be drawn from the findings. Like other behavioural addictions, the primary research design used to study problematic smartphone use (PSU) and smartphone addiction (SA) is the cross-sectional survey. The use of this design has important implications for assessing the impact of smartphone use. A reliance on cross-sectional studies is particularly limiting for identifying causal mechanisms or relationships. This drawback has been seen extensively when trying to explain the relationship between smartphone use, smartphone addiction, and mental health. Numerous studies have shown that the volume of smartphone use and smartphone addiction severity correlate with anxiety and depression (Busch & McCarthy, 2021; Augner et al., 2023; Yang et al., 2020). However, less is known about the reason why this correlation occurs. Many studies using these designs have concluded that smartphone use is associated with psychological harm. However, the opposite could be true, as distress often acts as a vulnerability marker for developing addictive behaviours, including PSU. Alternatively, a third factor might causally affect or interact with both smartphone use/addiction and mental health. When these causal associations are incorrectly specified (i.e. by omitting this third factor), this effect is erroneously attributed to technology use (Sewall & Parry, 2024).

Cross-sectional data are inherently limited in their ability to discriminate between these different explanations. By definition, the measures are collected at the same time. Most scales, especially in mental health, instruct participants to respond over a specific period (e.g. two weeks, a month, a year). Even when this is not instructed, and many PSU scales do not specify a time period, people tend to rely on recent experience. Consequently, these research designs provide almost no information about whether one variable causes the other. This problem cannot be overcome by asking about these retroactively, as such questions are subject to significant self-report and recall biases.

These limitations become especially constraining when trying to understand links between multiple variables. For example, does smartphone addiction indirectly increase depression because it reduces sleep quality? Questions like these are often asked in papers that use mediation analysis or structural equation modelling (e.g. Xie et al., 2018). This methodological approach is common in SA/PSU research and is frequently applied to cross-sectional data. However, this comes with significant limitations. Without temporal distance between variables, the specification of causal relationships (e.g. PSU -> depression or depression -> SU) is left to the researcher's choice and interpretation. This selection can be justified by theory, but as Chap. 2 explored, most theoretical accounts of PSU are underspecified. This flexibility means there are many ways of modelling relationships between a set of variables, with no way of telling which one is appropriate. Winer et al. (2016) show how it is possible to get statistically significant mediating relationships with the same variables in the same dataset specified in opposite directions, and the problems this poses for clinical research. This is equally relevant for SA/PSU research. Figure 4.1 demonstrates this using data from Hitcham et al. (2023) to show oppositional mediation effects between self-reported smartphone use, smartphone addiction severity, and depression severity (see https://osf.io/6e8n3/).

In short, cross-sectional research often precludes strong conclusions about the relationship between two or more constructs. The difficulty in explaining the correlation between depression and PSU exemplifies this. Depression could be either a risk factor or a consequence of PSU. Both could share a common cause, or the relationship could be illusory,

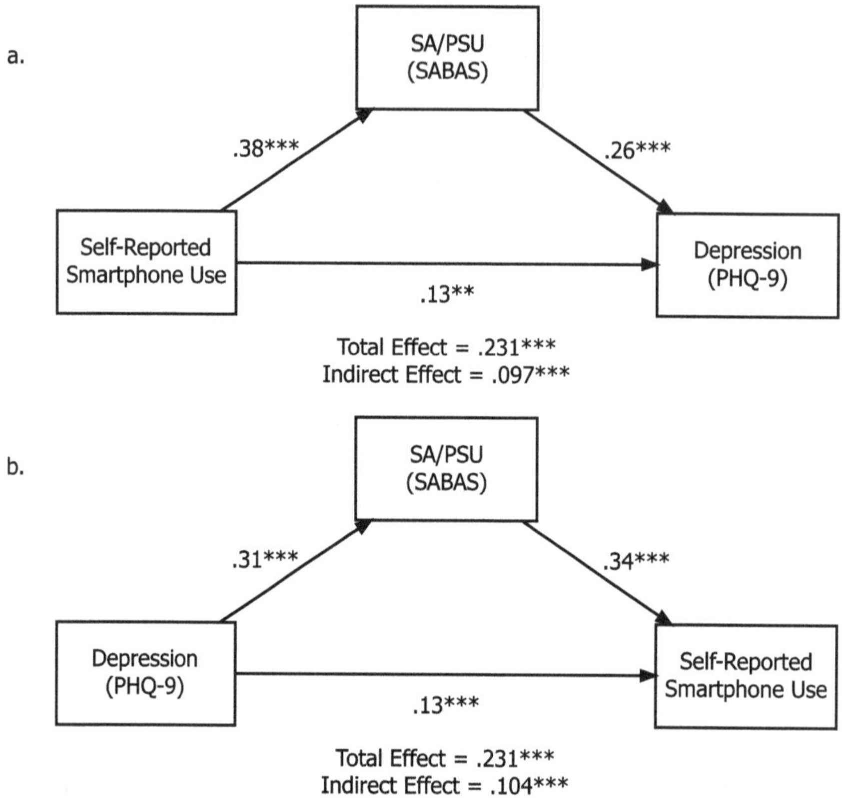

Fig. 4.1 Contrasting mediation models using the same cross-sectional data (data from Hitcham et al., 2023), modelling self-reported smartphone use, SA/PSU, and depression

created by omitting critical variables. This limitation becomes vividly illustrated when using mediation analyses that frequently produce multiple plausible, statistically viable, yet mutually exclusive conclusions about a set of common variables. As Fig. 4.1 shows, the indirect effects on this cross-sectional mediation analysis are essentially equivalent when swapped around. In any event, there is mounting evidence that when compared against longitudinal analyses, findings from cross-sectional mediation analyses are also biased (e.g. Maxwell & Cole, 2007). Although cross-sectional mediation analyses frequently warn against drawing causal conclusions, mediation is fundamentally grounded in establishing causal, directional relationships between variables (Rohrer et al., 2022).

The main way to overcome these obstacles is to conduct longitudinal research. Longitudinal studies allow potential explanations to be rejected because the passage of time precludes certain pathways from being plausible and is consistent with mediation as a causal process (Maxwell & Cole, 2007). Using the mediation example in Fig. 4.1, we can begin making directional statements about the relationship between smartphone use, SA/PSU, and depression when these measures are separated over time. Nonetheless, longitudinal research should not be seen as a magic bullet. Longitudinal studies are replete with methodological and analytical pitfalls that require caution, similar to any other piece of research. Any longitudinal research, even over a short period, is at risk of attrition (e.g. Banks et al., 2011). It may not be possible to re-contact participants because their contact information is incorrect, they don't wish to continue participating, or they cannot continue participating for other reasons (e.g. health issues). Accounting for this when using longitudinal data is vital, as only analysing participants with complete data carries a substantial risk of bias. It is especially important because attrition is seldom completely random. For example, it is plausible that more intense smartphone users are both more and less likely to drop out. However, many of these problems are not unique to longitudinal data. For example, handling missing data is an important issue in cross-sectional studies, especially with using larger samples or longer surveys. The latter is of greater significance when questions are asked in a major national survey, as is common in countries such as South Korea.

Cross-cultural Research

What is striking about SA/PSU research is its highly international and diverse composition. This diversity stands in contrast to academic psychology, where Western countries are systematically overrepresented among publications and research samples. This tendency has been summarised as psychology being 'WEIRD': White, Educated, Industrialized, Rich, and Democratic (Henrich et al., 2010), with a tendency to sample from populations that have at least one, but often many, of these characteristics. Specifically, countries that are culturally closer to the United

States not only feature more frequently in psychological research, but the cross-cultural dimensions that are given the greatest weight are ones (e.g. individualism-collectivism) that correlate with this cultural similarity (Muthukrishna et al., 2020). In our review of the empirical literature (James et al., 2023), the countries where studies were most frequently conducted were China, South Korea, Turkey, the United States of America, and India. Some features of WEIRD still apply; almost all studies sample educated populations, with high school and university students disproportionately sampled. But otherwise, a greater swathe of the world's population is represented in a way that is often absent from many other research fields.

With these strengths, there are also opportunities where critical research gaps exist. Some parts of the world, especially African countries, are less well represented. This absence is important because smartphones are more likely to be the main internet-connected device in these countries (Okano et al., 2022). The implications of this have largely gone unexplored. Additionally, there are substantial between- and within-country differences in phone ownership and greater variation in the types of devices used in African countries. Current estimates place phone ownership in Africa at close to 85%, with the kind of device owned roughly equally split between smartphones and older feature phones. These splits between countries will likely represent a mixture of societal, economic, and geographic factors worth additional consideration in understanding the positive and negative impacts of smartphone use.

The second is the relative absence of cross-cultural research. Although addictive/problematic smartphone use research is diverse, these studies tend to focus on a single population. We only found a handful of multinational studies, comprising 6–7% of the published empirical literature (James et al., 2023). Most of these focused on two or perhaps three countries (e.g. Panova et al., 2020), and the multinational component was incidental in a few cases. For example, some multinational studies recruited participants from countries such as Germany, Switzerland, and Austria due to common linguistic ties without explicitly looking at cross-cultural differences (e.g. Rozgonjuk et al., 2020). With some notable exceptions, discussed below, there are still substantial, unanswered questions about whether levels of PSU differ between countries, or if assessments of PSU are comparable across different countries or languages.

Cross-national Studies

Several major studies have collected multinational data to examine cross-cultural differences in PSU. These have indicated substantial cross-cultural differences in the presence and severity of smartphone addiction, but most have expressed methodological concerns about the comparability of scores between countries.

Olson et al. (2023) recruited over fifty thousand adults from nearly two hundred regions and administered the Smartphone Addiction Scale - Short Version (SAS-SV) (Kwon et al., 2013) to test international differences in smartphone addiction severity. This study found substantial geographic differences in PSU severity, with the greatest severity observed in Asian countries and the lowest in Europe. However, they also reported that their data did not meet the criteria for measurement invariance, which qualifies these conclusions. Measurement invariance is frequently promoted as a desirable property of assessment scales because it indicates whether scores on a measure are comparable across different groups (i.e. different ages, genders, countries). When invariance has not been demonstrated or tested, caution is needed when comparing measures across groups, as scores may be biased. In this instance, it isn't clear whether this means testing was infeasible because the study consisted of many small subsamples, invariance was rejected, or there were structural issues with the SAS-SV. Using multilevel confirmatory factor analysis (CFA) Blachnio et al. (2021) tested whether the Phubbing Scale was invariant across a sample drawn from 20 countries. In this case, problems with the Phubbing Scale emerged before invariance testing. Two of the ten items were removed because the measurement model proposed in the original study (Karadag et al., 2015) didn't fit the whole sample. Even then, the revised model didn't fit in some country subsamples. Invariance analyses indicated that factor loadings were equivalent, but item intercepts were not, precluding direct comparisons between countries on the measure. Lopez-Fernandez et al. (2017) evaluated the cross-national invariance of their Problematic Mobile Phone Use Questionnaire - Short Version (PMPUQ-SV) across eight countries using a multiple group CFA (MG-CFA). This study supported strict invariance but with important caveats. Three populations were excluded from invariance testing; two were removed for inadequate baseline model fit, and the model could not be estimated in one population because some items had categories that no participants endorsed. Zhang et al. (2024) conducted a secondary analysis of responses to the Nomophobia Questionnaire (NMP-Q) (Yildirim & Correia, 2015) from 11 countries to examine measurement invariance using MG-CFA. Zhang et al. (2024) concluded in favour of partial invariance when invariance constraints were relaxed on two items. Baseline models also indicated misfit in several of the country-specific samples. Kalaitzaki et al. (2024) investigated cross-cultural differences in PSU prevalence with the Mobile Phone Problem Use Scale (MPPUS) (Bianchi & Phillips, 2005) and the consistency of psychological risk factors across 14 countries. Although this did not test for invariance, the study identified numerous risk factors that were common between countries. Finally, García-Manglano et al. (2021) compared optimal cutoffs of the SAS-SV across 11 Spanish-speaking countries. Without clinical assessment, García-Manglano et al. (2021) compared cutoffs for the SAS-SV with and without comorbid psychological distress and intensive social media use. Their analysis identified substantial variation in optimal cutoffs across countries, determined using Receiver Operating Characteristic (ROC) analyses.

Several lessons can be drawn from these studies. Notably, the studies that tested cross-national or cross-linguistic invariance failed to support measurement invariance, meaning that many of the most popular scales are not easily comparable between the different populations included in these studies. Clearly, caution should be exercised when comparing means and prevalence statistics between countries and languages. This caution is specifically highlighted in three of them (Blachnio et al., 2021; García-Manglano et al., 2021; Olson et al., 2023). The second is that, despite critiques of measurement invariance as a practice, these studies reveal systematic differences in how people in different countries respond to items assessing PSU, and that there is a need to understand why that occurs. Additionally, several of these studies highlight issues with structural validity that occur before testing for invariance. This invalidity echoes many of the messages that are explored in Chap. 3.

Cross-national Meta-analyses

Despite a lack of cross-cultural research, other methods can be used to compare differences between populations. The main alternative to a multinational study is to conduct a systematic review to collate studies, assess their risk of bias, and undertake a meta-analysis to compare differences between countries or regions. Several meta-analyses have estimated the international prevalence of PSU in the general population (Meng et al., 2022; Lu et al., 2024), in children and adolescents (Sohn et al., 2019), and in specific populations such as medical students (Zhong et al., 2022).

Meng and colleagues (2022) collated estimates from 507 studies to calculate the global prevalence of 'digital addictions': internet, smartphone, gaming, social media, and cybersex. Smartphone addiction was the most prevalent, with 26.99% of participants from 82 studies exceeding scale cutoffs. Meng et al. (2022) also tested moderators of higher prevalence. They found that SA was more prevalent in less affluent countries, that prevalence was higher in more recent studies, within university student and adult samples, and in studies that used the SAS-SV as their classification measure. In contrast, geographic region, gender, questionnaire administration mode, sample size, and sample representativeness did not affect estimates. Several studies have examined changes over time to test whether smartphone addiction has become more prevalent as devices have proliferated. Olson et al. (2022) did this by synthesising scores from studies that used the SAS-SV to examine trends in smartphone addiction severity over time, and also found an increase in severity. Recently, Lu et al. (2024) conducted a further meta-analysis focusing on PSU prevalence and found a similar trend, with PSU increasing over time.

Some substantial challenges currently impede this approach. The most pressing issue is the lack of consistent measurement. As explored earlier, there are cultural and geographic differences in the popularity of SA/PSU scales. Meta-analyses comparing multiple scales have found that studies using the SAS/SAS-SV estimate higher prevalence rates (Meng et al., 2022; Lu et al., 2024). Even when incorporating these moderators, this approach still underestimates the risk of bias from combining these studies. The few multinational studies undertaken have found evidence of measurement biases, but because they have been under-investigated, the extent of these biases is unknown. This uncertainty is especially troubling because one implication of non-invariance is that comparing raw estimates between groups, as with meta-analysis, is inappropriate.

Several actions can be taken to address these problems. The first is to conduct multigroup and multinational research to assess measurement equivalence. This research would allow the determination of the presence and degree of measurement bias. However, achieving this is much easier said than done. Conducting these studies is a major time and resource-intensive undertaking. Another possibility is encouraging open data practices, with researchers sharing primary data from their research upon project completion (see Chap. 6). This data can be used to promote collaborative studies that pool data from multiple separate studies to assess invariance. Individual data also opens up the possibility of conducting an individual patient data (or IPD) meta-analysis. This has drawbacks, especially if demographic or other covariates are measured differently, but the benefits of doing so vastly outweigh these challenges.

Lack of Clinical Samples

Another limiting feature of the smartphone addiction literature is the lack of clinically focused research. Much of the smartphone addiction research is dedicated to assessing the clinical relevance of smartphone addiction as a disorder and establishing prevalence rates. Yet most of these studies rely on smartphone addiction scales designed to assess prevalence in the general population. This tendency means there is inconclusive evidence that smartphone behaviour meets this clinical threshold to be classified as an addiction (Panova & Carbonell, 2018). Despite the vast number of measurement scales (Harris et al., 2020), no agreed criterion has been developed to determine the clinical level of functional impairment for smartphone use and behaviour (Ting & Chen, 2020). This has led to considerable differences in self-report scale items, criteria, and "cut-off" thresholds to establish any consensus in this matter (see Chap. 3). Common screening questionnaires are frequently developed based on inconsistent criteria adapted from other addictions and not compared against clinical judgement. Few are suitable for clinical samples (Ting & Chen, 2020). This results in the measurement of smartphone addiction being considerably less standardised compared to clinical disorders such as depression and disordered gambling, which have widely tested and validated scales such as the Patient Health Questionnaire (PHQ9, Kroenke et al., 2001), the Beck Depression Inventory (Beck et al., 1961), and the Problem Gambling Severity Index (PGSI, Ferris & Wynne, 2001). To put these problems in perspective, measurement in both domains has undergone substantial scrutiny and refinement over time despite far better practices than smartphone use (e.g. Fried et al., 2022). By using scales that have not been clinically validated and only testing these amongst general population samples, it is difficult to determine whether the groups identified in these studies experience levels of harm that meet the threshold for 'addiction' and warrant clinical intervention. Instead, smartphone-related harm might be better suited as a spectrum of problematic use across different levels of severity (Panova & Carbonell, 2018) or integrated into an overarching internet or digital addiction (see Chap. 2). To effectively study clinical levels of impairment, including the possibility of addiction, this needs to be assessed in clinical settings with clinical (e.g. treatment seeking, those that exceed measurement "cut offs") samples facilitated by health professionals instead of through surveys with healthy general population samples (Kardefelt-Winther et al., 2017). However, this is lacking in the current smartphone addiction literature and limits our understanding of clinical treatment and interactions with clinical disorders, both physical and mental, or other adverse outcomes.

Instead of clinical samples, the literature largely relies on samples of school or university students (Ting & Chen, 2020; Pavona & Carbonell, 2018; James et al., 2023). In our review of 1305 studies, we found that around 75% recruited school or university-age students, with the mean age of participants across all studies being 20 years old (James et al., 2023). This is likely due to several different factors. Firstly, it has been previously identified that younger ages may be more at risk of developing problematic smartphone use (Olson et al., 2023; Liu et al., 2022; Csibi et al., 2021) and have higher rates of smartphone ownership (Newzoo,

2018; Olson et al., 2022). This focus has narrowed attention away from other age groups and resulted in disproportionately more research on how risk can be mitigated and assessed for younger populations, including possible government policies and treatments. Secondly, there has been concern about the growing rates of poor mental health among young people more generally, including rates of anxiety, depression, and self-harm (The Lancet, 2024; McGorry et al., 2024). Some have suggested that this increase is directly due to smartphones and social media (Twenge et al., 2018, 2022; Haidt, 2024). Coupled with the 'moral panic' around emerging technology developments (see Chap. 1), this has led to many wanting to understand these mental health associations while ignoring other contextual factors that may explain these trends (see Chaps. 5 and 6). Clinical research samples with those who meet the criteria for disordered use, along with other mental health disorders, would shed light on these associations and bring clarity to this fuzzy relationship. Lastly, university and college students have historically been an easy population to recruit through convenience sampling. This tendency has meant that smartphone addiction research has favoured studying children and young people while neglecting research using clinical populations, and working-age or elderly adults who may also be at risk of online harm.

This focus on children and young people has led to key gaps in our knowledge about smartphone use in other populations. A large international study of 41 countries found that rates of smartphone addiction (measured using the SAS-SV, Kwon et al., 2013) are often higher in younger adults (starting at 20 years old) and decline with age (Olson et al., 2023). But there is also considerable variation in this decline depending on the country, and elevated rates of problematic smartphone use in some countries were still present up to the age of 90. Other studies have also found evidence of problematic use among older populations (Csibi et al., 2021; Jeong & Bae, 2022) but the true prevalence is unclear due to limited research. These older populations are underrepresented in smartphone addiction literature, despite still being at risk of problematic smartphone use, making it difficult to know whether and in what ways this population is impacted differently from younger people. Problematic smartphone use may present very differently or have different contextual factors to explore in this case. This means these populations will also be missed when it comes to appropriately tailored measurement scales, introducing policies, assessing appropriate interventions and understanding the associations their smartphone use may have with mental health outcomes or any other adverse effects.

The field needs greater representation of more diverse samples and methods: older populations, clinical samples, longitudinal studies and other methodologies such as qualitative, mixed methods and multidisciplinary investigations. For example, Bye et al. (2024) report on their prospective longitudinal cohort study of 13–25-year-olds in a clinical population, including measures of self-harm, anxiety, depression and PSU. Their baseline data suggest that rates of problematic use may be higher among these clinical populations, and their future analysis may provide helpful insights into the mechanisms and associations that exist with clinical mental health outcomes. Their inclusion of Public and Patient Involvement (PPI), a focus on problematic use instead of addiction, and the use of objective data and clinical samples are all strengths of the prospective study that other researchers may benefit from. Further suggestions of how to move forward are presented in Chap. 6, but for research to understand what constitutes clinical levels of impairment and the best measurements to use, clinical samples are of greater value compared to studies that only includes general populations.

Self-Report Versus Logged Use

While the concentrated focus on non-clinical, student populations leaves gaps in our knowledge, there is also an issue with how smartphone behaviour is commonly measured in these studies. Smartphone addiction studies frequently rely on self-report smartphone addiction scales (see Chap 3.) or usage estimates to make conclusions about the impact on mental health and well-being but overlook other variables or methods to measure smartphone behaviour.

As discussed previously (see Chap. 1), 'screen time' is a poorly defined concept (Kaye et al., 2020; Livingstone, 2021) but this is further complicated by measurement using self-reported methods. While it is agreed that screen time refers to the volume of time spent on a device, much of the literature asks participants to estimate this usage. For instance, they may be asked to estimate how long they spend on their phone or how long they spend doing each activity. However, behavioural measures such as overall phone use, phone pickups, notifications, and time spent on certain apps can be collected from smartphones (Hitcham et al., 2023). Smartphone operating systems record this information, often by default through features such as Screen Time (iOS) or Digital Wellbeing (Android) but this method of collecting logged data is uncommon. In our recent review (James et al., 2023), we investigated what behavioural data is being collected in the existing smartphone addiction literature. Of the 1305 studies examined, only 10% collected data from participants' phones. Worse, this is becoming less common over time. While some studies have used this method to collect information on daily usage (e.g. Ryding & Kuss, 2020; Elhai et al., 2021; Hodes & Thomas, 2021) or event-level data (e.g. Noe et al., 2019; Andrews et al., 2015), logged data is unfortunately under-utilised in research. This oversight marks a missed opportunity to understand how objective data, instead of subjective estimates, relates to smartphone addiction and any possible harmful effects of use. Addressing this is particularly important when previous research demonstrates that associations with mental health outcomes differ between self-reported and logged measures of use (Shaw et al., 2020). Logged data can provide insights into how smartphone addiction could be identified or clinically monitored, and has been used successfully in many other health disorders. Behavioural data, properly utilised, could help define the markers of problematic usage patterns and identify how these can be tracked and monitored to mitigate harm or relapses. Behavioural trace data could further our understanding of what constitutes smartphone or other behavioural addictions (e.g. internet addiction) and more clearly define clinical "cut-offs." Therefore, it is recommended that logged data should be used where possible (Kaye et al., 2020).

Furthermore, of the 1305 studies included in our review, only half (49.89%) reported any behavioural data at all (James et al., 2023). The types of behavioural data were divided into different categories and behaviours as shown in Table 4.1. As mentioned, only 10% of these

Table 4.1 Categories and example behaviours of behavioural data (James et al., 2023)

Domain	Behaviours
Screen Time	Average daily or weekly smartphone use, including distinctions between weekday and weekend use
Type of use	Type of apps used, time spent on certain apps and frequency of use, number of calls or texts
Preferred type of use	Most used smartphone apps, purpose of smartphone use
Context of use	Using a smartphone before sleep or after waking; use while driving, walking, or during school or work hours; phone related accidents; 'phubbing'
Length of ownership	Number of ownership years, age of first smartphone
Expenditure	Number of phones owned, money spent on use (e.g. mobile data)
Pick ups	Number of times the smartphone was used each day or week, frequency of phone checks

studies used logged data, meaning that the rest elicited this behavioural data via self-report. While self-report data is valuable, it must be weighed against evidence demonstrating that self-reports are systematically biased (Parry et al., 2021; Sewall & Parry, 2021). There are a couple of key limitations to be aware of. Firstly, while there was consistency in the categories of data collected, there was no consensus on how to query smartphone use. For instance, screen time was especially variable. Studies frequently ask about different time periods (e.g. daily vs weekly usage), require different responses (e.g. free text vs questionnaire items), or use different response categories (e.g. increments of half hours, hours or multiple hours), which may bias how participants respond. Similar variation was also found with the type of use measured (e.g. categories such as messaging, gaming, or social media apps). Issues with the validity of self-report estimates are attributable both methodological choices and respondent bias. Secondly, participants frequently overestimate (Kobayashi & Boase, 2012) and underestimate (Felisoni & Godoi, 2018; Junco, 2013; Lin et al., 2015) their smartphone usage compared to logged data. This inaccuracy creates a mismatch in the data and potentially means that these measures of subjective and objective behaviour capture different constructs. This is supported by the findings of a meta-analysis and cubic response surface analysis, which demonstrated that self-reported estimates of usage were only moderately linked with logged behaviour (Parry et al., 2021) and that depression was more associated with estimated than logged phone use (Sewall & Parry, 2021). This means that self-report is more likely measuring people's perceptions of their use (Sewall et al., 2020) and therefore includes their attitudes and feelings about their smartphone use (Ellis, 2019). This differs from the objective data that can be obtained from devices. These estimates and self-reported use will, therefore, have different associations with self-reported smartphone addiction and mental health whereby perceptions have stronger associations to these negative outcomes (Sewall & Parry et al., 2021; Hitcham et al., 2023). For example, associations with depression were greater when people perceived their use to be more than it was compared to those who underestimated (Sewall & Parry, 2021). Given the reliance on self-report measures and estimates, it is important to understand the relationships between these constructs to understand smartphone-related harms. This provides further evidence that using self-reported screen time alone misses important associations that are vital in understanding smartphone addiction. It is important to consider other factors which provide more context such as how and when the phone is used (Griffiths, 2018) and how people think about their smartphone use (e.g. feeling they use their phone too much). This gap means that policies and interventions aimed at reducing overall screen time will likely be ineffective since greater screen time does not simply equate to higher levels of smartphone addiction or distress.

Logged data and self-reported behavioural data both provide valuable contributions to our understanding of smartphone addiction, but many studies continue to rely on smartphone addiction scales to assess smartphone use and engagement. This overreliance on problematic use scales (Harris et al., 2020) means that important information about the context and patterns of smartphone use is missed, thereby skewing our understanding towards negative effects. The lack of behavioural data used in smartphone research may bias prevalence rates and lead to inaccurate conclusions about the impact of smartphone usage on mental health. Future research should prioritise the collection of logged behaviour, incorporating measures into cross-cultural and longitudinal studies or large cohort studies such as those supported by the Department of Education (James & Hitcham, 2023). Research could also extend these efforts with the use of additional app-based studies to collect real-time data or by using time diaries or ecological momentary assessment (EMA), but much of this data is already available without the need for app development (Hodes & Thomas, 2021). There is still value in collecting self-report data, especially when logged data collection is infeasible, when self-reports can contextualise and explain beyond logged estimates, or to understand the differences between tracking and self-report estimates. Ultimately, it is important to understand the different types of conclusions we can draw from logged vs self-reported data and to recognise the value of logged, objective data in our assessment of smartphone addiction.

Conclusion

The focus of this chapter has been to discuss methodological concerns in studying smartphone addiction. Empirical studies rely heavily on cross-sectional survey designs. This approach is especially limited when testing structural (i.e. mediation) models and causal hypotheses. Smartphone addiction research is internationally diverse. However, a mixture of measurement problems with few cross-national studies threatens the validity of comparing different groups or cultures directly, or by using meta-analysis. Across populations, there are notable gaps in coverage, particularly in treatment-seeking, non-student adult, and elderly populations. Finally, there are critical problems with measuring phone use and engagement. Besides a lack of data collection, the field relies on inconsistently used self-report measures, when logged data of various kinds is feasible and easily accessible. There are solutions to each of these issues, primarily by adopting a broader range of methodologies and sampling techniques, and specifically by using passively collected logged data.

References

Andrews, S., Ellis, D. A., Shaw, H., & Piwek, L. (2015). Beyond self-report: Tools to compare estimated and real-world smartphone use. *PLoS One, 10*(10), e0139004. https://doi.org/10.1371/journal.pone.0139004

Augner, C., Vlasak, T., Aichhorn, W., & Barth, A. (2023). The association between problematic smartphone use and symptoms of anxiety and depression—A meta-analysis. *Journal of Public Health, 45*(1), 193–201. https://doi.org/10.1093/pubmed/fdab350

Banks, J., Muriel, A., & Smith, J. P. (2011). Attrition and health in ageing studies: Evidence from ELSA and HRS. *Longitudinal and Life Course Studies, 2*(2), 10.14301/llcs.v2i2.115.

Beck, A. T., Ward, C. H., Mendelson, M., Mock, J., & Erbauch, J. (1961). An inventory for measuring depression. *Archives of General Psychiatry, 4*(6), 561–571.

Bianchi, A., & Phillips, J. G. (2005). Psychological predictors of problem Mobile phone use. *Cyberpsychology & Behavior, 8*(1), 39–51. https://doi.org/10.1089/cpb.2005.8.39

Błachnio, A., Przepiórka, A., Gorbaniuk, O., Bendayan, R., McNeill, M., Angeluci, A., Abreu, A. M., Ben-Ezra, M., Benvenuti, M., & Blanca, M. J. (2021). Measurement invariance of the phubbing scale across 20 countries. *International Journal of Psychology, 56*(6), 885–894. https://doi.org/10.1002/ijop.12790

Busch, P. A., & McCarthy, S. (2021). Antecedents and consequences of problematic smartphone use: A systematic literature review of an emerging research area. *Computers in Human Behavior, 114*, 106414. https://doi.org/10.1016/j.chb.2020.106414

Bye, A., Carter, B., Leightley, D., Trevillion, K., Liakata, M., Branthonne-Foster, S., Cross, S., Zenasni, Z., Carr, E., Williamson, G., Vega Viyuela, A., & Dutta, R. (2024). Cohort profile: The social media, smartphone use and self-harm in young people (3S-YP) study–a prospective, observational cohort study of young people in contact with mental health services. *PLoS One, 19*(5). https://doi.org/10.1371/journal.pone.0299059

Csibi, S., Griffiths, M. D., Demetrovics, Z., & Szabo, A. (2021). Analysis of problematic smartphone use across different age groups within the 'components model of addiction'. *International Journal of Mental Health and Addiction, 19*(3), 616–631. https://doi.org/10.1007/s11469-019-00095-0

Elhai, J. D., Sapci, O., Yang, H., Amialchuk, A., Rozgonjuk, D., & Montag, C. (2021). Objectively-measured and self-reported smartphone use in relation to surface learning, procrastination, academic productivity, and psychopathology symptoms in college students. *Human Behavior and Emerging Technologies, 3*(5), 912–921. https://doi.org/10.1002/hbe2.254

Ellis, D. A. (2019). Are smartphones really that bad? Improving the psychological measurement of technology-related behaviors. *Computers in Human Behavior, 97*, 60–66. https://doi.org/10.1016/j.chb.2019.03.006

Felisoni, D. D., & Godoi, A. S. (2018). Cell phone usage and academic performance: An experiment. *Computers & Education, 117*, 175–187. https://doi.org/10.1016/j.compedu.2017.10.006

Ferris, J., & Wynne, H. (2001). *The Canadian problem gambling index: Final report*. Canadian Centre on Substance Abuse.

Fried, E. I., Flake, J. K., & Robinaugh, D. J. (2022). Revisiting the theoretical and methodological foundations of depression measurement. *Nature Reviews Psychology, 1*(6), 358–368. https://doi.org/10.1038/s44159-022-00050-2

García-Manglano, J., López-Madrigal, C., Sádaba-Chalezquer, C., Serrano, C., & Lopez-Fernandez, O. (2021). Difficulties in establishing "truth" conditions in the assessment of addictive smartphone use in young adults. *International Journal of Environmental Research and Public Health, 19*(1), 358. https://doi.org/10.3390/ijerph19010358

Griffiths, M. D. (2018). Conceptual issues concerning internet addiction and internet gaming disorder: Further critique on Ryding and Kaye (2017). *International Journal of Mental Health and Addiction, 16*(1), 233–239. https://doi.org/10.1007/s11469-017-9818-z

Haidt, J. (2024). *The anxious generation: How the great rewiring of childhood is causing an epidemic of mental illness*. Random House.

Harris, B., Regan, T., Schueler, J., & Fields, S. A. (2020). Problematic Mobile phone and smartphone use scales: A systematic review. *Frontiers in Psychology, 11*, 672. https://doi.org/10.3389/fpsyg.2020.00672

Henrich, J., Heine, S. J., & Norenzayan, A. (2010). The weirdest people in the world? *Behavioral and Brain Sciences, 33*(2–3), 61–83. https://doi.org/10.1017/S0140525X0999152X

Hitcham, L., Jackson, H., & James, R. J. E. (2023). The relationship between smartphone use and smartphone addiction: An examination of logged and self-reported behavior in a pre-registered, two-wave sample. *Computers in Human Behavior, 146*, 107822. https://doi.org/10.1016/j.chb.2023.107822

Hodes, L. N., & Thomas, K. G. (2021). Smartphone screen time: Inaccuracy of self reports and influence of psychological and contextual factors. Computers in Human Behavior, 115, Article 106616. https://doi.org/10.1016/j.chb.2020.106616.

James, R. J. E., Dixon, G., Dragomir, M.-G., Thirlwell, E., & Hitcham, L. (2023). Understanding the construction of 'behavior' in smartphone addiction: A scoping review. *Addictive Behaviors, 137*, 107503. https://doi.org/10.1016/j.addbeh.2022.107503

James, R. J. E., & Hitcham, L. (2023). *DESC evidence call response on screen time*. Retrieved December 29, 2024, from https://osf.io/3tmub

Jeong, J.-H., & Bae, S.-M. (2022). The relationship between types of smartphone use, digital literacy, and smartphone addiction in the elderly. *Psychiatry Investigation, 19*(10), 832–839. https://doi.org/10.30773/pi.2021.0400

Junco, R. (2013). Comparing actual and self-reported measures of Facebook use. *Computers in Human Behavior, 29*(3), 626–631. https://doi.org/10.1016/j.chb.2012.11.007

Kalaitzaki, A., Laconi, S., Spritzer, D. T., Hauck, S., Gnisci, A., Sergi, I., Vally, Z., Tudorel, O., Vintila, M., & Malik, S. (2024). The prevalence and predictors of problematic mobile phone use: A 14-country empirical survey. *International Journal of Mental Health and Addiction, 22*(1), 746–765. https://doi.org/10.1007/s11469-022-00901-2

Karadağ, E., Tosuntaş, Ş. B., Erzen, E., Duru, P., Bostan, N., Şahin, B. M., Çulha, İ. and Babadağ, B. (2015). Determinants of phubbing which is the sum of many virtual addictions: A structural equation model. Journal of Behavioral Addictions 4(2) 60–74. https://doi.org/10.1556/2006.4.2015.005

Kardefelt-Winther, D., Heeren, A., Schimmenti, A., Van Rooij, A., Maurage, P., Carras, M., Edman, J., Blaszczynski, A., Khazaal, Y., & Billieux, J. (2017). How can we conceptualize behavioural addiction without pathologizing common behaviours? *Addiction, 112*(10), 1709–1715. https://doi.org/10.1111/add.13763

Kaye, L. K., Orben, A., Ellis, D. A., Hunter, S. C., & Houghton, S. (2020). The conceptual and methodological mayhem of "screen time". *International Journal of Environmental Research and Public Health, 17*(10), 3661. https://doi.org/10.3390/ijerph17103661

Kobayashi, T., & Boase, J. (2012). No such effect? The implications of measurement error in self-report measures of mobile communication use. *Communication Methods and Measures, 6*(2), 126–143. https://doi.org/10.1080/19312458.2012.679243

Kroenke, K., Spitzer, R. L., & Williams, J. B. W. (2001). The PHQ-9. *Journal of General Internal Medicine, 16*(9), 606–613. https://doi.org/10.1046/j.1525-1497.2001.016009606.x

Kwon, M., Kim, D.-J., Cho, H., & Yang, S. (2013). The smartphone addiction scale: Development and validation of a short version for adolescents. *PLoS One, 8*(12), e83558. https://doi.org/10.1371/journal.pone.0083558

Lin, Y.-H., Lin, Y.-C., Lee, Y.-H., et al. (2015). Time distortion associated with smartphone addiction: Identifying smartphone addiction via a mobile application (app). *Journal of Psychiatric Research, 65*, 139–145. https://doi.org/10.1016/j.jpsychires.2015.04.003

Liu, H., Soh, K. G., Samsudin, S., Rattanakoses, W., & Qi, F. (2022). Effects of exercise and psychological interventions on smartphone addiction among university students: A systematic review. *Frontiers in Psychology, 13*, 1021285. https://doi.org/10.3389/fpsyg.2022.1021285

Livingstone, S. (2021). The rise and fall of screen time. In V. C. Strasburger (Ed.), *Masters of media: Controversies and solutions: Controversies and solutions, volume 1* (pp. 89–104). Rowman and Littlefield.

Lopez-Fernandez, O., Kuss, D. J., Romo, L., Morvan, Y., Kern, L., Graziani, P., Rousseau, A., Rumpf, H. J., Bischof, A., Gässler, A. K., Schimmenti, A., Passanisi, A., Männikkö, N., Kääriänen, M., Demetrovics, Z., Király, O., Chóliz, M., Zacarés, J. J., Serra, E., et al. (2017). Self-reported dependence on mobile phones in young adults: A European cross-cultural empirical survey. *Journal of Behavioral Addictions, 6*(2), 168–177. https://doi.org/10.1556/2006.6.2017.020

Lu, X., An, X., & Chen, S. (2024). Trends and influencing factors in problematic smartphone use prevalence (2012–2022): A systematic review and meta-analysis. *Cyberpsychology, Behavior, and Social Networking, 27*(9), 616–634. https://doi.org/10.1089/cyber.2023.0548

Maxwell, S. E., & Cole, D. A. (2007). Bias in cross-sectional analyses of longitudinal mediation. *Psychological Methods, 12*(1), 23. https://doi.org/10.1037/1082-989x.12.1.23

McGorry, P. D., Mei, C., Dalal, N., Alvarez-Jimenez, M., Blakemore, S.-J., Browne, V., Dooley, B., Hickie, I. B., Jones, P. B., McDaid, D., Mihalopoulos, C., Wood, S. J., El Azzouzi, F. A., Fazio, J., Gow, E., Hanjabam, S., Hayes, A., Morris, A., Pang, E., et al. (2024). The lancet psychiatry commission on youth mental health. *The Lancet Psychiatry, 11*(9), 731–774. https://doi.org/10.1016/S2215-0366(24)00163-9

Meng, S.-Q., Cheng, J.-L., Li, Y.-Y., Yang, X.-Q., Zheng, J.-W., Chang, X.-W., Shi, Y., Chen, Y., Lu, L., Sun, Y., Bao, Y.-P., & Shi, J. (2022). Global prevalence of digital addiction in general population: A systematic review and meta-analysis. *Clinical Psychology Review, 92*, 102128. https://doi.org/10.1016/j.cpr.2022.102128

Muthukrishna, M., Bell, A. V., Henrich, J., Curtin, C. M., Gedranovich, A., McInerney, J., & Thue, B. (2020). Beyond Western, educated, industrial, rich, and democratic (WEIRD) psychology: Measuring and mapping scales of cultural and psychological distance. *Psychological Science, 31*(6), 678–701. https://doi.org/10.1177/0956797620916782

Newzoo, B. V. (2018). Global mobile market report.

Noe, B., Turner, L. D., Linden, D. E. J., et al. (2019). Identifying indicators of smartphone addiction through user-app interaction. *Computers in Human Behavior, 99*, 56–65. https://doi.org/10.1016/j.chb.2019.04.023

Okano, J. T., Ponce, J., Krönke, M., & Blower, S. (2022). Lack of ownership of mobile phones could hinder the rollout of mHealth interventions in Africa. *eLife, 11*, e79615. https://doi.org/10.7554/elife.79615

Olson, J. A., Sandra, D. A., Colucci, É. S., Al Bikaii, A., Chmoulevitch, D., Nahas, J., Raz, A., & Veissière, S. P. L. (2022). Smartphone addiction is increasing across the world: A meta-analysis of 24 countries. *Computers in Human Behavior, 129*, 107138. https://doi.org/10.1016/j.chb.2021.107138

Olson, J. A., Sandra, D. A., Veissière, S. P. L., & Langer, E. J. (2023). Sex, age, and smartphone addiction across 41 countries. *International Journal of Mental Health and Addiction*. https://doi.org/10.1007/s11469-023-01146-3

Panova, T., & Carbonell, X. (2018). Is smartphone addiction really an addiction? *Journal of Behavioral Addictions, 7*(2), 252–259. https://doi.org/10.1556/2006.7.2018.49

Panova, T., Carbonell, X., Chamarro, A., & Puerta-Cortés, D. X. (2020). Specific smartphone uses and how they relate to anxiety and depression in university students: A cross-cultural perspective. *Behaviour & Information Technology, 39*(9), 944–956. https://doi.org/10.1080/0144929X.2019.1633405

Parry, D. A., Davidson, B. I., Sewall, C. J., Fisher, J. T., Mieczkowski, H., & Quintana, D. S. (2021). A systematic review and meta-analysis of discrepancies between logged and self-reported digital media use. *Nature Human Behaviour, 5*(11), 1535–1547. https://doi.org/10.1038/s41562-021-01117-5

Rohrer, J. M., Hünermund, P., Arslan, R. C., & Elson, M. (2022). That's a lot to process! Pitfalls of popular path models. *Advances in Methods and Practices in Psychological Science, 5*(2), 25152459221095827. https://doi.org/10.1177/25152459221095827

Rozgonjuk, D., Sindermann, C., Elhai, J. D., & Montag, C. (2020). Fear of missing out (FoMO) and social media's impact on daily-life and productivity at work: Do WhatsApp, Facebook, Instagram, and snapchat use disorders mediate that association? *Addictive Behaviors, 110*, 106487. https://doi.org/10.1016/j.addbeh.2020.106487

Ryding, F. C., & Kuss, D. J. (2020). Passive objective measures in the assessment of problematic smartphone use: A systematic review. Addictive Behaviors Reports, 11, Article 100257.

Sewall, C. J. R., Bear, T. M., Merranko, J., & Rosen, D. (2020). How psychosocial well-being and usage amount predict inaccuracies in retrospective estimates of digital technology use. *Mobile Media & Communication, 8*(3), 379–399. https://doi.org/10.1177/2050157920902830

Sewall, C. J. R., & Parry, D. A. (2021). The role of depression in the discrepancy between estimated and actual smartphone use: A cubic response surface analysis. *Technology, Mind, and Behavior, 2*(2). https://doi.org/10.1037/tmb0000036

Sewall, C. J. R., & Parry, D. A. (2024). Social media and youth mental health: Simple narratives produce biased interpretations. *Journal of Psychopathology and Clinical Science, 133*(7), 507–514. https://doi.org/10.1037/abn0000950

Shaw, H., Ellis, D. A., Geyer, K., Davidson, B., Ziegler, F., & Smith, A. (2020). Quantifying smartphone "use": Choice of measurement impacts relationships between "usage" and health. *Technology, Mind, and Behavior, 1*(2). https://doi.org/10.1037/tmb0000022

Sohn, S. Y., Rees, P., Wildridge, B., Kalk, N. J., & Carter, B. (2019). Prevalence of problematic smartphone usage and associated mental health outcomes amongst children and young people: A systematic review, meta-analysis and GRADE of the evidence. *BMC Psychiatry, 19*(1), 356. https://doi.org/10.1186/s12888-019-2350-x

The Lancet. (2024). Unhealthy influencers? Social media and youth mental health. *The Lancet, 404*(10461), 1375. https://doi.org/10.1016/S0140-6736(24)02244-X

Ting, C. H., & Chen, Y. Y. (2020). Smartphone addiction. In *Adolescent addiction* (pp. 215–240). Elsevier. https://doi.org/10.1016/B978-0-12-818626-8.00008-6

Twenge, J. M., Haidt, J., Lozano, J., & Cummins, K. M. (2022). Specification curve analysis shows that social media use is linked to poor mental health, especially among girls. *Acta Psychologica, 224*, 103512. https://doi.org/10.1016/j.actpsy.2022.103512

Twenge, J. M., Joiner, T. E., Rogers, M. L., & Martin, G. N. (2018). Increases in depressive symptoms, suicide-related outcomes, and suicide rates among U.S. adolescents after 2010 and links to increased new media screen time. *Clinical Psychological Science, 6*(1), 3–17. https://doi.org/10.1177/2167702617723376

Winer, E. S., Cervone, D., Bryant, J., McKinney, C., Liu, R. T., & Nadorff, M. R. (2016). Distinguishing mediational models and analyses in clinical psychology: Atemporal associations do not imply causation. *Journal of Clinical Psychology, 72*(9), 947–955.

Xie, X., Dong, Y., & Wang, J. (2018). Sleep quality as a mediator of problematic smartphone use and clinical health symptoms. *Journal of Behavioral Addictions, 7*(2), 466–472.

Yang, J., Fu, X., Liao, X., & Li, Y. (2020). Association of problematic smartphone use with poor sleep quality, depression, and anxiety: A systematic review and meta-analysis. *Psychiatry Research, 284*, 112686.

Yildirim, C., & Correia, A.-P. (2015). Exploring the dimensions of nomophobia: Development and validation of a self-reported questionnaire. *Computers in Human Behavior, 49*, 130–137. https://doi.org/10.1016/j.chb.2015.02.059

Zhang, Y., Pan, X., & Ma, Z. (2024). Cross-cultural psychometric evaluation of the nomophobia questionnaire (NMP-Q): Examining measurement invariance and psychological network structure across 11 countries. *International Journal of Mental Health and Addiction.* https://doi.org/10.1007/s11469-024-01408-8

Zhong, Y., Ma, H., Liang, Y.-F., Liao, C.-J., Zhang, C.-C., & Jiang, W.-J. (2022). Prevalence of smartphone addiction among Asian medical students: A meta-analysis of multinational observational studies. *International Journal of Social Psychiatry, 68*(6), 1171–1183.

5

Treatment

Abstract The present chapter considers the issue of how smartphone addiction could be treated if it were to be classed as a disorder. Various types of interventions have been proposed from academic literature to treat smartphone addiction, including CBT, exercise, and mindfulness. Meanwhile, popular literature (e.g. self-help books) is broader in scope and focus on practices of self-care and abstinence. This chapter will review different types of interventions and compare how academic and popular literature approach this issue. We then explore how smartphone and other technology addictions are currently treated in the UK, primarily by private clinics and the third sector, the role of policy, and the smartphone applications marketed as supports or treatments for smartphone addiction.

Keywords Smartphone addiction • Treatment • Cognitive Behavioural Therapy • Exercise • Interventions • Applications

R. James, L. Hitcham, *Critical Perspectives on Smartphone Addiction*, Palgrave Studies in Cyberpsychology, https://doi.org/10.1007/978-3-031-96188-5_5

Introduction

There are many ways in which the conceptualisation and measurement of smartphone addiction is flawed and there is considerable debate about whether it should be classified as a disorder, which poses the question: if smartphone addiction is a diagnosable addiction, how is it meant to be treated?

As with all mental health disorders, the Diagnostic and Statistical Manual (DSM) and International Classification of Disease (ICD) only exist to provide clinicians with the criteria and symptoms for the purpose of diagnosis (American Psychological Association, 2013; World Health Organisation, 2024). Given the variability and inconsistency of criteria and measurement scales for smartphone addiction (see Chap. 3), this corresponds with significant variation in the proposed treatment options. Existing academic literature often focuses on treatment approaches that are common to other mental health disorders, or repurpose concepts used for other addictions, such as gambling and alcohol. Meanwhile, popular literature often takes a contrasting approach by offering guidance around self-care or abstinence. However, in practice, professional treatment in the UK is not commonplace despite the rising concern over smartphone addiction prevalence.

This chapter aims to provide a critical overview of the proposed treatments for smartphone addiction across different domains of literature by focusing on:

(1) The different interventions for smartphone addiction from academic literature
(2) How popular literature positions smartphone addiction and possible treatments
(3) How technology addictions are currently treated in the UK
(4) The smartphone applications aimed at treating smartphone addiction

Within these areas, it is important to consider whether such treatments are targeting smartphone addiction specifically or rather the associated symptoms of anxiety or distress that may either precede smartphone use or be a consequence of it. Such considerations and proposed treatments will vary across the different stakeholders involved in this area, including academics, popular media authors, practitioners, and third-sector parties. Therefore this chapter will draw on issues covered in Chaps 2 and 3 on how smartphone addiction is conceptualised and measured, and explore what we can learn from other proposed technology addictions to understand how we could move forward.

Interventions from Academia

Aims of Interventions

As discussed in previous chapters, there are various models and symptoms ascribed to smartphone addiction or problematic smartphone use (PSU) resulting in issues such as an excess of measurement scales, lack of validity, and reliance on self-report measures, meaning there is a general lack of consensus on how to "diagnose" smartphone addiction. However, along with the efforts to define and measure smartphone addiction comes research and literature aimed at exploring how such problems should be treated.

There are a variety of interventions that have been proposed to treat smartphone addiction in academic literature, including Cognitive Behaviour Therapy (CBT), exercise, mindfulness, and 12-step addiction programmes. These interventions have often proven to be effective in treating other mental health disorders or addictions, therefore academic studies have sought to assess whether such methods also reduce symptoms of smartphone addiction.

The aims of such interventions often vary according to which model or criteria is being used to assess smartphone addiction, but success is often measured according to improvements in (1) symptoms, (2) activities, and (3) well-being (Sharma & Palanichamy, 2018; Malinauskas & Malinauskiene, 2019). For example, studies assessing interventions for digital addictions look for reductions in depression, anxiety, and addiction (internet, gaming, smartphone) scores, reductions in screen time, or improvements in self-esteem or self-control (Lu et al., 2024). This can also include changes in physical activity, life satisfaction, peer and familial relationships, and improved performance in work or school activities (Sharma & Palanichamy, 2018). However, such studies and academic reviews have often focused on internet addiction (IA) or internet gaming disorder (IGD) as opposed to smartphone addiction specifically. There is frequent reference to all digital addictions within treatment studies, which adds further complications in understanding the distinctions between these proposed addictions and how they should be treated, particularly smartphone addiction.

Cognitive Behaviour Therapy

Cognitive Behaviour Therapy (CBT) is one of the most popular forms of psychosocial treatment for a variety of mental health problems, including depression, anxiety, and obsessive-compulsive disorder (OCD). Both group and individual CBT aim to challenge unhelpful or negative thoughts and address unhelpful patterns of behaviours or coping strategies (National Institute of Care Excellence (NICE), 2022; Royal College of Psychiatrists, 2022). In the case of smartphone addiction, it has been suggested that pre-existing psychosocial problems and maladaptive cognitions may lead to addiction symptoms (Wu-Ouyang, 2022). In turn, smartphone use may contribute to unhelpful thinking or behaviour by providing an escape mechanism, which then becomes maladaptive (Davis, 2001; Young, 1998). Therefore, CBT aims to help a person reflect on the connection between their thoughts and behaviours and develop more helpful responses (Liu et al., 2017a). For example, CBT may help in identifying which negative emotions or thoughts (e.g. anxiety, low self-esteem) trigger maladaptive smartphone use and work to reframe them and provide more helpful coping strategies.

This model has proven popular with CBT being the most common psychotherapy model used for digital addictions (Lu et al., 2024; Ding and Li, 2023). CBT offers many advantages as a possible treatment option given that it is widely available in existing services, is non-invasive and could be adapted based on the model for existing conditions. However, evidence for CBT as a treatment of smartphone addiction is mixed and is often studied in parallel with internet addiction making it difficult to ascertain clear results. While some studies have found CBT in general to be effective in reducing addiction scores and levels of depression and anxiety (Liu et al., 2017a; Ding & Li, 2023), other studies looking at individual and group CBT separately did not find the same improvements (Malinauskas & Malinauskiene, 2019). A further umbrella review of CBT for digital addictions concluded that while some studies showed positive associations and improvements from CBT treatment, the studies only provide weak evidence (Lu et al., 2024). Consequently, while CBT may be a popular candidate treatment, there are gaps in how effective it may be for smartphone addiction as opposed to internet addiction and how it may differ across populations (e.g. ages, clinical samples) and symptom severity. It is also important to consider whether this treatment targets smartphone addiction symptoms specifically or rather underlying psychosocial problems, such as depression and anxiety. As a result, while CBT may be the most popular and studied option, more research is needed to understand how it can be appropriately adapted for smartphone addiction treatment.

Exercise

Exercise-based interventions are also commonly used for mental health disorders to benefit mood, physical health, and overall well-being. Group exercise is recommended for mild to moderate depression to boost mood and encourage peer support (NICE, 2022) and is generally well tolerated and effective (Noetel et al., 2024). Given the relative accessibility, safety, and possible effectiveness of exercise as a treatment, this has been suggested for other problems including smartphone addiction. The mechanisms of this have been explored with substance use disorders. Exercise may offer positive effects by (1) alleviating cravings and urges, (2) reducing rates of relapse by decreasing negative affect, (3) offering an alternative behaviour when triggered, and (4) increasing neurotransmitters (Linke & Ussher, 2015). These mechanisms may similarly apply to smartphone addiction by offering an alternative activity and improving any negative affect from smartphone use or co-morbid depression or anxiety symptoms.

Evidence suggests that exercise-based interventions, broadly speaking, are effective in reducing smartphone or internet addiction scores as a primary outcome and anxiety, depression, and loneliness as secondary outcomes (e.g. Kim, 2013; Liu et al., 2019; Azam et al., 2020; Li et al., 2023; Zhang et al., 2023; Lu et al., 2024). However, there are various variables at play here that can impact this. Firstly, review studies (i.e. systematic reviews, meta-analyses) collate the effects of all exercise interventions when, in truth, such exercise-based interventions include a diverse range of sports and exercises. Sports such as badminton, yoga, tennis, volleyball, running, football, basketball, cycling, tai chi, and others are all included in such reviews, either independently or as a combination (Liu et al., 2019, 2022) making it difficult to draw out conclusions as to the best type or combination of exercise. This is further complicated by distinctions between group or individual exercise interventions and the duration or level of intensity of these (e.g. twice a week for 60 minutes). Additionally, such interventions can also either be guided by a coach or practitioner or self-guided (Liu et al., 2022), all of which makes it difficult to identify the best exercise intervention to recommend. Secondly, the majority of these studies are focused on student populations because they are argued to be more at-risk of smartphone addiction (Liu et al., 2022; Csibi et al., 2021). Across different reviews, the age range of participants in exercise interventions is typically between 18 and 23 (Liu et al., 2022; Pirwani & Szabo, 2024). This particular concentration on a narrow age range causes issues with the applicability of exercise-based interventions to other populations and provides little information for how they should be adapted appropriately. This aligns with the observations and criticisms made in Chap. 4 that recommend the inclusion of greater representation of other populations (i.e. working age, older adults) in future studies investigating smartphone addiction and by extension, the treatment of it. Lastly, it has been argued that the effects of exercise interventions are more successful when combined with psychological treatments, such as group counselling and mindfulness-based or CBT-based therapies (Liu et al., 2022). For other disorders such as depression or substance abuse disorders, exercise is sometimes considered an adjunctive intervention (Noetel et al., 2024; Linke & Ussher, 2015) and this may also apply with smartphone addiction. Therefore, while exercise may be an engaging, safe, adaptable, and effective option for smartphone addiction intervention, there are unresolved questions around the type and frequency of exercise, whether it should be supervised, how it should be tailored and how it may fit with existing treatments (Linke & Ussher, 2015).

Mindfulness

Mindfulness is a meditation practice that encourages awareness of one's emotions and thoughts and is considered as a method of self-regulation that emphasises consciously perceiving and focusing our attention on the present moment (Kabat-Zinn, 2005; Gaur & Kohli, 2024). The practice originates in traditional Buddhist practice but has been introduced into psychological practice as a possible intervention for various mental health problems. Mindfulness and meditation are currently recommended as a treatment option for depression which involves focusing on the present moment, observing thoughts and feelings and breathing exercises to increase awareness and recognition (NICE, 2022). Likewise, mindfulness is regarded as a possible therapeutic option that is suitable for smartphone addiction (Cheng et al., 2020; Liu et al., 2017b; Yang et al., 2019). Mindfulness interventions may act as standalone interventions but are also used in conjunction with other psychotherapies such as Mindfulness-Based Cognitive Therapy (MBCT) (Segal et al., 2001), Mindfulness-Based Stress Reduction (MBSR) (Kabat-Zinn, 1990), and Acceptance and Commitment Therapy (ACT) (Hayes et al., 1999) and may be broadly grouped as "Mindfulness-Based Interventions" (MBIs). When specifically used for smartphone addiction, MBIs aim to regulate addiction-related distress, identify the intrinsic value of life, reduce the salience of smartphone use urges, and mitigate withdrawal and relapse symptoms (Van Gordon et al., 2017; Lan et al., 2018).

There are several studies investigating MBIs. Lan et al. (2018) conducted a pilot study with 27 college students using a group mindfulness-based cognitive-behavioural intervention and found significant differences in smartphone addiction scores and 'screen time'. Yang et al. (2019) also found mindfulness to have a moderating effect on anxiety, depression, and smartphone addiction among adolescents. Furthermore, a review by Fendel et al. (2024) investigating MBIs for internet addiction found positive effects on problematic internet use and screen time. However, all of these studies were rated low to very low in quality, and MBIs were mainly compared against waiting list or inactive control groups, which diminish any conclusions into their effectiveness. MBIs also vary significantly in duration, format, setting, included practices, and measurement scales used, but face-to-face and guided interventions showed greater positive effects (Fendel et al., 2024). Consequently, while mindfulness may help to reduce the desire for smartphone use and relieve withdrawal symptoms (Lan et al., 2018), the evidence for MBIs for smartphone addiction is mixed and complicated by differing practices. Nonetheless, MBIs may be helpful for prevention or relapse purposes. For example, mindfulness may help to address risk factors for problematic use, such as nomophobia and boredom proneness, but other factors like trait impulsivity may mediate this (Regan et al., 2020). Future research should explore the different variations involved with MBIs to understand the best practices needed to treat problematic smartphone use. Importantly, since research often focuses on student populations, MBIs and training for smartphone and other behavioural addictions need to be developmentally appropriate for the age group due to distinctive age differences (Fendel et al., 2024), which should be considered for all interventions.

Pharmacological

The majority of proposed treatments for smartphone addiction use psychosocial approaches to address behaviours, harms, and underlying mood or anxiety problems. However, in keeping with the treatment of other addictions and disorders, there have been investigations into pharmacological treatments of internet and smartphone addiction. These medications have been proposed and tested in response to suggestions that there is a biological element to smartphone addiction. Specifically, it has been suggested that there are changes to neurotransmitters (Seo et al., 2020;

Chun et al., 2018) and dopamine or "reward" pathways (Oprea et al., 2021; Sharma et al., 2021; Greenfield, 2021) in the brain in those with internet or smartphone addiction. This line of investigation is in keeping with the adaption of addiction conceptualisations and treatments from alcohol and substances to technology and behavioural addictions (see Chap. 2).

As a consequence, the use of pharmacotherapy such as antidepressants and medications used to treat ADHD (attention deficit hyperactivity disorder) have been tested for their efficacy in treating internet and smartphone addiction symptoms. Yang et al. (2024) found thirteen reviews investigating pharmacological treatments for internet addiction. Of these, five found evidence of positive effects of pharmacotherapy, four reported insufficient evidence, and a further four, which combined pharmacotherapy and other interventions, were inconclusive. However, the studies that report positive effects included multiple different medications (e.g. bupropion, methylphenidate) and were often studied in conjunction with comorbidities such as ADHD, depression, and OCD. All such reviews were only reported for internet addiction, with none finding positive effects for smartphone addiction. Consequently, evidence for pharmacological treatments for smartphone addiction or other technology addictions is not currently supported by academic evidence and, as such, would likely be included in treatment plans to address co-morbidities as opposed to any addiction symptoms.

Abstinence and Limits

Many other addictions, such as alcohol, substance use, and gambling, centre on the role of sobriety or abstinence in recovery and treatment. However, smartphones and other technologies have become ubiquitous in daily life making this harder to achieve in the modern era for such candidate addictions. Smartphones and the internet are now commonplace for work, study, and social reasons and, therefore, abstinence is often less achievable or is defined differently.

For treatment, Sharma and Palanichamy (2018) state that therapeutic interventions for technology addictions are often done under two contexts: total abstinence or controlled use. However, these authors recognise that total abstinence is impractical and suggest that 'moderate and controlled use' should be the guiding advice. Controlled use may take different meanings depending on the smartphone user. For example, Young (1999) suggests that abstinence may be applied specifically to applications that contribute to compulsive use, such as certain websites, games, or messaging apps. This abstinence may extend to other potentially problematic behaviours that are facilitated through smartphones, such as gambling, gaming, shopping, or pornography to minimise harm. The identification of the compulsive activities and triggers may form part of the treatments listed previously, such as CBT or mindfulness treatments, to complement the treatment intervention. This will be individual for each person and the boundaries of controlled use could be defined with or without a therapist, such as the bare minimum technology use that is still needed to live functionally (see *ITAA*). This process may involve establishing certain applications that are not to be used during certain hours of the day (i.e. during working hours), are only to be used for a limited amount of time each day or those that should not be used at all. Many people use additional applications to manage such smartphone use (see *Apps to Treat Smartphone Addiction*). This process of setting limits or defining abstinence may improve the effectiveness of other psychosocial interventions, be used as a preventative or self-help method of treatment, or potentially incorporated into everyday life in the long-term following treatment to prevent relapse. Research investigating treatment options should be clear about whether such limit setting or abstinence forms part of the interventions or aim to understand what strategies find most useful in this regard.

In addition, users may employ other coping strategies to limit or control their use. These may include activating smartphone features such as silent mode or greyscale, or non-technology solutions such as leaving the phone in a different room or having someone take the phone away (Kalk et al., 2024; Carter et al., 2024). Such coping strategies have been investigated in adolescent populations. Kalk et al. (2024) found that of these strategies, using 'Do not disturb', turning off notifications, and leaving the phone in another room overnight were the most effective in reducing smartphone usage in 16–18-year-olds compared to activating grayscale settings, using restriction apps, or parents taking the phone away. Similar findings were found by Sohn et al. (2021) with 92.1% of participants using at least one use reduction strategy, particularly those that met the criteria for smartphone addiction. However, Dekker et al. (2024) found that coping or reduction strategies were more commonly adopted by those who perceived their smartphone use to be excessive, but this perception did not always lead to adoption or prove that strategies were effective over time. While some of these strategies focus particularly on reducing screen time, which has different associations with harm compared to smartphone addiction (see Chap. 1), the introduction of controlled use, restrictions, or coping strategies may be adjunctive to the psychosocial therapies or may be helpful in preventing relapses. However, total abstinence is proving harder to achieve due to the increasing technology advancements and societal expectations to be online.

Popular Literature

Heightened public concern about smartphone use has led to several books being published that are designed to help people prevent or overcome their smartphone addictions. In contrast to the academic literature, which is equivocal on the diagnostic merit of smartphone addiction and the appropriate treatment options (Hogan et al., 2024), books designed for public consumption are not circumspect in their characterisation of smartphone use. It is common for popular books to describe smartphone addiction in lurid terms. Smartphone use is frequently compared to other addictions, especially gambling (Hansen, 2023; Alter, 2017), but also cocaine (Price, 2018) and other drugs (Hansen, 2023). Comparisons like these are often based on principles taken from behavioural neuroscience, such as dopamine release, random reinforcement, and variable magnitude of reward. Many of these analogies are fallacious and misleading (Etchells, 2024).

In contrast, the guidance proffered in self-help books is notably restrained in comparison to the problems being discussed. Many self-help approaches focus on themes encountered in academic research, such as exercise, meditation, and mindfulness. Exercise is especially noteworthy because reduced exercise is attributed to increased screen time (Twenge et al., 2018). Some form of exercise, mainly walking, is featured in most self-help books (e.g. Price, 2018; Goodin, 2018; Wrighton, 2022). The same applies to mindfulness (e.g. Brewer, 2017; Price, 2018), where impaired attention has been highlighted as a psychological harm (Hansen, 2023). The behavioural strategies proposed in these books frequently align with cognitive-behavioural principles. These measures include monitoring phone use and setting boundaries on when (e.g. eating) or where (i.e. the bedroom) phones can be used. Further boundaries are intended to delineate different types of time, e.g. preventing interruptions by disabling notifications and creating barriers to distracting content such as social media or games. Other suggestions include organising and 'decluttering' phone apps to focus on necessary ones and making the phone less salient by putting it in grayscale and removing colour. More drastic interventions include introducing locks on phone use or app/website blockers to prevent access to certain content.

For example, *How to Break up with Your Phone* by Catherine Price (2018) outlines a thirty-day program organised around four themed weeks. The first week, called 'technology triage', centres on assessing phone use, engaging in mindfulness skills, restricting social media, and building up displacement activities (e.g. exercise). The second week, 'Changing Your Habits', mainly consists of changing the physical (i.e. bedroom) and digital (e.g. notifications, apps) environment to promote behaviour change. Other activities are designed to set boundaries around when phones can be used and prevent phubbing in conversations. The next week, 'Reclaiming Your Brain', is mindfulness-themed, gearing up for a weekend separation from the smartphone. The final week, 'Your New Relationship', builds on the previous guidance, reinforcing and finessing the habit changes covered in the second chapter.

Similarly, *Stop Staring at Screens* by Tanya Goodin (2018) is designed around digital detox, referring to screen time and addictive smartphone use. The book is structured around seven themes that are potential intervention points to promote balanced, healthy technology use. These seven themes broadly correspond to communication, boundaries, healthy screen use, physical health, positive psychology, mindfulness, and displacement activities. Each section begins with a flowchart signposting potential issues, with four strategies proposed in each theme.

Clear themes emerge from the popular literature. Although smartphone use is treated as a harmful addiction, the self-help strategies outlined in these books are not commensurate with treating a potential addiction disorder. These resources do not typically mention or indicate where professional support is available or suitable. It is notable that the measures suggested in these books are actions that would successfully tackle and change unhealthy habits. The advice in these books mostly has a low risk of harm and, in many cases, will probably be beneficial even if it is not appropriate for treating excessive or addictive use. Activities such as exercise and mindfulness have been shown to improve mood. The main cause for concern is that they exaggerate and reinforce narratives about smartphone addiction.

Treatment in the UK

NHS

Given that smartphone addiction is not a recognised disorder, there are limited treatment venues in the UK that address it. The UK's public-funded healthcare system, the National Health Service (NHS) does not advertise (i.e. does not have a dedicated information page) nor widely offer treatment for smartphone addiction. However, as part of the NHS Long Term Plan 2019 (NHS England, 2019a) which is a nationwide strategy for the next 10 years that sets out the areas of priority, actions and goals, there has been an increased focus on mental health. This strategy includes goals to increase funding for mental health services each year, the roll out of gambling clinics across the UK and the adoption of more digital solutions into services. Alongside this, there was an acknowledgement of potential issues related to gaming, gambling, and social media as a public health issue (NHS England, 2019b). This prompted the launch of a National Centre for Behavioural Addictions. Based in London, this includes a National Centre for Gaming Disorders and a

National Gambling Clinic (Central and North West London (CNWL), 2024a). This is the only NHS-provided service to treat a technology addiction following the World Health Organization and DSM recognising Gaming Disorder as an addiction in 2013 (APA, 2013; WHO, 2024). The Centre for Gaming Disorders treats 13–25-year-olds for gaming disorders using many of the options mentioned above, including individual and/or group therapy, parent workshops, peer support groups and family therapy for gaming disorders specifically (CNWL, 2024b). Since opening in 2019, the Centre had received 236 referrals and offered treatment to 84 gamers by June 2021 (Sharman et al., 2022) and by March 2023, it had received 745 referrals from gamers or their family members (NHS England, 2023). While this Centre specifically targets gaming disorders, this offers an example of how treatment could extend to smartphone addiction if the disorder were to become formally classified. However, public services are often slow to adopt and provide such treatment services, and services are often limited to cities such as London, meaning national provision for any future technology addictions would likely be complicated and sparse. For now, treatment is primarily offered by private and third-sector organisations.

Private Clinics and Third Sector

While smartphone addiction is not publicly treated in the UK, several private clinics or third-sector organisations offer treatments such as rehabilitation programmes and counselling. The existing private clinics offer treatments for a wide range of addictions and mental health issues, including drug, alcohol, gambling, and sex addictions (e.g. UK Addiction Treatment Centres (UKAT), Gladstone Clinic, Nightingale Hospital, Recovery Trust). More recently these clinics have begun to provide information and possible treatment for technology addictions which are grouped differently depending on the provider, with some specifying internet addiction, smartphone addiction, or social media addiction. There is some consensus among clinics but each offers its definition or set of criteria for the addictions (e.g. distressed when away from the device, neglecting responsibilities and hygiene, unlimited device use, reduced sleep) and they often mention co-morbidities or the effects of problematic use such as depression, anxiety, low self-esteem, and social isolation. Each clinic also differs in its approach to treatment, with some offering inpatient and outpatient treatment across the UK using psychosocial therapies such as CBT, interpersonal therapy, and mindfulness. There is also a focus on education around technology hygiene, boundaries, and management for users and family members. For the clinics that specifically mention the treatment of children and adolescents, family therapy is also offered which may address relational problems that may have contributed to or resulted from internet addictions that have disrupted the family unit (Young, 1999; Sharma & Palanichamy, 2018). However, these private clinics do not declare their referral or treatment rates or state the evidence behind their information on their websites, therefore it is hard to determine how these treatment services are currently utilised.

There are also various charities and third-sector organisations that offer advice on how to manage technology addictions. For example, the UK charity Mind offers information on both the positives and risks of online activity while offering advice on online safety, alternative activities, and online relationships (Mind, 2023). Another charity, Young Minds, also advises young people on how to manage their social media and online use specifically and offers a guide for parents (Young Minds, n.d.-a; Young Minds, n.d.-b). However, neither mentions smartphone addiction specifically. Similarly, there are several grassroots organisations created by parents and/or professionals, such as teachers, that offer workshops and talks to students and parents on children's technology use (Papaya Parents, n.d.) and campaign to raise awareness of smartphone and social media harms (Smartphone Free Childhood, n.d.). While such charities and organisations do not give specific advice on the treatment of smartphone addiction, many concerned users may turn to such websites for information on how to manage their use or their child's use. Therefore, in the UK, the combination of these resources and the private clinics offer the main source of information on the treatment or management of problematic technology use, including smartphone addiction.

Internet and Technology Addicts Anonymous (ITAA)

Following in the footsteps of the well-known Alcoholics Anonymous (AA) and Gamblers Anonymous (GA) groups comes the smartphone addiction equivalent, Internet and Technology Addicts Anonymous (ITAA). This operates similarly to AA or GA but offers a community focused on technology addiction recovery, including smartphones, social media, gaming, and the Internet, for those whose digital use has become compulsive and problematic. This group has adopted the 12-step programme and traditions developed for alcohol addiction (ITAA, 2024a), but unlike these disorders, the focus is not on complete sobriety or abstinence. The group acknowledges that the goal of abstinence is less achievable and is not the primary goal, given how incorporated technology has become in today's work and social lives (also see *Abstinence and limits*). Instead, ITAA encourages individuals in their community to establish their own behaviours and intentions defined as their top, middle, and bottom line (ITAA, 2023a, 2023b). The intention of this is to prevent compulsive smartphone and technology use by developing an intentional, positive relationship by setting limits, finding offline alternatives, abstaining altogether temporarily, or permanently from certain online activities or devices (ITAA, 2023a). To support this, ITAA offers guides and resources to support recovery and operate using a sponsor system and holding meetings both online and in-person (ITAA, 2023c, 2024b). Interestingly, ITAA meetings initially began over the phone in 2017, but as the community has become more established, meetings are held daily online and are also now held in-person across various cities in the UK, USA, Europe and select other countries (e.g. Australia, Argentina) (ITAA, 2023c). Although there is not currently any evidence for the effectiveness of ITAA groups and meetings, research has shown that AA groups improve the long-term rates of abstinence (Kelly et al., 2020) and are helpful as a free, easily accessible and tailorable option for those looking to manage their addiction (Kelly et al., 2009). Such groups may aid recovery for individuals by improving self-efficacy, coping skills, and motivation and by offering peer support (Kelly et al., 2009). Therefore, ITAA may prove helpful for individuals looking to manage their compulsive technology use or at least provide a community for those looking for support.

Government Policy and Guidance

While psychosocial treatments are mostly offered by private clinics and third-sector organisations, the UK government and other organisations also aim to address or prevent harm through policy change. Similarly to much of the research into treatment and interventions, a majority of this policy focuses on school-age children and young people. 'Bans' and restrictions on smartphones in particular are some of the more frequent government and school policy suggestions to prevent harm. For example, the UK government issued non-statutory guidance for schools on how to prohibit or limit smartphones (Department of Education, 2024), which advises on different methods for restricting phone use (e.g. phones kept in lockers, handed in on arrival to school) and the role that various stakeholders (i.e. parents, staff) play in this. A review of UK policy found that outright bans in schools (i.e. not allowed on premises) are rare but rather phones are to be kept in lockers ('effective ban'), present but kept in student's bags ('ban but phone present') or banned in some locations or during class time but otherwise allowed ('partial ban') (Mansfield et al., 2024; Randhawa et al., 2024). Globally, one in seven countries have also introduced laws, policies, or guidelines restricting smartphone use in schools (UNESCO, 2023; Rahali et al., 2024). These bans often focus on improving attainment, behaviour, and safeguarding (Randhawa et al., 2024) as opposed to concerns about smartphone addiction specifically. However, there is conflicting evidence on the impact such smartphone bans have and much of the policy aimed at tackling this issue neglects to capture the views of the young people being impacted. A report by the DCU Anti-Bullying Centre explored the views of students' experiences of smartphone bans and found that bans have little impact on education, cyberbullying or wellbeing and may inhibit the skills students need later in life (Reynolds et al., 2025). It was also found that stricter bans led to students trying harder to undermine them and students wanted a greater say in the decision-making on smartphone restrictions, but this is overlooked (Reynolds et al., 2025). Article 12 of the UN Convention on the Rights of the Child protects children and young people's right to have their views heard in matters impacting them (United Nations, 1990) and yet their opinions are often excluded from both school and national policy on smartphone restrictions and laws. Much of this concern is also extended to 'screen time' and social media for young people. In 2023, the UK Government began an inquiry into screen time to understand possible impacts on education and wellbeing and published their report in 2024 (Education Committee, 2024). This report recommended measures such as the introduction of tougher bans in schools, the inclusion of digital literacy in school curriculums, commissioning revised guidance for parents and carers, and conducting a risk assessment on technology in education. Despite the report being titled 'screen time', a wide range of online harms and effects are investigated and these recommendations will work alongside the protections of the Online Safety Act (2023), which will come into full effect by 2026. Other countries are also looking at similar policies for smartphones and social media, notably the social media ban for under 16s which has recently come into effect in Australia (UNICEF Australia, 2025). While a focus on screen time specifically may be less helpful, measures to prevent online harms are needed for all ages. Attempts to address this should include the views of different stakeholders, including children, young people and researchers, and work to understand the benefits that technologies can provide, instead of just the risks.

Smartphone Applications

Lastly in this chapter, applications (apps) are often used to manage smartphone use and minimise harmful effects. Since many forms of treatment for smartphone addiction in the UK are provided by private or third-party sectors, people may often attempt to manage their use and symptoms themselves first or prevent the relapse of symptoms. There are many apps that have been marketed as treatments or "detoxes" for smartphone use, smartphone addiction, or nomophobia that are available in public app stores. These apps offer popular solutions that share the principles and mechanisms of self-care and abstinence raised in popular literature (see *Popular Literature*). There are several news articles and blogs that promote certain apps as cures for smartphone addiction or ways to break unhealthy habits and 'excessive' screen time (Dredge, 2018; Whillans, 2019; Willis, 2019; Smith, 2024). Such articles often begin with statistics about screen time and its possible effects to provoke worry before listing different apps to manage this along with personal accounts from the general public. Popular apps such as *Forest*, *Moment*, *Screen Time*, and *Mute*, which employ features including self-tracking, limit setting, and blocking, are frequently mentioned for readers to manage their screen time and smartphone addictions. However, as discussed previously, screen time specifically is less informative when it comes to addiction, depression, and anxiety, but much of the popular conversation continues to centre around this concept.

Meanwhile, academic literature exploring applications for the treatment or management of smartphone addiction is scarce. A review by Rahmillah et al. (2023) investigated 13 existing apps designed to reduce and prevent problematic mobile use and found minimal evidence of their effectiveness. Of the 13, only four apps (*Screen Time (iOS)*, *Forest*, *Screen Time*, and *AntiSocial*) showed effectiveness in reducing mobile use, but the results for *Forest* and *Screen Time* are limited by a small sample ($n = 26$). These apps used several strategies and features to reduce use with grayscale mode, app limit features, and mixed interventions being the most effective, and self-tracking and goal-setting features also being popular. As found by Kalk et al. (2024, see *Abstinence and limits*), activating limiting or blocking features was found to lower problematic use (Rahmillah et al., 2023), but these apps are still likely to fail without user motivation and commitment (Throuvala et al., 2020). Similarly, Bychkov and Young (2018) reviewed 125 apps for iOS and Android and found no apps to treat nomophobia that rely on evidence-based research. They found that reminders and tracking were the most popular features used, but apps also attempted to adopt behaviour-change methods such as goal setting, gamification, commitment, and self-tracking. However, many of these apps fell into the categories of productivity, lifestyle, or health and fitness apps, as opposed to marketed treatments specifically for smartphone addiction. Löchtefeld et al. (2013) developed and tested *AppDetox* as a potential mobile app to allow users to control their usage using blocking and rule setting features to directly treat mobile addiction. Users could opt to set rules for certain apps under three different conditions: restrict use for specific times, restrict use at all times or restrict according to a countdown timer. They found that users did attempt to restrict their usage, mostly with social networking and messaging apps and often starting in the mornings, but users also "broke" these rules frequently. While such apps may not justify being classed as a treatment, they may be helpful as an adjunct to other treatment options, such as therapy, to either prevent or manage symptoms or relapse. Examples of this can be found with alcohol and gambling addictions where smartphone applications can be used to provide brief psychological therapies (e.g. Staiger et al., 2020; Magwood et al., 2024; Mehta et al., 2024; McCurdy et al., 2023) or limit access to online gambling apps or sites or block adverts (e.g. Gamban, BetBlocker). Since many of these apps are through public app stores, they offer an easily accessible option for people worried about their use to take control and limit access to certain apps, despite limited evidence of their effectiveness for smartphone addiction. However, considerations around privacy, security, and management of personal data need to be included to ensure protection for users.

Conclusion

The majority of the proposed treatments for smartphone addiction or other technological addictions are psychosocial interventions such as CBT, mindfulness, or exercise. While there is some mixed evidence that these interventions may improve evaluations of addiction severity and mental health, in combination with strategies such as restricting certain apps and establishing individual limits, there are several factors that impact these conclusions. Firstly, the majority of the treatments discussed are also used for mood disorders and are evidenced for internet addiction instead of smartphone addiction. This further complicates the conceptualisation issues that surround distinctions between IA and SA. It is difficult to say whether treatments for IA will translate to SA if they are seen to be different disorders with distinct symptoms and behaviour. Arguably, these psychosocial interventions may be treating underlying anxiety, depression, or distress that potentially drives problematic smartphone use, as opposed to treating smartphone addiction itself. It is important to recognise that many societal factors contribute to poor mental health rates, such as inequalities, structural threats, and other health behaviours (The Lancet, 2024; Sewall & Parry, 2024), despite smartphones often being positioned as the culprit for this decline, especially for children and young people. Therefore, it is important to consider the role of society and mental health in the treatment of smartphone addiction. Secondly, the majority of the research into smartphone addiction does not use clinical samples, including research into potential treatments, which limits the conclusions that can be drawn. This is discussed further in Chaps. 4 and 6 but using convenience samples that do not meet the "cut-offs" for smartphone addiction or overfocusing on adolescent student samples diminishes the evidence for proposed interventions. Results from studies using clinical samples may yield different results and give greater insight into the most effective types, intensity, and duration of treatments for problematic use. Thirdly, there are considerable differences between how academic versus popular literature approach the treatment of smartphone addiction. Although both treat smartphone use as an addictive disorder, the measures proposed in self-help books lean towards habit change rather than significant treatment. Lastly, many of the treatment studies also measure effectiveness according to reductions in screen time instead of self-reported or behavioural measures of smartphone addiction. As discussed in Chap. 1, screen time does not always equate to smartphone addiction and associated issues in the same way, therefore interventions targeting or measuring screen time as a proxy may not be as effective. Overall, if smartphone addiction is declared an official disorder in future, there is a need for more robust evidence on how to treat it and other technology addictions. While we do not advocate for any of the treatments discussed in this chapter, there are implications for future policy, research, and treatment venues to ensure interventions are safe and evidence-based.

References

Alter, A. (2017). *Irresistible: Why you are addicted to technology and how to set yourself free*. Penguin Random House.

American Psychiatric Association. (2013). *Diagnostic and statistical manual of mental disorders, (DSM-5®)*. American Psychiatric Publishing.

Azam, M., Ali, A., Mattiullah, J., & Perveen, N. (2020). Physical activity, sports participation, and smartphone addiction in adolescent students: A systematic review. *Journal of Evidence-Based Psychotherapies, 20*(1), 25–41. https://doi.org/10.24193/jebp.2020.1.2

Brewer, J. (2017). *The craving mind: From cigarettes to smartphones to love - why we get hooked and how we can break bad habits*. Yale University Press.

Bychkov, D., & Young, S. D. (2018). Facing up to nomophobia: A systematic review of Mobile phone apps that reduce smartphone usage. In S. S. Roy, P. Samui, R. Deo, & S. Ntalampiras (Eds.), *Big data in engineering applications* (Vol. 44, pp. 161–171). https://doi.org/10.1007/978-981-10-8476-8_8

Carter, B., Payne, M., Rees, P., Sohn, S. Y., Brown, J., & Kalk, N. J. (2024). A multi-school study in England, to assess problematic smartphone usage and anxiety and depression. *Acta Paediatrica, 113*(10), 2240–2248. https://doi.org/10.1111/apa.17317

Central and North West London. (2024a). National Centre for Behavioural Addictions. https://www.cnwl.nhs.uk/services/addictions/our-sites/national-centre-for-behavioural-addictions

Central and North West London. (2024b.) National Centres for Gaming Disorders. https://www.cnwl.nhs.uk/national-centre-gaming-disorders

Cheng, S., Zhang, C., & Wu, J. (2020). Mindfulness and smartphone addiction before going to sleep among college students: The mediating roles of self-control and rumination. *Clocks & Sleep, 2*(3), 354–363. https://doi.org/10.3390/clockssleep2030026

Chun, J.-W., Choi, J., Cho, H., Choi, M.-R., Ahn, K.-J., Choi, J.-S., & Kim, D.-J. (2018). Role of Frontostriatal connectivity in adolescents with excessive smartphone use. *Frontiers in Psychiatry, 9*, 437. https://doi.org/10.3389/fpsyt.2018.00437

Csibi, S., Griffiths, M. D., Demetrovics, Z., & Szabo, A. (2021). Analysis of problematic smartphone use across different age groups within the 'components model of addiction'. *International Journal of Mental Health and Addiction, 19*(3), 616–631. https://doi.org/10.1007/s11469-019-00095-0

Davis, R. A. (2001). A cognitive-behavioral model of pathological internet use. *Computers in Human Behavior, 17*(2), 187–195. https://doi.org/10.1016/S0747-5632(00)00041-8

Dekker, C. A., Sumter, S. R., & Baumgartner, S. E. (2024). Unraveling the dynamics of perceived smartphone overuse and disconnection strategies: Longitudinal insights. *New Media & Society*, 14614448241303113. https://doi.org/10.1177/14614448241303113

Department of Education. (2024). *Mobile phones in schools: Guidance for schools on prohibiting the use of mobile phones throughout the school day.* https://www.gov.uk/government/publications/mobile-phones-in-schools

Ding, K., & Li, H. (2023). Digital addiction intervention for children and adolescents: A scoping review. *International Journal of Environmental Research and Public Health, 20*(6), 4777. https://doi.org/10.3390/ijerph20064777

Dredge, S. (2018, January 27). Mobile phone addiction? It's time to take back control. *The Guardian.* https://www.theguardian.com/technology/2018/jan/27/mobile-phone-addiction-apps-break-the-habit-take-back-control

Education Committee. (2024). *Screen time: Impacts on education and wellbeing. Fourth Report of Session 2023–24* (HC 118). UK Parliament.

Etchells, P. (2024). *Unlocked: The real science of screen time (and how to spend it better)*. Piatkus.

Fendel, J. C., Vogt, A., Brandtner, A., & Schmidt, S. (2024). Mindfulness programs for problematic usage of the internet: A systematic review and meta-analysis. *Journal of Behavioral Addictions, 13*(2), 327–353. https://doi.org/10.1556/2006.2024.00024

Gaur, D. T., & Kohli, R. (2024). Mindfulness as an intervention for smartphone addiction in adolescents. *International Journal of Interdisciplinary Approaches in Psychology, 2*(10), 163–196.

Goodin, T. (2018). *Stop staring at screens: A digital detox for the whole family.* Hachette Publishing Group.

Greenfield, D. N. (2021). Digital distraction: What makes the internet and smartphone so addictive? In *Human capacity in the attention economy* (pp. 27–47). American Psychological Association. https://doi.org/10.1037/0000208-003

Hansen, A. (2023). *The attention fix: How to focus in a world that wants to distract you.* Penguin Random House.

Hayes, S. C., Strosahl, K. D., & Wilson, K. G. (1999). *Acceptance and commitment therapy: An experiential approach to behaviour change.* Guilford Press.

Hogan, J. N., Heyman, R. E., & Smith Slep, A. M. (2024). A meta-review of screening and treatment of electronic "addictions". *Clinical Psychology Review, 113*, 102468. https://doi.org/10.1016/j.cpr.2024.102468

Internet and Technology Addicts Anonymous. (2023a, December 9). *Tools of recovery—Internet and technology addicts anonymous*. https://internetaddictsanonymous.org/resources/tools-of-recovery/

Internet and Technology Addicts Anonymous. (2023b, December 9). *A guide for newcomers—internet and technology addicts anonymous*. https://internetaddictsanonymous.org/guide-for-newcomers

Internet and Technology Addicts Anonymous. (2023c, November 18). *About—internet and technology addicts Anonymous*. https://internetaddictsanonymous.org/about/

Internet and Technology Addicts Anonymous. (2024a, November 16). *The Twelve Steps and Twelve Traditions of ITAA—Internet and Technology Addicts Anonymous*. https://internetaddictsanonymous.org/12-steps-of-itaa/

Internet and Technology Addicts Anonymous. (2024b, August 26). *The importance of sponsorship—Internet and technology addicts anonymous*. https://internetaddictsanonymous.org/sponsorship/

Kabat-Zinn, J. (1990). *Full catastrophe living: Using the wisdom of your body and mind to face stress, pain, and illness*. Random House.

Kabat-Zinn, J. (2005). *Coming to our senses: Healing ourselves and the world through mindfulness*. Hyperion.

Kalk, N. J., Downs, J., Clark, B., & Carter, B. (2024). Problematic smartphone use: What can teenagers and parents do to reduce use? *Acta Paediatrica, 113*(10), 2177–2179. https://doi.org/10.1111/apa.17365

Kelly, J. F., Humphreys, K., & Ferri, M. (2020). Alcoholics anonymous and other 12-step programs for alcohol use disorder. *Cochrane Database of Systematic Reviews, 3*, CD012880. https://doi.org/10.1002/14651858.CD012880.pub2

Kelly, J. F., Magill, M., & Stout, R. L. (2009). How do people recover from alcohol dependence? A systematic review of the research on mechanisms of behavior change in alcoholics anonymous. *Addiction Research & Theory, 17*(3), 236–259. https://doi.org/10.1080/16066350902770458

Kim, H. (2013). Exercise rehabilitation for smartphone addiction. *Journal of Exercise Rehabilitation, 9*(6), 500–505. https://doi.org/10.12965/jer.130080

Lan, Y., Ding, J.-E., Li, W., Li, J., Zhang, Y., Liu, M., & Fu, H. (2018). A pilot study of a group mindfulness-based cognitive-behavioral intervention for smartphone addiction among university students. *Journal of Behavioral Addictions, 7*(4), 1171–1176. https://doi.org/10.1556/2006.7.2018.103

Li, Z., Xia, X., Sun, Q., & Li, Y. (2023). Exercise intervention to reduce mobile phone addiction in adolescents: A systematic review and meta-analysis of randomized controlled trials. *Frontiers in Psychology, 14*, 1294116. https://doi.org/10.3389/fpsyg.2023.1294116

Linke, S. E., & Ussher, M. (2015). Exercise-based treatments for substance use disorders: Evidence, theory, and practicality. *The American Journal of Drug and Alcohol Abuse, 41*(1), 7–15. https://doi.org/10.3109/00952990.2014.976708

Liu, H., Soh, K. G., Samsudin, S., Rattanakoses, W., & Qi, F. (2022). Effects of exercise and psychological interventions on smartphone addiction among university students: A systematic review. *Frontiers in Psychology, 13*, 1021285. https://doi.org/10.3389/fpsyg.2022.1021285

Liu, J., Nie, J., & Wang, Y. (2017a). Effects of group counseling programs, cognitive behavioral therapy, and sports intervention on internet addiction in East Asia: A systematic review and meta-analysis. *International Journal of Environmental Research and Public Health, 14*(12), 1470. https://doi.org/10.3390/ijerph14121470

Liu, Q., Zhou, Z., Yang, X., Kong, F., Niu, G., & Fan, C. (2017b). Mobile phone addiction and sleep quality among Chinese adolescents: A moderated mediation model. *Computers in Human Behaviour, 72*, 108–114. https://doi.org/10.1016/j.chb.2017.02.042

Liu, S., Xiao, T., Yang, L., & Loprinzi, P. D. (2019). Exercise as an alternative approach for treating smartphone addiction: A systematic review and meta-analysis of random controlled trials. International Journal of Environmental Research and Public Health, 16(20), Article 20. https://doi.org/10.3390/ijerph16203912

Löchtefeld, M., Böhmer, M., & Ganev, L. (2013). AppDetox: Helping users with mobile app addiction. In *Proceedings of the 12th international conference on Mobile and Ubiquitous Multimedia*, 1–2. https://doi.org/10.1145/2541831.2541870

Lu, P., Qiu, J., Huang, S., Wang, X., Zhu, S., Zeng, F., & Yuan, Y. (2024). *Interventions to digital addiction: An umbrella review of meta-analyses* (Preprint). https://doi.org/10.2196/preprints.59656

Magwood, O., Saad, A., Ranger, D., Volpini, K., Rukikamirera, F., Haridas, R., Sayfi, S., Alexander, J., Tan, Y., & Pottie, K. (2024). Mobile apps to reduce depressive symptoms and alcohol use in youth: A systematic review and meta-analysis. *Campbell Systematic Reviews, 20*(2), e1398. https://doi.org/10.1002/cl2.1398

Malinauskas, R., & Malinauskiene, V. (2019). A meta-analysis of psychological interventions for internet/smartphone addiction among adolescents. *Journal of Behavioral Addictions, 8*(4), 613–624. https://doi.org/10.1556/2006.8.2019.72

Mansfield, I., Phillips, S., & Webb, N. (2024). Disconnect: The case for a smartphone ban in schools. *Policy Exchange.* https://policyexchange.org.uk/wp content/uploads/Disconnect.pdf

McCurdy, L. Y., Loya, J. M., Hart-Derrick, V. R., Young, G. C., Kiluk, B. D., & Potenza, M. N. (2023). Smartphone apps for problem gambling: A review of content and quality. *Current Addiction Reports, 10*(2), 178–186. https://doi.org/10.1007/s40429-023-00479-2

Mehta, G., Lin, S., Nadar, A., Pv, B., Kumar, R., Balaji, A., Macdonald, S., Sheikh, M. F., Saeidinejad, M., Sharma, S.-R., King, J. J., Mookerjee, R. P., McDonagh, L., Afuwape, S. A., Moore, K., & Jalan, R. (2024). AlcoChange: A digital therapeutic for patients with alcohol-related liver disease. *JHEP Reports, 6*(4), 100993. https://doi.org/10.1016/j.jhepr.2023.100993

Mind. (2023). *Looking after your mental health online.* https://www.mind.org.uk/information-support/tips-for-everyday-living/looking-after-your-mental-health-online/about-your-mental-health-online/

National Institute of Care Excellence (NICE). (2022). *Depression in adults: Treatment and management* (NICE Guideline NG222). https://www.nice.org.uk/guidance/ng222/chapter/Recommendations

NHS England. (2019a). *The NHS Long Term Plan.* www.longtermplan.nhs.uk/publication/nhs-long-term-plan

NHS England. (2019b, October 8). *Children treated for computer gaming addiction under NHS Long Term Plan.* https://www.england.nhs.uk/2019/10/children-treated-for-computer-gaming-addiction-under-nhs-long-term-plan/

NHS England. (2023, March 28). *NHS treats hundreds with gaming disorders.* https://www.england.nhs.uk/2023/03/nhs-treats-hundreds-with-gaming-disorders/

Noetel, M., Sanders, T., Gallardo-Gómez, D., Taylor, P., Del Pozo-Cruz, B., van den Hoek, D., Smith, J. J., Mahoney, J., Spathis, J., Moresi, M., Pagano, R., Pagano, L., Vasconcellos, R., Arnott, H., Varley, B., Parker, P., Biddle, S., & Lonsdale, C. (2024). Effect of exercise for depression: Systematic review and network meta-analysis of randomised controlled trials. *BMJ, 384,* e075847. https://doi.org/10.1136/bmj-2023-075847

Online Safety Act. (2023, c. 50). https://www.legislation.gov.uk/ukpga/2023/50/enacted

Oprea, D.-C., Moldovan, M.-A., Chirija, R., & Bolos, A. (2021). Behavioural addictions and the role of dopamine. *Bulletin of Integrative Psychiatry, 27*(4), 63–70.

Papaya Parents. (n.d.). *Workshops.* https://www.papayaparents.com/new-page-1

Pirwani, N., & Szabo, A. (2024). Could physical activity alleviate smartphone addiction in university students? A systematic literature review. *Preventive Medicine Reports, 42*, 102744. https://doi.org/10.1016/j.pmedr.2024.102744

Price, C. (2018). *How to break up with your phone: The 30-day plan to take Back your life.* Orion Publishing Group.

Rahali, M., Kidron, B., & Livingstone, S. (2024). Smartphone policies in schools: What does the evidence say? *Digital Futures for Children.*. https://eprints.lse.ac.uk/125554/1/Smartphone_policies_in_schools_Rahali_et_al_2024_002_.pdf

Rahmillah, F. I., Tariq, A., King, M., & Oviedo-Trespalacios, O. (2023). Evaluating the effectiveness of apps designed to reduce Mobile phone use and prevent maladaptive Mobile phone use: Multimethod study. *Journal of Medical Internet Research, 25*, e42541. https://doi.org/10.2196/42541

Randhawa, A., Pallan, M., Twardochleb, R., Adab, P., Al-Janabi, H., Fenton, S., Jones, K., Michail, M., Patterson, P., Sitch, A., Wade, M., & Goodyear, V. A. (2024). Secondary school smartphone policies in England: A descriptive analysis of how schools rationalize, design, and implement restrictive and permissive phone policies. *Journal of Research on Technology in Education, 0*(0), 1–20. https://doi.org/10.1080/15391523.2024.2363204

Regan, T., Harris, B., Van Loon, M., Nanavaty, N., Schueler, J., Engler, S., & Fields, S. A. (2020). Does mindfulness reduce the effects of risk factors for problematic smartphone use? Comparing frequency of use versus self-reported addiction. *Addictive Behaviors, 108*, 106435. https://doi.org/10.1016/j.addbeh.2020.106435

Reynolds, M., Esfandiari, M., & O'Higgins Norman, J. (2025). Restriction or Resilience? Smartphone Bans in Schools: A Qualitative Study of the Experiences of Students. Dublin: Anti-Bullying Centre. https://antibullyingcentre.ie/wp-content/uploads/2025/06/Restriction-or-Resilience_Report_June_2025_ABC.pdf

Royal College of Psychiatrists. (2022). *Cognitive Behavioural Therapy (CBT).* https://www.rcpsych.ac.uk/mental-health/treatments-and-wellbeing/cognitive-behavioural-therapy-(cbt)

Segal, Z. V., Williams, J. M. G., & Teasdale, J. D. (2001). *Mindfulness-based cognitive therapy for depression, First Edition: A New Approach to Preventing Relapse*. Guilford Press.

Seo, H. S., Jeong, E.-K., Choi, S., Kwon, Y., Park, H.-J., & Kim, I. (2020). Changes of neurotransmitters in youth with internet and smartphone addiction: A comparison with healthy controls and changes after cognitive behavioral therapy. *American Journal of Neuroradiology, 41*(7), 1293–1301. https://doi.org/10.3174/ajnr.A6632

Sewall, C. J. R., & Parry, D. A. (2024). Social media and youth mental health: Simple narratives produce biased interpretations. *Journal of Psychopathology and Clinical Science, 133*(7), 507–514. https://doi.org/10.1037/abn0000950

Sharma, B., Kumar, P., & Sharma, P. (2021). Smartphone is it "behaviour addiction or substance abuse disorder": A review to find chemistry behind. *International Journal of Pharmaceutical Sciences and Research, 12*(1), 57–64. https://doi.org/10.13040/IJPSR.0975-8232

Sharma, M. K., & Palanichamy, T. S. (2018). Psychosocial interventions for technological addictions. *Indian Journal of Psychiatry, 60*(Suppl 4), S541. https://doi.org/10.4103/psychiatry.IndianJPsychiatry_40_18

Sharman, S., Roberts, A., Harris, B., Lockwood, R., & Bowden-Jones, H. (2022). The National Centre for gaming disorders (UK) - who is accessing this service? *Journal of Behavioral Addictions, 11*(2), 147–149. https://doi.org/10.1556/2006.2022.00010

Smartphone Free Childhood. (n.d.). *About us.* https://smartphonefreechildhood.co.uk/about

Smith, S. (2024, January 4). 6 ways to cure your crippling phone addiction. *Dazed Digital.* https://www.dazeddigital.com/life-culture/article/61683/1/how-to-cure-your-crippling-phone-addiction-screen-time-new-years-resolution-2024

Sohn, S. Y., Krasnoff, L., Rees, P., Kalk, N. J., & Carter, B. (2021). The association between smartphone addiction and sleep: A UK cross-sectional study of Young adults. *Frontiers in Psychiatry, 12*, 629407. https://doi.org/10.3389/fpsyt.2021.629407

Staiger, P. K., O'Donnell, R., Liknaitzky, P., Bush, R., & Milward, J. (2020). Mobile apps to reduce tobacco, alcohol, and illicit drug use: Systematic review of the first decade. *Journal of Medical Internet Research, 22*(11), e17156. https://doi.org/10.2196/17156

Throuvala, M. A., Griffiths, M. D., Rennoldson, M., & Kuss, D. J. (2020). Mind over matter: Testing the efficacy of an online randomized controlled trial to reduce distraction from smartphone use. *International Journal of Environmental Research and Public Health, 17*(13), 4842. https://doi.org/10.3390/ijerph17134842

Twenge, J. M., Joiner, T. E., Rogers, M. L., & Martin, G. N. (2018). Increases in depressive symptoms, suicide-related outcomes, and suicide rates among US adolescents after 2010 and links to increased new media screen time. Clinical Psychological Science, 6(1), 3–17. https://doi.org/10.1177/2167702617723376

UNESCO. (2023). Global education monitoring report 2023: Technology in education—a tool on whose terms? https://unesdoc.unesco.org/ark:/48223/pf0000385723

UNICEF Australia. (2025). Social media ban. UNICEF Australia. https://www.unicef.org.au/unicef-youth/staying-safe-online/social-media-ban-explainer

United Nations (1990). Convention on the Rights of the Child (UNCRC). https://www.ohchr.org/en/instruments-mechanisms/instruments/convention-rights-child

Van Gordon, W., Shonin, E., Dunn, T. J., Garcia-Campayo, J., Demarzo, M. M. P., & Griffiths, M. D. (2017). Meditation awareness training for the treatment of workaholism: A controlled trial. *Journal of Behavioral Addictions, 6*(2), 212–220. https://doi.org/10.1556/2006.6.2017.021

Whillans, A. (2019, April 30). Our smartphone addiction is killing us—Can apps that limit screen time offer a lifeline? *The Conversation.* https://theconversation.com/our-smartphone-addiction-is-killing-us-can-apps-that-limit-screen-time-offer-a-lifeline

Willis, J. (2019, December 5). How I broke my smartphone addiction. *GQ Magazine.* https://www.gq-magazine.co.uk/lifestyle/article/forest-app

World Health Organisation. (2024). *ICD-11.* Retrieved December 24, 2024, from https://icd.who.int/en

Wrighton, T. (2022). *Stop scrolling: 30 days to healthy screen time habits.*

Wu-Ouyang, B. (2022). Are smartphones addictive? Examining the cognitive-behavior model of motivation, leisure boredom, extended self, and fear of missing out on possible smartphone addiction. *Telematics and Informatics, 71*, 101834. https://doi.org/10.1016/j.tele.2022.101834

Yang, X., Zhou, Z., Liu, Q., & Fan, C. (2019). Mobile phone addiction and adolescents' anxiety and depression: The moderating role of mindfulness. *Journal of Child and Family Studies, 28*(3), 822–830. https://doi.org/10.1007/s10826-018-01323-2

Yang, H., Guo, H., Zhu, Z., Yuan, G., Zhang, H., Zhang, K., Lu, X., Zhang, J., Du, H., Shi, H., Jin, G. & Zhang, Z. (2024) Intervention of Internet Addiction and Smartphone Addiction: an Umbrella Review of Systematic Reviews and Meta-Analyses Current Addiction Reports 11(1) 125–148 https://doi.org/10.1007/s40429-023-00536-w

Young, K. S. (1998). Internet Addiction Test (IAT). http://www.netaddiction.com/resources/Internetaddiction test.htm.

Young, K. S. (1999). Internet addiction: Symptoms, evaluation and treatment. In L. VandeCreek & T. Jackson (Eds.), *Innovations in clinical practice: A source book*. Professional Resource Press.

YoungMinds. (n.d.-a). *Social media and mental health.* https://www.youngminds.org.uk/young-person/coping-with-life/social-media-and-mental-health/

Young Minds. (n.d.-b). *Social media.* https://www.youngminds.org.uk/parent/parents-a-z-mental-health-guide/social-media/

Zhang, Y., Li, G., Liu, C., Chen, H., Guo, J., & Shi, Z. (2023). Mixed comparison of interventions for different exercise types on students with internet addiction: A network meta-analysis. *Frontiers in Psychology, 14*. https://doi.org/10.3389/fpsyg.2023.1111195

6

Addressing the Problems in Smartphone Addiction Research

Abstract This book has critically examined the conceptualisation, measurement, research practices, and proposed treatment of smartphone addiction to highlight ongoing tensions and debates. In this final chapter, we draw together these key issues and messages and offer practical solutions for how to move forward in research and policy. We focus on five recommendations: to abandon screen time (and other general measures of phone use), a need for greater methodological diversity, the adoption of open scientific practices wherever possible, to refine and improve measurement practices, and to urge caution when applying an addictions perspective to everyday, technology based behaviours.

Keywords Screen Time • Open practices • Smartphone Addiction • Measurement • Methodology

R. James, L. Hitcham, *Critical Perspectives on Smartphone Addiction*, Palgrave Studies in Cyberpsychology, https://doi.org/10.1007/978-3-031-96188-5_6

Introduction

Throughout this book, we have critically examined the key issues and arguments that form the conceptual and empirical basis for smartphone addiction research. Chapter 1 introduced the concept of smartphone addiction and its value as a medium for understanding the relationship between ourselves, society, and technological change. This is important because smartphone addiction is proposed as one of several potential technology-mediated addictions and is a source of intense public concern alongside 'screen time'. Chapter 2 reviewed conceptual issues with smartphone addiction as a construct, discussing whether smartphone use meets the criteria for an addiction, whether the focus of the disorder should be on the device or the content on the device, and how smartphone addiction relates to other behavioural addictions and technology use constructs. Chapter 3 deconstructed the process of translating these concepts into measurement scales and the problematic practices that compromise their validity and introduce bias. Chapter 4 reflected on issues with common research practices in empirical research. Smartphone addiction studies rely on cross-sectional designs and self-report measures while neglecting certain populations and more powerful methodological designs. Chapter 5 focused on the proposed treatment options for smartphone addiction found in the academic and popular literature, including the current context in the UK and how smartphone applications are used in this respect. Together, these illustrate a chain of complications and frustrations throughout the entire process of understanding smartphone addiction. These problems originate in conceptualisation and then feed into measurement, research, and the possibility of treatment.

At present, smartphone addiction is not considered a psychiatric disorder. This is unlikely to change in the immediate future. In the longer term, emerging evidence could shift consensus towards or against the codification of a smartphone disorder. Smartphone use may find consideration as a subtype of certain behavioural addictions or as part of a wider overarching digital or technology-based addiction (e.g. Montag et al., 2021). Alongside academic concerns, the continued pace of technological development and changing policy attitudes are likely to drive structural changes that shape how smartphone use continues to be conceptualised.

This final chapter draws together the key themes and messages from our analysis and exploration of these issues and distils them into recommendations and guidance for future practice. We acknowledge at the outset that these are not an exhaustive list, nor can they address every problem that has been explored. However, these recommendations are intended to encourage research that can meaningfully test whether an addiction model is viable and appropriate. If so, this enables the core ambitions of smartphone addiction research to be examined, if not fulfilled: to identify behaviours symptomatic of clinical disorder; develop valid measurement instruments; assess population prevalence, risk factors, consequences, and mechanisms; and implement suitable intervention strategies.

Abandon Generalized 'Screen Time'

Our first suggestion for future research is to move away from 'screen time' and generalised measures of smartphone use. There is a growing consensus in research that the concept of screen time is no longer a helpful construct (Kaye et al., 2020; Livingstone, 2021; James & Hitcham, 2023), especially in connection with smartphone addiction. We argue that there are several reasons for this.

Firstly, screen time is often poorly measured and subject to bias. Many studies rely on self-report estimates of screen time with significant variation in how participants are asked to report this (e.g. free text or varying time increments) (James et al., 2023). This overreliance on self-reported estimates persists despite smartphones organically collecting logged data on screen time habits, including other behaviours such as notifications, pickups and app usage, which offer more objectively accurate measurements. These estimates are often mismatched with logged data with people often over- or underestimating their usage, which leads to inaccurate conclusions about their impact on negative outcomes such as depression (Shaw et al., 2020; Parry et al., 2021; Sewall & Parry, 2021; Hitcham et al., 2023). This is likely because the data collected using self-report estimates also captures what people believe they do on their smartphones and the perceptions of their use. This subjective screen time data will have different relationships to smartphone addiction and mental health compared to logged data (Shaw et al., 2020; Sewall & Parry, 2021), but this is still the predominant way that screen time data is collected. Future research needs to either account for these discrepancies in their research design and conclusions or abandon screen time as a measure. There is also limited longitudinal data with either self-reported or logged data that would provide information on how screen time may change over time and how this relates to other variables of interest such as smartphone addiction, depression, and anxiety. Longitudinal data is often necessary to establish any meaningful casual relationships, especially when measuring such complex constructs (Kaye et al., 2020). These issues with self-reported versus logged screen time and other limitations in research design mean that screen time is often poorly measured and biased.

Secondly, there is little evidence that screen time alone negatively impacts mental health and indicates smartphone addiction. Studies which have used more robust research practices (e.g. longitudinal, logged data) have found that the impact of screen time on mental health and wellbeing is much smaller than suggested (Orben & Przybylski, 2019; Houghton et al., 2018; Jensen et al., 2019). Despite claims that smartphones are a significant factor behind cohort effects of worsening mental health (Twenge et al., 2018, 2022; Haidt, 2024), there is little conclusive evidence to justify this. Screen time is often studied as a proxy or measure of smartphone addiction, and while there is evidence that the two are correlated (Olson et al., 2022), they are likely two different constructs and have different impacts on mental health.

Lastly, screen time combines several positive, negative, and neutral behaviours into one generalised term. Focusing on overall usage includes positive activities such as online socialising, the building of digital skills, education, navigation, and entertainment, despite much of the focus being drawn to the negative effects of screen usage. By combining all such activities and behaviours into one term, some nuances are missed. For example, there are differences between active and passive use, the use of multiple devices, when and how these devices are used, and the type of content that is being accessed. These important contextual factors are ignored by focusing on screen time and distract from other legitimate online harms such as access to harmful content, exploitation, and cyberbullying (Education Committee, 2024). The use of screen time as a scapegoat for mental health problems also ignores other socioeconomic factors and determines which are known to contribute to negative outcomes. Factors such as poverty, community inequalities, difficult job markets, familial mental health and environment, school staff shortages and policies, and wider societal politics all contribute to mental health effects (Sewall & Parry, 2024; The Lancet, 2024; Rahali et al., 2024). All of these contextual factors should not be ignored when trying to determine the effect of technology on mental health and therefore, focusing on generalized screen time is of little value. Policies should avoid blanket policies centred on screen time, but instead, concentrate on specific harmful behaviours, such as online gambling, gaming, and exposure to distressing content (e.g. self-harm, pornography), and introduce measures such as increased digital literacy skills for all ages, allowing greater control over online content and developing an effective, representative evidence base.

Greater Methodological Diversity

For our second recommendation, we urge greater methodological diversity in future smartphone addiction research. Much of the current literature relies on cross-sectional self-report surveys of the general population, often focused on children and young people and specific to only one country or culture (see Chap. 4). The aim of many studies in the field is to develop a measurement scale, test prevalence rates, identify correlations with other outcomes, or prove that smartphone addiction should be considered a clinical addiction. Considering research on smartphone use more broadly, there is similarly an intense focus on how smartphones negatively impact mental health. This means that a lot of the research into smartphones focuses on the negative outcomes of use but less weight is given to the many benefits that smartphones afford to us. While online harms pose a real threat and can be facilitated by smartphones, these specific harms (e.g. online gambling, harmful content, exploitation, cyberbullying, online scams) should be the focus. Research that examines how smartphones may enable these harms ought to be encouraged, rather than focusing on volumes of 'screen time' and measurements of addiction. We believe that the use of a greater range of samples and methodologies can provide valuable insights into our understanding of smartphone use and online harms. Such methodologies should include longitudinal studies, clinical studies, logged data methods, qualitative studies and mixed methods studies. There is also a deleterious absence of multidisciplinary and interdisciplinary research that would foster a balanced, nuanced understanding of the benefits and risks associated with specific technology uses. Each of these can be used to disentangle different issues that exist in the smartphone literature.

Firstly, longitudinal studies would allow researchers to understand how smartphone use and behaviour change over time. Addictions are generally chronic conditions that transition between regular usage, problematic and risky usage, and during recovery may include stages of withdrawal and relapse. If smartphone addiction is to be classified as an addiction, there is a need to understand how behaviour and symptoms change over time through the use of longitudinal studies to justify this burden of proof. However, the current literature is scarce, providing very little evidence to confirm the stability and durability of smartphone addiction as a disorder (Pavona & Carbonell, 2018). This is important for both the measurement and potential treatment of smartphone addiction, including what interventions would be helpful and at what point. The same argument is made for smartphone use and behaviours in general. Much research focuses on 'screen time', and yet there is little evidence to show how this also changes over time. However, our research showed that screen time varied even over a period of two weeks (Hitcham et al., 2023). Consequently, it is difficult to know how the associations between smartphone use and mental health outcomes may fluctuate and what this means for diagnosis and recovery. Therefore, we encourage future research to consider longitudinal study designs. One possibility is to include measures of smartphone behaviour in existing cohort studies, such as those led by the Department of Education in the UK (James & Hitcham, 2023) and equivalent population studies in other countries.

Secondly, to effectively study whether smartphone use can reach clinical levels of impairment, including addiction, more studies need to be conducted with clinical samples (e.g. treatment seeking, those that meet measurement "cut offs" or have other diagnosed mental health disorders). This means assessing smartphone use, in combination with mental health outcomes, in clinical settings with clinical samples and health professionals instead of through surveys with the general population (Kardefelt-Winther et al., 2017). However, this is lacking in the current smartphone addiction literature (Ting & Chen, 2020), making it difficult to determine whether smartphone use can be classified as severe as an addiction (Pavona & Carbonell, 2018). Clinical samples would allow investigation into the crossovers with diagnosed mental health disorders, how interventions should be tailored to account for smartphone use, and again, understand the trajectories of this. For smartphone addiction to potentially be classified as an addiction, there needs to be greater evidence of impairment using clinical samples. Bye et al.'s (2024) prospective study may serve as a good example with their use of both clinical samples and longitudinal methodology that also includes Patient and Public Involvement (PPI) input to understand the best way for the study to be conducted. If prevalence rates for smartphone addiction are as high as reported using measurement scales, future research needs to focus on populations that exceed these "cut-offs" to understand the harms this group experiences and why.

Thirdly, much of the existing literature relies on measurement scales and quantitative measures of smartphone use. Qualitative studies would add valuable insights to our understanding of this phenomenon. For example, qualitative studies could investigate how people perceive these different measurement scales. Mason et al. (2023) investigated lay perceptions of three commonly used psychological measures for self-esteem, personality, and desire to engage in cognitive effort and found that lay people find it difficult to complete such measurement scales and say that they lack nuance. The same may apply to smartphone addiction scales, and with such a variety of different scales (Harris et al., 2020), it may be helpful to understand what items or behaviours people feel are relevant to problematic use. Indeed, some items may seem outdated, irrelevant, or more associated with different constructs. It is also important that our measurements of smartphone addiction are also age and culturally appropriate, and therefore perceptions of these scales, or views on treatment options and other contextual issues, are valuable. This investigation of scale items and behaviours could also be investigated using a content analysis of the popular measurement scales or other analytical methods. This type of qualitative data may provide insights into why people may think their screen time is too high or what online activities or behaviours different groups of people (e.g. parents, family members, teachers) worry about the most to identify what harms to focus on. Investigations into these perceptions will also provide some clarity to the data being collected by self-reported estimates of use. These estimates may be capturing people's perceptions, attitudes, and feelings about their smartphone use instead of their actual use (Ellis, 2019; Sewall et al., 2020). Qualitative data may be able to add understanding to this measurement of smartphone use and how it may relate to measures of addiction and mental health. Additionally, with much of the current literature being conducted with samples of children and young people, it is important to understand their perspectives on smartphone use, particularly problematic use. This is especially relevant given that policies are generally enacted upon this group without much consultation, such as bans and restrictions. There is a need to include the voices of children and young people in this field of research since they are also digital citizens and will have valuable views and opinions. The rich data that can be obtained from qualitative data could make many significant contributions to our understanding of smartphone use and addiction.

Lastly, as discussed in Chap. 4, logged smartphone use data is only used in 10% of current studies (James et al., 2023). Self-reported methods are commonly used in psychology, but this misses the opportunity to analyse data which is already organically recorded by many smartphones and can be easily collected for research use. Data such as what apps are used most, how long they are used for, pickups and notifications are commonly tracked by operating systems and provide insights into the type and context of smartphone use. However, this is not frequently used by researchers. Logged data can provide insights into what behaviour is linked to smartphone addiction or harm and how this could be identified or monitored clinically. This would help define what is meant by terms like problematic or addiction levels of use using behavioural markers and allow researchers to track this over time or intervene if needed. Therefore, it is recommended that logged data should be used where possible (Kaye et al., 2020) but currently represents a missed opportunity. Since smartphone addiction would fall under the umbrella of behavioural addiction, it is important that we include measures of actual behaviour in our research. Logged data, in combination with qualitative methods, offers interesting future insights in this area of study.

This is not to say that current studies and methods are not valuable to our understanding, but the approaches outlined above would allow researchers to disentangle different issues that have been discussed in this book. With smartphones being so prominent in our lives, and with that being unlikely to change, it is important to understand our smartphone use using as many research methods as possible.

Adopt Pre-registration and Open Science Practices

Our third reflection is to promote open scientific practices to increase transparency in published research. Open science refers to a collection of activities, including making manuscripts (open access), experimental materials (open materials), data, analytic code, and statistical outputs available to the scientific community, alongside pre-registering hypotheses, methods, and analysis plans before conducting a study. Open scientific practices are not a remedy on their own, but each practice contributes to improving the rigour, robustness, replicability, and reproducibility of research. Incrementally, these encourage the production of higher quality research that overcomes many of the threats encountered in this book, especially in Chaps. 3 and 4. The current state of open scientific practices, their utility, and recommendations for practice in behavioural addiction research have been recently reviewed by Eben et al. (2023). Many of these points are relevant to smartphone use. Adopting these practices not only helps improve the quality of published research, but each practice has specific benefits pertinent to problematic smartphone use (PSU) or smartphone addiction (SA) research.

Pre-registration is rarely applied in SA research but has benefits both in general and for specific research questions. Generally, a pre-registered hypothesis and study plan guard against the risk of Type I error, which has been the source of sustained concern in behavioural sciences. Pre-registration requires researchers to think about and declare how variables are operationalised (e.g. frequency of smartphone use) and decide how the data is analysed before the study is initiated. For studies that are testing mechanisms, for example, using mediation or structural equation modelling (SEM), pre-registration can guard against the risk of specification bias discussed in Chaps. 3 and 4. A clear analysis plan, including contingency plans if the data fails to meet certain criteria or assumptions, is the strongest protection against specification bias. Pre-registration allows readers to distinguish between confirmatory hypothesis testing and exploratory analysis. If model adjustments are required, transparent reporting of these deviations will enable other researchers to assess the generalisability of findings.

The public availability of materials makes it easier for other researchers to understand exactly what research has been conducted. In our review of how smartphone use behaviours were conceptualised in the research literature (James et al., 2023), we found these converged on several common domains (see Table 4.1). However, within each of these domains, there was little consistency in how each behaviour was measured. There are dozens of ways to ask how long someone uses their phone for, and the specific question and response options are seldom reported. Response categories might be reported in a table, but whether these represent the original categories or a combination of multiple groups is often unclear. Most research uses validated questionnaires, but contextual, behavioural, and demographic indicators are commonly left unreported or assumed. This represents one of the most serious threats to the reproducibility of SA/PSU research. Self-reported estimates of smartphone use are demonstrably unreliable (Parry et al., 2021). However, it is unclear if this represents a fundamental inaccuracy or poor methodological practice. These questions, which ultimately concern engagement with the primary addictive behaviour of interest, are unstandardised and left to individual discretion. Otherwise, it is uncommon, but not unheard of, to find papers reporting the development or revision of an instrument without reporting the scale or the modifications, both in smartphone addiction research (James et al., 2023) and in general (Flake & Fried, 2020). In this instance, transparency has the added benefit of encouraging the use of the developed scale.

Open analysis code and output serve many of the same purposes as open materials but for statistical analysis rather than methodology. Because the most popular techniques are highly flexible, a transparent record of the analytic technique and output means that researchers and peer reviewers can understand the analytic procedure and assess whether it is appropriate. The reporting of specific analytic choices is often incomplete or omitted due to space constraints. The issues discussed in Chap. 3 should highlight that this ambiguity is dangerous, either due to ill-advised specifications or bias. Open code and output allow transparent assessment of this risk of bias and can guard against inconsistent findings emerging due to hidden differences in analytic procedure. Open analysis code can become a resource for other researchers wanting to apply complex techniques, indirectly promoting their use and acting as a citable document.

Open data is the most controversial practice but has the greatest upside. It allows researchers to verify whether the published findings can be independently reproduced. Studies that are well-cited frequently become the basis for selecting methodologies, instruments, and analytic approaches in future studies. Several studies have demonstrated that published research findings in high-profile journals are difficult to computationally reproduce when other researchers try to do so using the original data (Crüwell et al., 2023; Ellis et al., 2024). Open data, alongside other practices, enables transparent scrutiny of these choices. Open data can also act as a tool for collaboration. As discussed in Chap. 4, similar studies in different populations could be pooled to enable cross-cultural comparisons, or independent patient data (IPD) meta-analyses could be conducted. Similarly, there are many cases where there is scope to take a different analytic approach that might be of wider interest or focus on variables or effects unexplored in the published work as an exploratory analysis.

At the same time, open data is a sensitive issue. There are ethical considerations that must be kept in mind. Some ethical review boards may be uncomfortable with public data sharing or require explicit consent from participants. Sometimes, the data is a secondary analysis of an existing study or dataset and not the authors' data to share. There is a need to ensure that data is sufficiently anonymised to protect participants' privacy. This becomes more difficult with sensitive data (i.e. logged records, clinical data). Indeed, in these situations, sharing raw or processed data may not be feasible or ethical.

However, this type of data is the exception rather than the norm. As explored in Chap. 4, the primary research approach to study smartphone use is survey-based and focuses on subsets of the general population. By most standards, the risks associated with sharing this data are minimal. Where data is sensitive or there is a high risk of identification, measures can be put in place to enable sharing. The first option could be to omit sensitive variables or responses from a data deposit. This also applies to data with a risk of identification, that is, only a handful of respondents in a demographic group. Many data archives (e.g. UK Data Archive, GESIS, AILA) enable multiple levels of data access. More sensitive data might require an application or training for the data to be used responsibly.

Finally, if the data is so sensitive that any release is inappropriate, there are two possible pathways to reproducibility. Researchers can generate synthetic datasets that allow reproducibility without disclosing the raw data. This has recently been done in a study looking at gambling expenditure using financial records, where the data is highly sensitive and has a high risk of identification (Zendle & Newall, 2024). Another option would be to include enhanced reporting of the fundamental data. From frequencies, descriptive statistics, and correlation matrices, it is possible to approximately reproduce most statistical tests used in the literature, from chi-square tests to t-tests and multiple regressions to factor analysis and structural equation models. However, these are not usually reported at sufficient granularity to enable such reproduction.

The Importance of Measurement

The third and fourth chapters highlight serious, pervasive issues with measurement. One of the dominant themes of research on problematic, excessive, addictive, or dependent smartphone use is the persistent development of new measurements. Our appraisal is that this fixation is a consequence of fundamental issues with how technology use scales work, which is felt by practitioners in the field and researchers in affiliated areas. However, the attention given to assessment as it is currently harnessed is unlikely to achieve substantial progress on these issues. Although there are cases where substantive improvement can be evidenced, much of the focus here is likely to recapitulate the same problems found with existing instruments.

The sheer volume of measures creates inertia and impedes deeper validation and improvement. It presents researchers, especially those unfamiliar with the area, with a daunting array of options and encourages defaulting to the most popular and well-known instruments, regardless of other factors. Even with such a variety of scales, our empirical work found problems with the widespread use of unvalidated measures or non-standard use of existing scales.

Despite the amount of assessment-focused research, there are clear problems with how these instruments are developed and validated. Many begin by adapting from an existing scale in another domain. This creates problems at the very outset, as these are often based on flawed or ambiguous conceptual models or are adapted for smartphone addiction without considering the context and nature of phone usage. This confirmatory, 'out of the box' approach also means little consideration is given to whether the questions are appropriately calibrated and elicited, whether they correspond to actual smartphone engagement, or the individual's perception of the impact on their wellbeing. This practice has proliferated across many forms of technology-mediated interaction. It is fundamentally harmful to the development of reasoned debate on the relevance of an addiction perspective to these behaviours.

The validation literature prioritises structural (factor) validity at the expense of almost all other forms of psychometric evidence. Despite this, there is significant ambiguity in how developed measures should be used. Most scales emerge as multidimensional inventories with highly correlated factors. Although many are suitable as a single score, this is seldom directly tested with appropriate models. The issues encountered here embed problems when these instruments are used in research studies. Analytic flexibility and ambiguity on how smartphone use constructs should be represented create a substantial risk of bias.

Major gaps in knowledge exist concerning the use of PSU scales between groups. A significant section of the research literature identifies group differences in categories such as age, gender, educational and socio-economic background. However, there is a general disregard for measurement bias in evaluating these differences. Because of the number of factors at play, it is impossible to determine the extent to which genuine differences, biases between scales, or specific differential item functioning drive these. These issues interact with attempts to understand smartphone use cross-culturally. The number of measures available has meant that there are geographic, cultural, and linguistic determinants of which scale has become popular in different parts of the world. Combined with limited testing of cross-cultural differences and the comparative validity of various measures, this also represents a major threat to the validity of comparisons using techniques such as meta-analysis.

These problems multiply further when these inventories are used to classify individuals. Many proposed cutoffs are not derived from external benchmarks, such as clinical assessment or a level of functional impairment. Instead, they come adapted from other constructs, simple heuristics, or are arbitrary. Few are robustly evaluated, and the performance of these across groups is rarely investigated. As a result, it is the norm for cutoffs to classify large proportions of the population (~20–30%) as potentially meeting clinical criteria for addiction. Rigorous testing of the external validity of these is notable in its absence. The use of cutoffs or scale (severity) scores is arbitrary.

Given the other problems discussed throughout the book, it is tempting to argue there is little that can be salvaged from the existing state of affairs. However, concrete steps could be taken that lay the groundwork for evaluating the scale of the problem and scoping possible solutions. The first is the need for a comprehensive, systematic examination of the current measurements. The most recent review in 2020 identified 78 measures (Harris et al., 2020). That number has almost certainly exceeded 100 at the time of writing. Although this might seem like a major undertaking, some features make this task seem more daunting than it is. The first is the relative use of these instruments. Many have seldom seen applications in published research. Moreover, while many instruments have been developed, we suspect that the vast majority originate from a handful of sources, and much of this variety is, in fact, illusory. Indeed, the Harris et al. (2020) review counts the shortened version of an instrument as a separate measure. Alongside the prevalent practice of creating new scales from existing inventories and models, we anticipate most of the variety in measurement can be summarised into five or six dominant sources. A detailed evaluation of these would determine which approaches would be more fruitful and identify specific gaps that can be feasibly addressed. There are also quick fixes, such as asking about functional impairment, that would go some way to stemming one of the more egregious concerns.

Otherwise, the main barrier is in current practice. There are a few areas of particular concern. The first is during theoretical and conceptual development when the construct is defined and mapped out. Continuing to develop instruments from clinical frameworks and other behavioural addictions has not been successful. Instead, a focus on identifying relevant indicators from a behavioural and context-specific perspective grounded in basic psychological or qualitative research to build a strong theoretical framework for adopting an addiction perspective. This also ties into proposed alternatives to the confirmatory approach to doing behavioural addiction research (Flayelle et al., 2023). The other is to encourage greater variety in scale validation. Many alternatives have already been expounded here. Harris et al. (2020) highlight an absence of test-retest reliability. One that deserves particular attention is the need for validation against multiple external indicators. Currently, the main tools used for convergent validity have been other addiction scales, mental health and personality indicators, and broad technology use measures. Validating instruments, or new items, against indicators of functional impairment, qualitative experiences of problematic use, clinical significance, and nuanced, detailed behaviour metrics would alleviate some of these problems.

The Use of the Addiction Lens

We urge caution when applying an addiction perspective to smartphone use. For devices, platforms, and mediums like smartphones or the internet, the classification of a distinct smartphone addiction disorder currently appears unlikely. Even if there is a consensus at some point that phone use can meet the criteria of addiction, there are reasons why an addiction-focused perspective has fundamental limitations when applied to emerging technologies. These limitations suggest that an addiction lens should not be considered the default choice for conceptualising our psychological relationships with technology.

The addiction narrative is very effective at drawing attention to an issue. When discussed by policymakers and in the media, this becomes a clear anchor that can help rally disparate concerns around technologies into a coherent entity. At the same time, a focus on this narrative can also draw attention away from more serious harms that may emerge or be facilitated by the behaviours analysed through an addiction lens. This was striking in recent Select Committee briefs on technology use (see James & Hitcham, 2023), which mentions addiction alongside serious, specific harms such as technology facilitating the grooming of children into gangs. This is harmful, made easier by technology, and has nothing to do with the affected individuals being addicted to smartphones or social media. Much of the research on risk factors indicates potential harm, particularly in the mental health domain, but there are fundamental limitations to the research approach behind these conclusions.

As explored in Chap. 2, the methodology used to determine behavioural addictions cannot distinguish credible from implausible candidates. The existing approach to labelling behaviours is narrow and has been described as confirmatory (Billieux et al., 2015). It essentially entails the conclusion that behaviour should be considered addictive by the nature of the research being conducted. It often gives limited insights into what is addictive or problematic about the behaviour itself and focuses on individual vulnerability. This quickly becomes entrenched and is difficult to shift. Evidence of this practice spreading can already be seen in emerging technologies like short-form videos and generative large language models (LLMs). The breadth and variety of interactions available with large language models have the potential to replicate many of the same problems that have plagued smartphone addiction, and internet addiction before that.

Defaulting to analysing technology through an addiction perspective is, at best, unlikely to affect public policy. At worst, it has the potential to distract from more serious harm. As we have seen with gambling, framing negative impacts in terms of addiction has often led to policies that have focused on a pathological minority of the population instead of addressing wider social and societal harms (Wardle et al., 2019). The proliferation of this narrative throughout different forms of technology has done little to affect public policy. The main motivating factor for policy intervention and regulation in addictive substances and behaviours has been the presence of harm rather than evidence in favour of addiction.

The other concern is the use of the term addiction, its related concepts and terminology. This comes with the risk of stigmatising and trivialising any potential harm from smartphone use. In mitigation, it is important to stress that the language used in the literature has tended not to be stigmatising in ways that have been evidenced in gambling or substance use (Blaszczynski et al., 2020). The risk of trivialisation is perhaps greater (e.g. Hugues et al., 2023). Notably, an increasing proportion of published papers explicitly using the term 'addiction' are focused on technological behaviours. A flawed approach to measurement that identifies around one in four as being at risk of addiction, as found in smartphone use and several other technology-focused behavioural addictions, is likely to feed into public perceptions over time and reshape or dilute how we think about addiction.

Combined, these give a strong rationale for taking a different approach. There are numerous different frameworks that can act as a more appropriate point for thinking about our relationship with technology. Etchells (2024) uses habits as a model for thinking about device behaviours. This is not prescriptive on the relationship between ourselves and our devices. It also does not necessitate an addiction perspective (Hogarth, 2020). Alternatively, others have proposed frameworks that mirror approaches for thinking about healthy eating, such as a digital diet (e.g. Orben, 2022;

Orben et al., 2024) or digital well-being (Vanden Abeele, 2021; Vanden Abeele et al., 2022). These perspectives distinguish between different activities, affordances, and motivations for engagement that might be beneficial or harmful. These also align with some of the models covered in Chap. 2, especially compensatory use models. For informing policy and public health, the metaphors of diet enable an obvious translation from healthy eating programmes where there is already a wealth of practical experience. Notably, many published 'treatment' books focus on activities designed to break bad habits and encourage mindful or positive use of technology (see Chap. 5). It is unlikely these on their own would be sufficient to treat an addiction disorder, but they are consistent with a worldview that takes a different approach to thinking about smartphone use.

Ultimately, conceptualising a behaviour as an addiction should be the culmination of a multidisciplinary, multimodal understanding of the behaviour in question. This might involve a functional analysis of features of the interaction that lead to impaired control (James & Tunney, 2017) or a detailed qualitative examination of the motivations, triggers, and consequences of the interaction (Flayelle et al., 2023). Positive evidence of clinically significant phenomena and demonstrable functional impairment are vital. Regardless of how this is pursued, the existing approaches and models that proliferate across smartphone use and many other behavioural addictions are unsuitable for the task (Grubbs & Boness, 2025). Proposing that something should be the basis of a clinical disorder should be the culmination of comprehensive examination rather than a starting point.

Final Remarks

The concern that new technologies could be dangerous, or even addictive, is an old phenomenon. Technological advances in computing and the Internet since the 1990s have made these ideas pervasive with each new development. Meanwhile, the growth and expansion of concepts in possible behavioural addictions, especially gambling and later gaming and the Internet, has created a set of tools and ideas that can be applied to almost any behaviour. The task of this book has been to critically examine the impact these have had when applied to smartphone use, and where to go from here.

The purpose of this chapter has been to reflect on possible paths forward. Underlying these recommendations are two central messages. The first is that applying an addiction perspective to a behaviour, especially everyday activities, should necessitate a substantial burden of proof. It is neither especially informative nor helpful as a default approach. Conceptualisations such as 'problematic use' can be more informative, but only when incorporating non-addictive harms and not used as a substitute for addiction. The second is a dire need for conceptual and methodological development in smartphone and technology use research to improve the evidence base. Existing limitations preclude drawing substantive conclusions concerning the relationship between smartphone use, other addictive behaviours, and mental health because they are conceptually indistinct. This especially applies to treatment or intervention in the event this is deemed appropriate.

Although the book has focused on critical issues, there are reasons for optimism that change can be achieved. These methodological and conceptual issues have been acknowledged elsewhere (e.g. Larsen et al., 2023). This has, in part, prompted a change of terminology and perspective from smartphone addiction to problematic smartphone use (e.g. Sun & Tang, 2024). Although many of the instruments for measuring smartphone addiction have been kept, it does suggest that better ways of thinking about our relationship with technology have the potential to be adopted. Similarly, there are encouraging signs that more rigorous methodologies and transparent research practices are being implemented in some studies. With the analysis and considerations highlighted in this book, we hope to promote critical and robust research into smartphone use and other current or emerging technologies.

References

Billieux, J., Schimmenti, A., Khazaal, Y., Maurage, P., & Heeren, A. (2015). Are we overpathologizing everyday life? A tenable blueprint for behavioral addiction research. *Journal of Behavioral Addictions, 4*(3), 119–123. https://doi.org/10.1556/2006.4.2015.009

Blaszczynski, A., Swanton, T. B., & Gainsbury, S. M. (2020). Avoiding use of stigmatising descriptors in gambling studies. *International Gambling Studies, 20*(3), 369–372. https://doi.org/10.1080/14459795.2020.1808774

Bye, A., Carter, B., Leightley, D., Trevillion, K., Liakata, M., Branthonne-Foster, S., Cross, S., Zenasni, Z., Carr, E., Williamson, G., Vega Viyuela, A., & Dutta, R. (2024). Cohort profile: The Social media, smartphone use and Self-harm in Young People (3S-YP) study–A prospective, observational cohort study of young people in contact with mental health services. PLOS ONE, 19(5). https://doi.org/10.1371/journal.pone.0299059

Crüwell, S., Apthorp, D., Baker, B. J., Colling, L., Elson, M., Geiger, S. J., Lobentanzer, S., Monéger, J., Patterson, A., & Schwarzkopf, D. S. (2023). What's in a badge? A computational reproducibility investigation of the open data badge policy in one issue of psychological science. *Psychological Science, 34*(4), 512–522. https://doi.org/10.1177/09567976221140828

Eben, C., Bőthe, B., Brevers, D., Clark, L., Grubbs, J. B., Heirene, R., Kräplin, A., Lewczuk, K., Palmer, L., & Perales, J. C. (2023). The landscape of open science in behavioral addiction research: Current practices and future directions. *Journal of Behavioral Addictions, 12*(4), 862–870. https://doi.org/10.1556/2006.2023.00052

Education Committee. (2024). *Screen Time: Impacts on Education and Wellbeing. Fourth Report of Session 2023–24* (HC 118). UK Parliament.

Ellis, D. A. (2019). Are smartphones really that bad? Improving the psychological measurement of technology-related behaviors. *Computers in Human Behavior, 97*, 60–66. https://doi.org/10.1016/j.chb.2019.03.006

Ellis, D. A., Towse, J., Brown, O., Cork, A., Davidson, B. I., Devereux, S., Hinds, J., Ivory, M., Nightingale, S., & Parry, D. A. (2024). Assessing computational reproducibility in behavior research methods. *Behavior Research Methods, 56*(8), 8745–8760. https://doi.org/10.3758/s13428-024-02501-5

Etchells, P. (2024). *Unlocked: The real science of screen time (and how to spend it better)*. Piatkus.

Flake, J. K., & Fried, E. I. (2020). Measurement schmeasurement: Questionable measurement practices and how to avoid them. *Advances in Methods and*

Practices in Psychological Science, 3(4), 456–465. https://doi.org/10.1177/2515245920952393

Flayelle, M., Brevers, D., King, D. L., Maurage, P., Perales, J. C., & Billieux, J. (2023). A taxonomy of technology design features that promote potentially addictive online behaviours. *Nature Reviews Psychology, 2*(3), 136–150. https://doi.org/10.1038/s44159-023-00153-4

Grubbs, J. B., & Boness, C. L. (2025). Thinking beyond substances: Why behavioral "addiction" research must move past substance use disorder paradigms. *Journal of Psychopathology and Clinical Science, in press.* https://doi.org/10.1037/abn0000970

Haidt, J. (2024). *The anxious generation: How the great rewiring of childhood is causing an epidemic of mental illness*. Random House.

Harris, B., Regan, T., Schueler, J., & Fields, S. A. (2020). Problematic mobile phone and smartphone use scales: A systematic review. *Frontiers in Psychology, 11*, 672. https://doi.org/10.3389/fpsyg.2020.00672

Hitcham, L., Jackson, H., & James, R. J. E. (2023). The relationship between smartphone use and smartphone addiction: An examination of logged and self-reported behavior in a pre-registered, two-wave sample. *Computers in Human Behavior, 146*, 107822. https://doi.org/10.1016/j.chb.2023.107822

Hogarth, L. (2020). Addiction is driven by excessive goal-directed drug choice under negative affect: Translational critique of habit and compulsion theory. *Neuropsychopharmacology, 45*(5), 720–735. https://doi.org/10.1038/s41386-020-0600-8

Houghton, S., Lawrence, D., Hunter, S. C., Zadow, C., Rosenberg, M., Wood, L., & Shilton, T. (2018). Reciprocal relationships between trajectories of depressive symptoms and screen media use during adolescence. *Journal of Youth and Adolescence, 47*(11), 2453–2467. https://doi.org/10.1007/s10964-018-0901-y

Hugues, J. C., Nogueira-López, A., Flayelle, M., von Hammerstein, C., & Billieux, J. (2023). Spilling the tea about milk tea addiction-a reply to Qu et al.(2023). *Journal of affective disorders*, S0165–S0327. https://doi.org/10.1016/j.jad.2023.10.155

James, R. J. E., & Hitcham, L. (2023). DESC Evidence Call Response on Screen Time. Retrieved 29/12/2024 from https://osf.io/3tmub

James, R. J. E., Dixon, G., Dragomir, M.-G., Thirlwell, E., & Hitcham, L. (2023). Understanding the construction of 'behavior' in smartphone addiction: A scoping review. *Addictive Behaviors, 137*, 107503. https://doi.org/10.1016/j.addbeh.2022.107503

James, R. J. E., & Tunney, R. J. (2017). The need for a behavioural analysis of behavioural addictions. *Clinical Psychology Review, 52*, 69–76. https://doi.org/10.1016/j.cpr.2016.11.010

Jensen, M., George, M., Russell, M., & Odgers, C. (2019). Young adolescents' digital technology use and mental health symptoms: Little evidence of longitudinal or daily linkages. *Clinical Psychological Science, 7*(6), 1416–1433. https://doi.org/10.1177/2167702619859336

Kardefelt-Winther, D., Heeren, A., Schimmenti, A., van Rooij, A., Maurage, P., Carras, M., Edman, J., Blaszczynski, A., Khazaal, Y., & Billieux, J. (2017) How can we conceptualize behavioural addiction without pathologizing common behaviours? Abstract Addiction, 112(10), 1709–1715. https://doi.org/10.1111/add.v112.10 https://doi.org/10.1111/add.13763

Kaye, L., Orben, A., Ellis, D. A., Hunter, S. C., & Houghton, S. (2020). The conceptual and methodological mayhem of "screen time". International Journal of Environmental Research and Public Health, 17(10), Article 10. https://doi.org/10.3390/ijerph17103661.

Larsen, H., Wiers, R. W., Su, S., & Cousijn, J. (2023). Excessive smartphone use and addiction: When harms start outweighing benefits. *Addiction, 118*(4), 586–588. https://doi.org/10.1111/add.16060

Livingstone, S. (2021). The rise and fall of screen time. In V. C. Strasburger (Ed.), *Masters of media: Controversies and solutions: Controversies and solutions* (Vol. 1, pp. 89–104). Rowman and Littlefield.

Mason, J., Pownall, M., Palmer, A., & Azevedo, F. (2023). Investigating Lay Perceptions of Psychological Measures: A Registered Report. Social Psychological Bulletin, 18, 1–32. https://doi.org/10.32872/spb.9383

Montag, C., Wegmann E., Sariyska R., Demetrovics, Z. & Brand, M. (2021) How to overcome taxonomical problems in the study of Internet use disorders and what to do with "smartphone addiction"? Journal of Behavioral Addictions, 9(4), 908–914. https://doi.org/10.1556/2006.8.2019.59

Olson, J. A., Sandra, D. A., Colucci, É. S., Al Bikaii, A., Chmoulevitch, D., Nahas, J., Raz, A., & Veissière, S. P. L. (2022). Smartphone addiction is increasing across the world: A meta-analysis of 24 countries. *Computers in Human Behavior, 129*, 107138. https://doi.org/10.1016/j.chb.2021.107138

Orben, A. (2022). Digital diet: A 21st century approach to understanding digital technologies and development. *Infant and Child Development, 31*(1), e2228. https://doi.org/10.1002/icd.2228/

Orben, A., Meier, A., Dalgleish, T., & Blakemore, S. J. (2024). Mechanisms linking social media use to adolescent mental health vulnerability. *Nature Reviews Psychology, 1–17*. https://doi.org/10.1038/s44159-024-00307-y

Orben, A., & Przybylski, A. K. (2019). Screens, teens, and psychological well-being: Evidence from three time-use-diary studies. *Psychological Science, 30*(5), 682–696. https://doi.org/10.1177/0956797619830329

Panova, T. & Carbonell, X. (2018) Is smartphone addiction really an addiction? Journal of Behavioral Addictions 7(2) 252–259 https://doi.org/10.1556/2006.7.2018.49

Parry, D. A., Davidson, B. I., Sewall, C. J. R., Fisher, J. T., Mieczkowski, H., & Quintana, D. S. (2021). A systematic review and meta-analysis of discrepancies between logged and self-reported digital media use. *Nature Human Behaviour, 5*(11), 1535–1547. https://doi.org/10.1038/s41562-021-01117-5

Rahali, M., Kidron, B., & Livingstone, S. (2024). Smartphone policies in schools: What does the evidence say? *Digital Futures for Children*. https://eprints.lse.ac.uk/125554/1/Smartphone_policies_in_schools_Rahali_et_al_2024_002_.pdf

Sewall, C. J. R., Bear, T. M., Merranko, J., & Rosen, D. (2020). How psychosocial well-being and usage amount predict inaccuracies in retrospective estimates of digital technology use. *Mobile Media & Communication, 8*(3), 379–399. https://doi.org/10.1177/2050157920902830

Sewall, C. J. R., & Parry, D. A. (2021). The role of depression in the discrepancy between estimated and actual smartphone use: A cubic response surface analysis. *Technology, Mind, and Behavior, 2*(2). https://doi.org/10.1037/tmb0000036

Sewall, C. J. R., & Parry, D. A. (2024). Social media and youth mental health: Simple narratives produce biased interpretations. *Journal of Psychopathology and Clinical Science, 133*(7), 507–514. https://doi.org/10.1037/abn0000950

Shaw, H., Ellis, D. A., Geyer, K., Davidson, B., Ziegler, F., & Smith, A. (2020). Quantifying smartphone "use": Choice of measurement impacts relationships between "usage" and health. *Technology, Mind, and Behavior, 1*(2). https://doi.org/10.1037/tmb0000022

Sun, H., & Tang, K. (2024). Psychometric evaluation and measurement invariance of the problematic smartphone use scale among college students: A national survey of 130 145 participants. *Addiction*. https://doi.org/10.1111/add.16699.

The Lancet. (2024). Unhealthy influencers? Social media and youth mental health. *The Lancet, 404*(10461), 1375. https://doi.org/10.1016/S0140-6736(24)02244-X

Ting, C H. & Chen, Y.Y. (2020). Smartphone addiction. In Adolescent Addiction. Elsevier. (pp. 215–240)

Twenge, J. M., Haidt, J., Lozano, J., & Cummins, K. M. (2022). Specification curve analysis shows that social media use is linked to poor mental health, especially among girls. *Acta Psychologica, 224*, 103512. https://doi.org/10.1016/j.actpsy.2022.103512

Twenge, J. M., Joiner, T. E., Rogers, M. L., & Martin, G. N. (2018). Increases in depressive symptoms, suicide-related outcomes, and suicide rates among U.S. adolescents after 2010 and links to increased new media screen time. *Clinical Psychological Science, 6*(1), 3–17. https://doi.org/10.1177/2167702617723376

Vanden Abeele, M. M. (2021). Digital wellbeing as a dynamic construct. *Communication Theory, 31*(4), 932–955. https://doi.org/10.1093/ct/qtaa024

Vanden Abeele, M. M., Halfmann, A., & Lee, E. W. (2022). Drug, demon, or donut? Theorizing the relationship between social media use, digital well-being and digital disconnection. *Current Opinion in Psychology, 45*, 101295. https://doi.org/10.1016/j.copsyc.2021.12.007

Wardle, H., Reith, G., Langham, E., & Rogers, R. D. (2019). Gambling and public health: we need policy action to prevent harm. BMJ, 365. https://doi.org/10.1136/bmj.l1807

Zendle, D. & Newall, P. (2024) The relationship between gambling behaviour and gambling-related harm: A data fusion approach using open banking data. Addiction, 119(10), 1826–1835. https://doi.org/10.1111/add.v119.10 https://doi.org/10.1111/add.16571

Glossary

Digital, device, gadget, screen, media, and technology addictions These terms are all used as umbrella concepts to refer to multiple different addictive behaviours. Device, gadget, and screen addictions specifically focus on devices, for example, smartphones, tablets, computers. Digital, media, and technology are non-specific with regard to devices and behaviours but include activities such as smartphone use, internet, gaming, social media, and online pornography.

Excessive, dysregulated smartphone use Excessive and dysregulated smartphone use are used interchangeably to refer to smartphone use at a volume beyond personal or socially accepted boundaries. In practice, both are used as synonyms for problematic smartphone use and smartphone addiction. In the context of screen time, excessive use is usually defined as exceeding a specific volume of phone use.

Internet addiction A proposed behavioural addiction characterised by impaired control, disordered engagement, and harm emerging from internet use in general. Models of internet addiction have tended to focus on generalised internet addiction instead of specific problematic behaviours.

Nomophobia A portmanteau of 'NO MObile PHOne PhoBIA'. Nomophobia describes a psychological dependence on one's phone, with excessive attachment leading to anxious and phobic responses when separated or unable to access the internet.

R. James, L. Hitcham, *Critical Perspectives on Smartphone Addiction*, Palgrave Studies in Cyberpsychology, https://doi.org/10.1007/978-3-031-96188-5

Phubbing Phubbing is ignoring ('snubbing') someone in a social situation and using one's phone instead. Despite referring to a specific behaviour, questionnaires measure individual differences in the tendency to 'phub' someone else. In this framework, phubbing is a consequence of smartphone addiction.

Problematic smartphone use Problematic smartphone use encompasses a wider continuum of harmful behaviour than addiction. PSU is wider in terms of both severity, that is, not just severe dependence, but also type of behaviour, that is, harmful behaviours that are not addiction-related. However, smartphone addiction scales are often used to assess PSU.

Ringxiety Ringxiety is a portmanteau of 'ringing' and 'anxiety'. Ringxiety has been used to refer to the attribution of phone ringing or other sounds from someone else's phone to their phone because of increased vigilance or salience. It has since included phantom vibration sensations (e.g. in pockets) due to texts or notifications.

Screen time Screen time describes the volume of time spent using screen-based technological devices. These varyingly include smartphones, tablets, TVs, computers, gaming consoles, e-readers, and other devices.

Smartphone addiction, smartphone use disorder Smartphone addiction is a proposed behavioural addiction characterised by disordered (excessive, compulsive, uncontrolled) interactions between the individual and their smartphone, leading to functional impairment in everyday life.

Smartphone dependence Dependence is often used ambiguously in both smartphone use and addiction. Psychological dependence is a symptom of addiction disorder. However, non-addictive emotional dependence is often used as a concept in smartphone use research (i.e. absence of harm, feelings of anxiety when unable to use or access the phone). Others have used dependence as a synonym for smartphone addiction, similar to the older use of dependence as a synonym for addictive disorders. Unrelated to problematic use, dependence is used to refer to the use of media to fulfil core needs (following media dependency theory), or being dependent upon the phone as the only device someone has as a means to access the internet.

Smartphone involvement Involvement has been proposed to encompass a continuum of non-disordered and non-problematic smartphone usage that measures adaptive use. Involvement is based on the Components Model of Addiction.

Smartphone pervasiveness Pervasiveness has been recently proposed as an alternative to addiction-focused accounts of problematic smartphone use, based on the volume of smartphone use in situations or contexts where usage could become problematic (i.e. during conversations, in situations where inattention could be harmful).

Smombies Smombies is a portmanteau of 'smartphone zombies'. The term Smombies has been recently used to describe the phenomenon of people using their phones while they are walking. This behaviour is associated with inattention leading to an increased risk of harmful or dangerous situations, such as walking into other people or traffic, tripping over, or falling down stairs.

Social media addiction A proposed behavioural addiction characterised by impaired control, disordered engagement, and harm emerging from social media usage. Models of social media addiction have tended to focus on generalised engagement instead of specific affordances or social media platforms.

Index

R. James, L. Hitcham, *Critical Perspectives on Smartphone Addiction*, Palgrave Studies in Cyberpsychology, https://doi.org/10.1007/978-3-031-96188-5